PENGUIN CLASSICS

HEDDA GABLER AND OTHER PLAYS

HENRIK IBSEN was born at Skien, Norway, in 1828. His family went bankrupt when he was a child, and he struggled with poverty for many years. His first ambition was medicine, but he abandoned this to write and to work in the theatre. Of his early verse plays, *The Vikings at Helgeland* is now best remembered. In the year of its publication (1858) he married Susannah Thoresen, a pastor's daughter.

A scholarship enabled Ibsen to travel to Rome in 1864. In Italy he wrote *Brand* (1866), which earned him a state pension, and *Peer Gynt* (1867), for which Grieg later wrote the incidental music. These plays established his reputation. Apart from two short visits to Norway, he lived in Italy and Germany until 1891.

From *The League of Youth* (1869) onwards, Ibsen renounced poetry and wrote prose drama. Though a timid man, he supported in his plays many crucial causes of his day, such as the emancipation of women. Plays like *Ghosts* (1881) and *A Doll's House* (1879) caused critical uproar. Other plays included *The Pillars of the Community*, *The Wild Duck*, *The Lady From the Sea*, *Hedda Gabler*, *The Master Builder*, *John Gabriel Borkmann* and *When We Dead Wake*.

Towards the end of his life Ibsen, one of the world's greatest dramatists, suffered strokes which destroyed his memory for words and even the alphabet. He died in 1906 in Kristiania (now Oslo).

UNA ELLIS-FERMOR was Professor of English at Bedford College, University of London until her death in 1958. She also translated *The Master Builder*, *Rosmerholm*, *Little Eyolf* and *John Gabriel Borkman*, which are published together in another volume of the Penguin Classics.

Henrik Ibsen

———— ✳ ————

HEDDA GABLER
AND OTHER PLAYS

———— ✳ ————

THE PILLARS OF THE
COMMUNITY

THE WILD DUCK

HEDDA GABLER

———— ✳ ————

TRANSLATED BY
UNA ELLIS-FERMOR

PENGUIN BOOKS

PENGUIN BOOKS

Published by the Penguin Group
Penguin Books Ltd, 80 Strand, London WC2R 0RL, England
Penguin Putnam Inc., 375 Hudson Street, New York, New York 10014, USA
Penguin Books Australia Ltd, 250 Camberwell Road, Camberwell, Victoria 3124, Australia
Penguin Books Canada Ltd, 10 Alcorn Avenue, Toronto, Ontario, Canada M4V 3B2
Penguin Books India (P) Ltd, 11 Community Centre, Panchsheel Park, New Delhi – 110 017, India
Penguin Books (NZ) Ltd, Cnr Rosedale and Airborne Roads, Albany, Auckland, New Zealand
Penguin Books (South Africa) (Pty) Ltd, 24 Sturdee Avenue, Rosebank 2196, South Africa

Penguin Books Ltd, Registered Offices: 80 Strand, London WC2R 0RL, England

www.penguin.com

First published under the title *Three Plays* 1950
Reprinted under the title *Hedda Gabler and Other Plays* 1961
41

Translation and editorial matter copyright 1950 by Penguin Books Ltd
All rights reserved

Printed in England by Clays Ltd, St Ives plc
Set in Monotype Bembo

All applications for licences to perform plays in this volume
should be made to the International Copyright Bureau Ltd,
25 Charing Cross Road, London WC2

ISBN-13: 978-0-140-44016-4

www.greenpenguin.co.uk

CONTENTS

INTRODUCTION

———————— * ————————

THIS is an attempt to translate into the English of today three plays written in Norwegian at the end of the nineteenth century. The original itself is no longer the speech that would be used by a contemporary dramatist such as Helge Krog or Nordahl Grieg; some words have slightly different associations and overtones and there are turns of phrase here and there that represent the conversation of that period rather than of the present day. Moreover, the Norwegian language has changed rather more in the last half-century than has English in the corresponding period. Yet, because Ibsen is a great dramatist, the presence of these faint but subtle differences does not date the dialogue as it would that of a man who was wholly of his age. His language (like his thought and his technique) has less in it that is old-fashioned to modern Norwegian ears than has Henry Arthur Jones's to modern Englishmen. Nevertheless, it poses some pretty problems for the translator, who must try to render that dialogue in an English which sounds natural to the modern reader and, without so using the ephemeral as to put the translation itself out of date in ten years, nevertheless avoid that safe and colourless neutrality which would do an even graver injustice to the original. I am all too keenly aware that I have not achieved this; only Ibsen, writing in English, could. I can only plead that this is what I believe should be done.

This is primarily a reader's translation. But it has been my intention throughout to write dialogue which could be spoken by the actor, the cadences and the word-order such as can be put across from the stage without undue effort.

This is more difficult in translation than in original writing; and the superb ease and power with which Ibsen does it in his own language is at once a stimulus and a responsibility. Nevertheless, this is not a 'stage version' or a free translation. No one who has lived for twenty years in close association with Ibsen's mind and thought would dare to tamper deliberately with the close-wrought and precise expression to which he gave the care and labour of constant revision. To the question of particular problems in the language of these three plays I shall return later.

Ibsen was the first Norwegian of modern times to lead the world in any of the arts; he is one of the five greatest dramatists of history. He inherited the stern moral tradition of a race accustomed to hardship and in love with liberty, a race of fine integrity and of a strenuous intellectual habit. His cultural heritage derived from the ancient and the modern world alike and, more immediately, from that of nineteenth-century Europe. But though the great age of Norwegian literature lay in the far past, its spirit was still potent; and in the Renaissance which he dominated he had Wergeland before him and Björnson beside him. The effect of Ibsen upon the European theatre and drama, and through them on European thought, is hard to calculate. He found the drama, in every literature but Germany's, moribund or fixed in its traditions; he left it vital and fertile. Apart from a few dramatists in Scandinavia and France, there was less attempt to imitate him than is sometimes supposed. Like Shakespeare, he affected his contemporaries by the stimulus and inspiration of his example, not by the conventions which found schools. There are no fixed traditions in Ibsen's work, though certain ideals persist from the beginning to the end. He left the world his integrity as a thinker and as an artist. And that can only be 'imitated' in the noblest, the Aristotelian sense.

The plays by which Ibsen is best known in this country are still the naturalistic studies of contemporary life, the work of his middle and late years, and three of those are presented here. But it is impossible to value Ibsen aright, even the Ibsen of the social problem plays, without an understanding of the poet who, like his contemporary Björnson, began with romantic historical verse plays and only gradually took upon himself the task of exposing the makeshift morality of his contemporaries in private and public life. To think of him solely as the great (though never undramatic) moralist of those middle plays is to forget the poet of *Peer Gynt* and its predecessors and of the late plays after *The Master Builder*, to lose sight of the slow and complex evolution of poet into moralist and of the moralist again into the individualist of the final years. Ibsen was no Shakespeare; he was never wholly an artist and never wholly a dramatist. But he was as much of both as was the great dramatic moralist, Aeschylus, before him. He was never, after the early years, content to contemplate the world as it is with the strange Shakespearian balance of eager affection, sympathy and non-critical detachment. His sympathies threw him headlong into criticism. He was a fighter, a prophet, an accuser of souls, and between this mood and the mood of the poet-dramatist there is perpetual conflict. But because of his power and integrity as an artist, he again and again subdued this conflict, so that only the clear runnings, the decantation of his thought, enter the plays; and it takes a knowledge of the whole of his work to see, beneath the flawless form, the volcanic forces that have moulded it. The poems give us the clues. And we are further helped by the letters, the posthumous papers and the passages in *Peer Gynt*, *The Master Builder* and *When We Dead Awaken* where the problems of the artist become themselves the matter of his art.

The three plays chosen for this volume, *The Pillars of the Community*, *The Wild Duck* and *Hedda Gabler*, cover the whole of the period during which Ibsen was preoccupied with the problems of personal and social morality in the world immediately about him. *The Pillars of the Community* initiates, almost with enthusiasm, the group of five which concentrate upon this theme; *The Wild Duck* ends the group in seeming disillusionment, and *Hedda Gabler* is a partial return to that world at a later period.

The Pillars of the Community, when it was finished in 1877, had cost Ibsen two years of unremitting labour and several re-writings.* The result is a play whose thought is so profound and clear, whose craftsmanship is so natural and easy, that it puts to shame alike the emptiness of the contemporary *pièce bien faite* in France and the turgidity of the serious British drama of the next two decades. His concern here is with the function of truth in life. This is, in fact, his concern throughout his life, and it links the early *Vikings at Helgoland* with the last play, *When We Dead Awaken*. But in the group of five upon which he now entered, *The Pillars of the Community*, *A Doll's House*, *Ghosts*, *An Enemy of the People* and *The Wild Duck*, Ibsen brings to the test of his ideal the society of his own times, observing it pitilessly, exactly and at close range, studying the immediate and the particular in terms of the universal and the continuing. He exposes in these five plays the effect of lies, shams and evasions, showing the tragedy and the degradation that accompany the forfeiting of integrity. In *The Pillars of the Community* he examines the lie in public life, the tragic struggle of Karsten Bernick to hide his sin and preserve his reputation at the expense of another man's good name. The lie in the soul so works upon him that,

* The rejected passages and variants occupy some seventy pages in the *Efterladte Skrifter* (vols. II, pp. 261–329 and III, pp. 449–56).

like Macbeth in a more primitive world, he is drawn step by step into actual crime and plans (and all but carries through) what is virtually a murder. Ibsen allows his Karsten Bernick to redeem himself by confession and to save his soul at the cost of his long-guarded reputation. But this is the first play of the series and it is, for Ibsen, optimistic. Lona Hessel's life-long love for Karsten saves him, as does Solveig's for Peer Gynt, by preserving the image of the man he should have been. In *A Doll's House* and in *Ghosts* the subject is the lie in domestic life; the first shows the destruction of a marriage by an unreal and insincere relationship between husband and wife, and the second the destruction of the lives and souls of the characters by the oppressive tyranny of convention. There is a ray of hope still in *A Doll's House*; in *Ghosts* there is no consolation but the integrity of mind to which Mrs Alving has won her way through the wreckage of her life. In *An Enemy of the People* Ibsen returns to the lie in public life; but here the odds are against the honest man, solitary, outmanoeuvred and overpowered by the corrupt community. The plays had stirred and shocked his contemporaries, and Ibsen had become more famous but less popular; it is his voice that speaks when Stockmann exclaims at the end of the play, 'The strongest man in the world is he who stands most alone'.

The Wild Duck ends this group and yet, at the same time, begins the next. The apprehension of truth, which had for Karsten Bernick been a relatively simple psychological process, is now something more difficult, more doubtful and more dangerous. Gone is Lona Hessel who, with her robust affection and good sense, lets in the fresh air from the American prairies, and in her place is Gregers Werle, whose conception of truth is like an icy, fanatical wind from the frozen fjelds. Under his ministration the unfortunate Hjalmar Ekdal, a weakling with none of Bernick's fighting pluck, makes shipwreck of his life and of those of his wife and child. It takes two to tell the truth: one to speak and one to hear. It is obvious from the first that Hjalmar is incapable of hearing it, and before the play is out we realize that Gregers is in fact incapable of speaking it. His self-imposed mission has nothing to do with the truth which is an attitude of mind, and his harsh presentation of destructive fact bankrupts the lives he touches. Ibsen has not lost his faith in truth. He has only seen that it sometimes demands a subtler service than the first two plays of the series had supposed.

These three plays, and the two that fall between them, are sometimes called realistic, fourth-wall dramas. This is true if we give a liberal connotation to the word 'realism', but not if we identify it with photography. In fact, as a study of his craftsmanship will make clear, Ibsen does anything but photograph. Even his material is seldom wholly naturalistic. In all five plays, and most clearly in our two, a part at least is used (and we must suppose introduced) for its symbolic value as well as for its contribution to the action. The coffin-ships in *The Pillars of the Community* offer us one of the most artistically exquisite pieces of functional symbolism in modern drama. They are simultaneously an important factor of the action, a clear representative instance of the corruption and greed of the shipowners and, finally – but only in addition to these two strictly dramatic functions – a symbol of the rottenness of society. The wild duck is not quite so finely subordinated, but it plays the same three parts in its play: the symbolism, though more insistent than that of *The Pillars of the Community*, has not broken faith with dramatic form, as it was to do in *The Master Builder* and some later plays.

Hedda Gabler, finished in 1890, six years after *The Wild Duck*, is separated from it by two plays, *Rosmersholm* and *The Lady from the Sea*, which form a natural sequence with the last four, *The Master Builder, Little Eyolf, John Gabriel Borkman* and *When We Dead Awaken*. These six are all concerned with the problems of the individual, not as a member of society, but as a spiritual being. Society, the world outside the mind, enters indeed into all of them, and in *Rosmersholm* it is the man's public life that is the chief issue of the outward action and of the inner debate. But the emphases have changed. Ibsen is no longer concerned, as in the five earlier plays that we have just considered, with the moral responsibility of a man to the society around him, but with the potency of the inner life of thought. Public life, his contact with the surrounding society and even with his family, are significant now because of their effect upon that world of thought, imagination or spiritual development. In the last two plays of all, the impact of that world is itself a thing of the past, and the mind's reading of its experience and discovery of itself make up the action of the play.

Now, in this sequence *Hedda Gabler* was a little out of place, for it is not, as all of these are in one way or another, the study of the progress of a soul. The sharp, distinct detail in the picture of the two societies, bourgeois and aristocratic, whose conflict forms the background of the play, appears to link it with the sequence from *The Pillars of the Community* to *The Wild Duck*. But in fact it is not entirely at home in this group either, for the action is initiated by the central character, and not until the end does the control pass out of her hands into those of the other characters. The play is a member of both groups and of neither. The figure of Hedda dominates the play as do those of the great individualists of the later group, and her society is important only in so far as it affects her mind and determines her thought and action. But it is not, as they are, a study of a mind's progress into self-discovery, because Hedda's mind remains the same at the end as at the beginning; it has merely gone round and round the cage she has built for herself, looking for a way of escape. And yet it offers the same kind of negative comment on the dominant thought of the later plays as parts of *The Wild Duck* do on the main theme of its four predecessors. For Hedda refuses to discover herself, and her conflict and her tragedy are the result of this refusal. Longing for life and yet afraid of it, she refuses to admit this fear and convert the energy of the conflict into action, and so, at the centre of the play, is a mind turning upon itself in a kind of vacuum. The other plays of this group are studies of spiritual explorations, *Hedda Gabler* of a refusal to embark.

No less interesting than the relations of material and thought in these three plays are their relations as works of art. We pass from the clear, firm, almost diagrammatic structure of *The Pillars of the Community*, with its superb articulation of theme and subject, to the complex organization of *The Wild Duck*, in which Ibsen reached the height of his power as a structural artist, handling several themes and the destinies of different characters with an almost Shakespearian balance. From this we come, in *Hedda Gabler*, to the bare, economical plotting characteristic of the late plays despite their great variety of form. In the binding together of the structure, irony and humour play an increasingly subtle part. The light-hearted comedy of Lona Hessel's arrival, with the slight but regrettable confusion as to the identity of the Fallen Sisters, the neat theatrical effects of entrances that give an ironical twist to the last speaker's words, all these characteristics of the first play give place, in *The Wild Duck*, to the graver irony that dares to introduce, in the flood of Hjalmar's false and sentimental emotion, the first reference to the pistol which is to be the instrument of pathos if not of tragedy, and faintly to foreshadow the catastrophe itself. Even the unfortunate rabbits run in and out of the dialogue like a brief comic motif on the wood-wind in the final and increasingly tragic movement of a symphony.

Nor are the modifications of Ibsen's technique in the drawing of character less remarkable. It is no longer, in any of the plays, a question of skill: Ibsen is a master-craftsman before he writes *The Pillars of the Community*. But the technique varies with the nature and purpose of the play: from the deliberately clear outlining of most of the characters in the first, so that the detailed drawing of Karsten stands out from the background; to the full and profound revelation of rounded personality in *The Wild Duck*, with its subtle implication and cross-bearing; to the limpid but, at first glance, colourless technique of *Hedda Gabler*, which deliberately focuses the attention of the reader upon the inner movements of the minds.

So close and economical is the relation of theme to subject in *The Pillars of the Community* that the play appears at times almost schematic, and even the chief character, Karsten Bernick, has something of this in him. He seems perhaps, at first reading, to explain himself too much and too clearly, to border upon an analysis of a character rather than the dramatic semblance of a living man. But as we look closer we see that, though this is in some sense a necessity of the play, of a play that must convey a moral problem and elucidate it, it is at the same time psychologically sound. Ibsen has not failed as an artist; for Karsten's habit of explaining his own motives, of explaining what kind of man he is, is at once a subtle piece of self-deception and the resultant of a life-long habit of arguing with his subdued but not yet silenced conscience. He must justify himself to himself, and so he continually calls for help in that continual effort; his admiring fellow-citizens and his adoring wife repeat faithfully what he dictates to them. The more dishonest his action, the nobler are the sentiments and motives he defines, until, at the moment of his conversion in the fifth act, he speaks for the first time soberly and plainly, humbly destroying the illusion he had so strenuously created. This is a special type of character-drawing, but it is not shallow or, in the end, undramatic.

Utterly unlike this treatment is that given to the people of *The Wild Duck*. Here each in turn calls out our sympathy and each is created for us as much by what is said of him and by the characters of those who say it as by his own words. There are the masterly background studies of Werle senior and of Mrs Sörby, of whom no one speaks well and who yet win upon us and command our respect because the cross-fire of bitter and vindictive comment subtly reveals them as better than their critics. So it is with other minor figures in the play, while in the foreground is the figure of Gina, as enigmatic in her silences as Jean Jacques Bernard's Martine. Is it impercipience, a slightly coarse-grained placidity, that gives her her tolerant patience with Hjalmar's selfish egotism, or is it an almost divine, inarticulate wisdom and charity? We do not know, and she herself is the last person to tell us. But Ibsen builds this characteristic into the grouping with a delicate sense of intricate balance. Her tolerance or obtuseness seems now a factor in the destruction and disintegration of the lives about her, now a binding and redemptive power. Sometimes, as in the discussion in Act III about Werle senior, we are persuaded that she has driven Hjalmar to escape into irresponsible, falsely heroic gestures. Sometimes, when she bears with equanimity his insults and injustice, we see how this very quality helps her to hold her little society together without rebellion and without thought of her own rights. Such is the balance of character with character and of both with action throughout the play.

Different again is the function of character in *Hedda Gabler*. But how subtle is not only the final effect, but

Ibsen's touch upon our sympathies, and how tightly inter-locked are all these human destinies, not by action but by psychological reaction! Jörgen Tesman, the despised and unworthy husband of Hedda, is in his way as inarticulate as Gina Ekdal, but he conceals his mind not in silence but in a stream of garrulous and insignificant chatter; for all his fussy, naïvely self-important talking, he comes no nearer to expressing what is there. The devotion, the genuine humil-ity, the good, bourgeois family affection reveal themselves as it were by accident; in spite of his words rather than through them. The most pitiless exposures of his character come not from the clever, cynical, worldly Brack or the contemptuous Hedda, but from the simple, devoted aunt who innocently believes that to collect a trunkful of notes is to be a great scholar and that the ability to sort and arrange another man's papers is proof of a master mind. Simple as he too is, Jörgen knows better; and the foolish little pedant slips suddenly into a gesture of unconscious greatness as, putting aside his own hopes and ambitions, he settles down, full of doubts and misgivings, to reconstruct the book of his dead rival. It is the ambivalent nature of the characterization in this play that links *Hedda Gabler*, in this aspect of its technique, with the plays of Ibsen's final period.

Ibsen, like all major dramatists, allows the differences be-tween the mental habits of his characters to reflect them-selves in their way of speech – in vocabulary, sentence structure, imagery. In *The Pillars of the Community* Aune, the shipwright, mixes plain workman's speech with the language learnt from political textbooks; Rörlund drifts into the vocabulary and rhythms of the pulpit when he becomes self-conscious, and Karsten Bernick into the lan-guage of the platform, with all its temptation to confused metaphor. In *The Wild Duck* each character speaks his own language. Gina's original illiteracy breaks through the sur-

face of that 'education' that Hjalmar had imparted, not in
moments of deep feeling, but, as might be expected, in
moments of irritation or embarrassment. It is then that she
misuses words that she has overheard in her husband's conversation and speaks ungrammatically. The speech of old
Ekdal shows the same process working in the opposite
direction: in him the speech of a gentleman has been gradually overlaid by the habits of Pettersen and his like, and
when his confidence is at its lowest these show most clearly.
But when he is happy and unselfconscious, showing off his
rabbits, his attic and his wild duck, he tends to revert to
what was native to him and the speech is that of an old-
fashioned army officer. These two individual ways of
speech, to go no farther, cross and recross like bells in
a change and make their slight but subtle contribution to
the pattern of the play. The same skill is at work in *Hedda
Gabler*; each character plays its own instrument, Berte, Miss
Tesman, Hedda, Brack, Thea and Eilert. Of them all,
Jörgen Tesman is perhaps the most obvious, for he seems to
keep about him relics of undergraduate slang, little more
than half-jocular turns of phrase, which nevertheless serve
to make his incessant chatter sound now pleasantly boyish
now rather foolish in a man of his years, but in either case
carry the merciless implication of undeveloped personality.

Beside the pattern given to the dialogue by this relation
of speakers to speech, there is, in most mature plays of
Ibsen, a running pattern of words that recur as imagery
might do in poetic drama. It is very seldom that this recur-
rence can be reproduced. The sequences 'fag', 'fagmen-
neske', 'fagskriften', etc., can never be fully preserved without endangering the naturalness of the dialogue, but great
loss is inflicted on every play by a translation that must
perforce abandon some of them.

Structure, characterization and dialogue such as this are

the despair of the translator, and perhaps the best justification for a translation is the hope that a proportion of its readers will think Ibsen worth the trouble of learning his language. But in order that the glass through which they see him may not be unnecessarily dimmed, I should like to explain some of the differences between his language and ours and show what lines I have tried to follow.

Some of the specific problems that trouble a translator arise at those points where one language is more precise than the other. If the facility for sharper distinction belongs to the original, it is often hard to render this in the translation; if the other way about, ambiguity which may be the source of intentional confusion is equally difficult to reproduce. An instance will make this clear. The Norwegian language, in common with many others, often uses the equivalent of the English 'thou', where modern English has lost the power of distinguishing, in everyday speech, between the singular and the plural of the second person. A translation can often avoid making any distinction, though there is always an appreciable loss when this is done, because the form 'du' conveys a certain degree of intimacy. This flavour may perhaps be conveyed by other means, but the problem becomes much more acute when the characters themselves discuss their own ways of addressing each other. In *Hedda Gabler* alone there are three such passages; in one Hedda invites Thea to use the intimate 'du' instead of the formal 'de', and in another she rebukes Eilert Lövberg for his presumption in doing so without her permission. The advocate of accurate translation will generally incorporate the actual word in the dialogue, generally in quotation marks and accompanied by a footnote, thus achieving the 'clingingly close' translation enjoyed, albeit disrespectfully, by Mark Twain. Even William Archer, to whom, for his services to Ibsen, all honour is due, could still, at the date at which he was writing, adopt some such method as this. But what would be the effect today, when prose drama is almost as widely read as the novel, if we presented Jörgen Tesman's appeal to Hedda, 'Hvis du bare kunde overvinde dig til at sige "du" til hende' in the form 'If you could only bring yourself to say "du" to her'? That 'du', with its reference number above it and its footnote at the bottom of the page, would kill the dialogue for the majority of modern readers. On the stage, shorn of its footnote, it would perhaps be less obtrusive, but it would certainly be more bewildering. Today we insist that the dialogue shall run continuously without the intervention of the commentator, and the modern translator must find his way as best he may through passages that refer explicitly to ways of speech, thought or customs that have no equivalent in modern English. We perhaps do Ibsen's art more injury by checking the flow of his dialogue to explain what he is at than by substituting an inadequate translation of the original for a conscientious annotation. If we have to choose between the run of the dialogue and the accurate presentation of one of its component sentences, the interests of the dialogue as a whole must win. Drama, in this, furnishes its own special set of problems.

There are, moreover, in modern Norwegian as in modern German, several words which from time to time do the work of particles. To translate these into separate English words would overweight them, for their function is to give a slight, delicate qualification to the sentence, to throw a shimmer of meaning over it that Englishmen find it hard to imagine, much less to translate. A Greek scholar, accustomed to the habits of μεν and δε, finds himself at home in the company of *ja, jo, nej, da, naa, nu, saa, ogsaa, altsaa, alt, bare, netop,* and so forth, but even he may wish they were not so numerous. And although the word-order in a Norwegian sentence does not differ so much from the English as does that of French, German, Latin, the factor of cadence subtly modifies the lighter forms of punctuation, so that the equivalent pace and timing in emotional passages must sometimes be supplied in other ways.

A few modifications in the text here presented should perhaps be made in production. Since Ibsen carefully prescribes the setting of these plays, it is essential to produce them in the costume of the period. But because the modern reader will naturally visualize the figures in modern dress, I have once or twice altered a reference and substituted its modern equivalent. In the first act of *Hedda Gabler* Miss Tesman produces Jörgen's slippers from her pocket, and in the last act Thea carries the rough notes of Lövberg's book there. No modern pocket would hold either of these, and so, in order not to confuse the reader or transport him suddenly to the Victorian world, I have substituted a handbag in each case. But in a costume production the pocket will be natural, and the literal translation should replace mine. In the same way, Miss Tesman's hat should become a bonnet, the proper head-dress for a lady of her years in 1890. I have taken a perhaps less warrantable liberty with Gina Ekdal's cloak in the first stage direction of Act III of *The Wild Duck* and substituted the modern coat.

The settings for these three plays are indoors. The garden room of *The Pillars of the Community* is a characteristic feature of a Norwegian house, a large room opening on to a veranda, much used during the summer months. In the other two plays the set consists of two rooms with folding or sliding doors between; in *Hedda Gabler* the main acting area is the outer room and the inner room lies at the back throughout; in the first Act of *The Wild Duck* the audience's position is reversed, and we look through the small inner room to the larger, outer one.

Finally, a word must be said about the text. I have used throughout the text of the *Samlede Digterverker* of 1930 (the seventh edition), edited by Didrik Arup Seip, except in one instance where, on the advice of a Norwegian colleague, I have preferred a reading from the Centenary Edition (1928 *seq.*) of Francis Bull, Halvdan Koht and Didrik Arup Seip. Readers who are interested in details of text and translation will find a note upon one or two other points at the end of the volume.

It remains to express my sense of the debt all modern translators owe to the work of William Archer for the first complete translation, published by Heinemann, and to R. Farquharson Sharp and his colleagues for the versions published by Dent (Everyman). The pioneer work was theirs. The present volume attempts the impossible task of pretending that Ibsen wrote his plays in the English of 1950. Four things have encouraged me to attempt it: the knowledge that the undying imagination of the greatest modern dramatist is as much alive today as it was in 1870 or 1890 and that there must therefore be some kind of modern equivalent for his speech; the heroic labours of those predecessors in this field that I have already named; a life-long devotion to Ibsen's thought and art; and, not least, the generous assistance of many Norwegian friends who are equally at home in both languages. Of these I would mention specially my friends Sofie Mess and Illit Gröndahl; the first for the elucidation of many references to Norwegian customs and ways of life, the second for a thorough examination of my versions and for many illuminating discussions on Norwegian language, literature and thought. For the faults that remain despite this assistance, I – and not they – am responsible.

July 1950   UNA ELLIS-FERMOR

THE PILLARS OF THE COMMUNITY

CHARACTERS

———— * ————

KARSTEN BERNICK, the head of a shipping firm and a consul

BETTY BERNICK, his wife

OLAF, their son, thirteen years old

MARTA BERNICK, Karsten's sister

JOHAN TÖNNESEN, Betty Bernick's younger brother

LONA HESSEL, her elder half-sister

HILMAR TÖNNESEN, her cousin

RÖRLUND, an assistant teacher in the State school; in Orders

RUMMEL, a wholesale merchant

VIGELAND, a merchant

SANDSTAD, a merchant

DINA DORF, a young girl living with the Bernicks

KRAP, Karsten Bernick's head clerk

AUNE, a shipwright

MRS RUMMEL

MRS HOLT, the postmaster's wife

MRS LYNGE, the doctor's wife

HILDA RUMMEL, Mrs Rummel's daughter

NETTA HOLT, Mrs Holt's daughter

Townsmen and other residents, foreign sailors, steamship passengers and so forth

The action takes place in Bernick's house in one of the smaller Norwegian coast-towns

ACT ONE

———————— * ————————

[*A large garden room in Bernick's house. In the foreground, to the left, a door leads into Bernick's room; farther back in the same wall is a similar door. In the middle of the opposite wall is a larger door leading to the entrance hall. The wall in the background is almost entirely of plate glass; an open door leading to broad steps down to the garden, with an awning spread over them. Below the steps is seen part of the garden, enclosed by a railing with a little entrance-gate. Outside and along the railing runs a street, the opposite side of which consists of small, brightly painted wooden houses. It is summer, and the sunshine is warm. Now and then somebody passes by along the street; people stop and talk, buy something at a little shop on the corner, and so forth.*

In the garden room, a group of women are sitting round a table. In the middle, facing the audience, sits Mrs Bernick. On her left sits Mrs Holt with her daughter, then Mrs Rummel and Miss Rummel. On Mrs Bernick's right sit Mrs Lynge, Miss Bernick and Dina Dorf. The women are all busy with needle-work. On the table are large piles of linen, cut out and half made-up, and other articles of clothing. Farther back, at a little table with two potted plants and a glass of sugar-water, sits Rörlund, the schoolmaster, reading aloud from a gilt-edged book, but so that only an occasional word is heard by the audience. Out in the garden Olaf Bernick is running about and shooting at things with a toy gun.

Presently Aune, the shipwright, comes quietly in by the door on the right. There is a moment's interruption in the reading; Mrs Bernick nods to him and points to the door on the left. Aune goes quietly across and knocks gently on Bernick's door, once or twice, pausing between the knocks. Krap, the head clerk, comes out of the room with his hat in his hand and some papers under his arm.]

KRAP. Oh, it's you knocking?

AUNE. The master sent for me.

KRAP. He did; but he can't see you. He's instructed me to –

AUNE. You? I'd really rather –

KRAP. – Instructed me to tell you this: you must stop these talks to the workmen on Saturdays.

AUNE. Must I? I thought I could use my free time –

KRAP. You can't use your free time to make the men useless in work-time. Last Saturday you were talking about the harm it would do the workers if we introduced the new machines and methods in the shipyard. Why do you do that?

AUNE. I do it in the interests of the community.

KRAP. That's odd! The chief says it's disrupting the community.

AUNE. My community is not the master's, Mr Krap. As head of the Workers' Association I must –

KRAP. You are first and foremost the head of Mr Bernick's shipyard. First and foremost comes your duty to the community known as Bernick and Co. For that's where we all get our living. Well, now you know what the chief had to say to you.

AUNE. The master wouldn't have said it like that, Mr Krap. But I can guess who's to thank for this. It's that damned American wreck. Those people want the work done the way they're used to over there, and that –

KRAP. Well, well; I can't go into details. You know now what the chief wants, and that's enough. So you go down to the shipyard again; you're probably needed. I'll be down there myself directly. If you'll permit me, ladies!

[*He bows and goes out through the garden and down the street. Aune goes quietly out to the right. Rörlund, who has gone on reading in lowered tones during this conversation, finishes the book soon after and shuts it up with a snap.*]

RÖRLUND. There we are, my dear listeners; that is the end.

MRS RUMMEL. What an instructive story!

MRS HOLT. And such a beautiful moral!

MRS BERNICK. A book like that certainly gives one a lot to think about.

RÖRLUND. Ah yes. It provides a wholesome contrast with what we unfortunately meet every day in our newspapers and periodicals. This gilded and painted façade that the big nations display – what does it actually conceal? Hollowness and rottenness, if I may put it so. No moral foundation to stand on. In short, these big communities of today are whited sepulchres.

MRS HOLT. Yes, that is certainly true.

MRS RUMMEL. We've only to look at the crew of the American boat that's lying here at the moment.

RÖRLUND. Ah, well, I won't discuss off-scourings of humanity like that. But even in the better classes – how are things with them? Doubt and unrest at work everywhere. No peace in men's minds and no security in any kind of relationship. The undermining of family life out there! The revolutionary audacity – the defiance of the most solemn truths!

DINA [*without looking up*]. But there are some great things done, too, aren't there?

RÖRLUND. Great things? I don't understand –

MRS HOLT [*in astonishment*]. But – good gracious, Dina!

MRS RUMMEL [*simultaneously*]. But, Dina, how can you – ?

RÖRLUND. I don't think it would be very good for us if things like that gained a footing here. No; we at home should thank God that things here are as they are. Of

course, here too tares sometimes grow among the wheat
– unfortunately. But we do our best to weed them out,
as far as we can. Our business is to keep society pure,
ladies; to keep out all these experimental notions that an
impatient age wants to force on us.

MRS HOLT. And there are more than enough of them,
unfortunately.

MRS RUMMEL. Why, last year the town was only saved by
a hair's breadth from having a railway.

MRS BERNICK. Ah, well, Karsten managed to prevent that.

RÖRLUND. Providence, Mrs Bernick. You may be sure
your husband was an instrument in a Higher Hand when
he refused to lend himself to that project.

MRS BERNICK. And yet he was so abused by the papers.
But we're quite forgetting to thank you, Mr Rörlund.
It is really more than kind of you to give us so much
time.

RÖRLUND. Oh no. Now, during the school holidays –

MRS BERNICK. Ah yes, but it's a sacrifice, all the same, Mr
Rörlund.

RÖRLUND [*moving his chair nearer*]. Don't mention it, my
dear lady. Aren't you all making a sacrifice in a good
cause? And don't you make it willingly and gladly?
These fallen sisters, for whose betterment we're working,
should be thought of as wounded soldiers on a battlefield.
You, ladies, are the First Aid Detachment, a Red Cross
Unit that prepares the lint for these unhappy victims, lays
the bandages gently upon their wounds, cures and heals
them –

MRS BERNICK. It must be a great blessing to be able to see
everything in such a beautiful light.

RÖRLUND. Much of it comes by nature; but much can also
be acquired. The great thing is to look at things by the
light of a serious purpose. Now what do you say, Miss

Bernick? Don't you find that you have, as it were, a firmer foundation to stand on since you took on your school-work?

MISS BERNICK. Well, I don't know what to say. Often when I'm down there in the school-room, I wish I were far out on the stormy sea.

RÖRLUND. Why, yes; we all have our temptations, my dear Miss Bernick. But we must bar the door against such disturbing guests. The stormy sea – of course you don't mean that literally; you mean the great surging world of humanity where so many are wrecked. And do you really set so much store by the life you hear seething and rushing past out there? Just look down into the street. The people there are going about in the burning sun, sweating and struggling over their petty concerns. Ah no; we're certainly better off, we who sit in here in the shade and turn our backs on the sources of distraction.

MISS BERNICK. Yes, of course, you're perfectly right, I'm sure. ...

RÖRLUND. And in a house like this, in a good and pure home, where family life is to be seen in its fairest form, where peace and concord rule – [*To Mrs Bernick.*] What is it you're listening to, Mrs Bernick?

MRS BERNICK [*who has turned towards the farther door on the left*]. How loud they're getting in there!

RÖRLUND. Is anything specially the matter?

MRS BERNICK. I don't know. I can hear someone in there with my husband.

[*Hilmar Tönnesen, with a cigar in his mouth, comes in by the door on the right, but stops at the sight of so many women.*]

HILMAR TÖNNESEN. Oh ... er ... I beg your pardon. [*Retreating.*]

MRS BERNICK. It's all right, Hilmar; come in. You aren't disturbing us. Did you want anything?

HILMAR TÖNNESEN. No, I just thought I'd look in. Good morning, ladies. [*To Mrs Bernick.*] Well, what's going to happen?

MRS BERNICK. Happen? About what?

HILMAR TÖNNESEN. Why, Karsten has summoned a meeting.

MRS BERNICK. Really? But what for, in particular?

HILMAR TÖNNESEN. Oh, it's this silly business about the railway again.

MRS RUMMEL. No! It can't be that, surely?

MRS BERNICK. Poor Karsten, has he got to have more bother still – ?

RÖRLUND. But this doesn't make sense, Mr Tönnesen? A year ago Mr Bernick gave it plainly to be understood that he would not have any railway.

HILMAR TÖNNESEN. Yes, I thought so too. But I met the head clerk, Krap, and he told me that the question of the railway had come up again and that Bernick was holding a meeting with three of our local capitalists.

MRS RUMMEL. Ah, that's just what I thought – that I heard my husband's voice?

HILMAR TÖNNESEN. Yes, Mr Rummel's there, naturally; and then there's Sandstad, giving his support, and Michael Vigeland – 'Holy Mike', as they call him.

RÖRLUND. Hm –

HILMAR TÖNNESEN. I beg your pardon, Mr Rörlund.

MRS BERNICK. And it was all so nice and peaceful here ...

HILMAR TÖNNESEN. Well, for my part, I shouldn't much mind if they did begin squabbling again. It would be a distraction, at any rate.

RÖRLUND. I think we can dispense with that kind of distraction.

HILMAR TÖNNESEN. It depends how people are made. Certain types need a desperate battle every now and then.

But small-town life doesn't offer much of that sort of thing, worse luck, and it's not given to everyone to – [*turning over the pages of Rörlund's book*] 'Woman as the Servant of the Community'. What sort of tosh is this?

MRS BERNICK. Oh, Hilmar, you mustn't say that. I'm sure you haven't read the book.

HILMAR TÖNNESEN. No, and I don't intend to, either.

MRS BERNICK. You can't be feeling very well today.

HILMAR TÖNNESEN. No, I'm not.

MRS BERNICK. Didn't you sleep well last night?

HILMAR TÖNNESEN. No, I slept very badly. I went for a walk yesterday evening, because I wasn't feeling well. I went up to the club and read a report of a polar expedition. There's something stimulating in following men in their battle with the elements.

MRS RUMMEL. But it doesn't seem to have been very good for you.

HILMAR TÖNNESEN. No, it was distinctly bad for me. I lay tossing about all night, half awake and half asleep, dreaming I was being chased by a horrible walrus.

OLAF [*who has come up on to the veranda*]. Have you been chased by a walrus, Uncle?

HILMAR TÖNNESEN. I dreamt it, you little idiot. Are you still going round playing with that ridiculous toy? Why don't you get hold of a proper gun?

OLAF. I only wish I could, but –

HILMAR TÖNNESEN. There's some point in having a real gun; there's always something stimulating about firing a gun.

OLAF. And then I could shoot bears, Uncle. But I can't get father to let me.

MRS BERNICK. You really mustn't put things like that into his head, Hilmar.

HILMAR TÖNNESEN. Hm. What a generation's growing up nowadays! All this talk about action – and, Lord bless you, it's nothing but play! No real desire for the discipline that comes of looking danger manfully in the face. Don't stand there pointing your gun at me, you little fool! It might go off.

OLAF. No, Uncle, it isn't loaded.

HILMAR TÖNNESEN. You don't know that. It may quite well be. Take it away, I tell you! Why the dickens haven't you ever gone to America in one of your father's boats? You might see a buffalo-hunt there or a battle with the redskins.

MRS BERNICK. Oh, but Hilmar –

OLAF. I only wish I could, Uncle. And then perhaps I could meet Uncle Johan and Aunt Lona.

HILMAR TÖNNESEN. Hm – stuff and nonsense!

MRS BERNICK. You can go out in the garden again now, Olaf.

OLAF. Mother, can I go out in the street, too?

MRS BERNICK. Yes. But you're to be sure not to go too far.

[Olaf runs out through the gate.]

RÖRLUND. You shouldn't put ideas like that into the child's head, Mr Tönnesen.

HILMAR TÖNNESEN. No, of course not. He's to turn into a stay-at-home, like the rest of them.

RÖRLUND. But why don't you go across yourself?

HILMAR TÖNNESEN. I? With my health? But of course, no one takes any notice of that here. ... There must be someone here, at any rate, to keep the flag of idealism flying. Ugh! Now he's shouting again!

THE WOMEN. Who's shouting?

HILMAR TÖNNESEN. Oh, I don't know. They're talking rather loudly in there and it gets on my nerves.

MRS RUMMEL. It's probably my husband, Mr Tönnesen.

You see, he's so accustomed to speaking at large meet-
ings –

RÖRLUND. The others hardly seem to be speaking in a
whisper.

HILMAR TÖNNESEN. No, Lord bless us, directly it's a question of fighting over money, why – ! Everything here
turns on petty, material considerations. Ugh!

MRS BERNICK. Anyhow, that's better than it was before,
when everything turned on the love of pleasure.

MRS LYNGE. Were things really so bad here before?

MRS RUMMEL. They certainly were, Mrs Lynge. You can
count yourself lucky you didn't live here in those days.

MRS HOLT. Oh yes; there have certainly been changes here.
When I look back over my girlhood ...

MRS RUMMEL. Well, you only need to look back fourteen
or fifteen years. God bless me, what goings on here! In
those days there was the Dance Club and the Music Club –

MRS BERNICK. And the Dramatic Club. I well remember
that.

MRS RUMMEL. Yes, your play was produced there, Mr
Tönnesen.

HILMAR TÖNNESEN [in the background]. Tck! Tck!

RÖRLUND. The play Mr Tönnesen wrote as a student?

MRS RUMMEL. Yes, it was long before you came here, Mr
Rörlund. Anyway, there was only one performance.

MRS LYNGE. Wasn't that the play you said you took the
heroine's part in, Mrs Rummel?

MRS RUMMEL [with a glance at Rörlund]. I? I really can't
remember, Mrs Lynge. But I well remember all the gay
social life that went on here.

MRS HOLT. Yes, I actually know houses where they had
two large dinner-parties a week.

MRS LYNGE. And there was even a theatre company on
tour here, I've heard.

MRS RUMMEL. Yes, that was the worst of all. Now –

MRS HOLT [*uneasily*]. Hm, hm –

MRS RUMMEL. Oh, a theatre company? No, I don't re-member that at all.

MRS LYNGE. Why, I heard they'd done all sorts of awful things. How much truth is there really in those stories?

MRS RUMMEL. Oh, there's nothing in it really, Mrs Lynge.

MRS HOLT. Dina, dear, pass me that piece of linen there.

MRS BERNICK [*simultaneously*]. Dina, darling, go out and ask Katrine to bring in the coffee, will you?

MISS BERNICK. I'll come with you, Dina.

[*Dina and Miss Bernick go out by the upper door on the left.*]

MRS BERNICK [*getting up*]. And if you will excuse me a moment, my friends, I think we will have our coffee outside.

[*She goes out on the veranda and lays the table; Rörlund stands in the doorway and talks to her. Hilmar Tönnesen is sitting outside smoking.*]

MRS RUMMEL [*in a low voice*]. Good gracious, Mrs Lynge, how you frightened me!

MRS LYNGE. I?

MRS HOLT. Well, you know, you began it yourself, Mrs Rummel.

MRS RUMMEL. Why, how can you say that, Mrs Holt? Not a single word passed my lips.

MRS LYNGE. But what *is* it all about?

MRS RUMMEL. How could you begin to talk about – ! Just think. Didn't you see Dina was there?

MRS LYNGE. Dina? But, my goodness, is there anything the matter with – ?

MRS HOLT. And in *this* house, too. Don't you know that it was Mrs Bernick's brother – ?

MRS LYNGE. What about him? I don't know a single thing. I'm an absolute newcomer –

MRS RUMMEL. Haven't you heard, then, that – ? Hm. [*To her daughter.*] You can go down into the garden for a little while, Hilda dear.

MRS HOLT. You go too, Netta. And be very nice to poor Dina when she comes back.

[*Miss Rummel and Miss Holt go out into the garden.*]

MRS LYNGE. Well, what about Mrs Bernick's brother?

MRS RUMMEL. Don't you know it was he who caused that shocking scandal?

MRS LYNGE. What! Hilmar Tönnesen cause a shocking scandal?

MRS RUMMEL. Good gracious, no! Our Mr Tönnesen is her cousin, Mrs Lynge. I am talking about the brother –

MRS HOLT. – The ne'er-do-well Tönnesen –

MRS RUMMEL. He was called Johan. He ran away to America.

MRS HOLT. Had to run away, you know.

MRS LYNGE. Then it was he who caused the scandal?

MRS RUMMEL. Yes, it was a kind of … er … what shall I call it? It was to do with Dina's mother. Ah! I remember it as if it was today. Johan Tönnesen was in the office then in old Mrs Bernick's business. Karsten Bernick was just back from Paris. He wasn't engaged yet.

MRS LYNGE. Yes, but what about the scandal?

MRS RUMMEL. Well, you see, that winter Möller's theatre company was here in town –

MRS HOLT. – And in the company was an actor, Dorf, and his wife. The young men all lost their heads over her.

MRS RUMMEL. Lord knows why they thought her attractive. Well, this actor, Dorf, comes home late one evening –

MRS HOLT. – Quite unexpectedly –

MRS RUMMEL. – And he finds – no; I really can't tell you …

MRS HOLT. He didn't find anything, actually, Mrs Rummel, because the door was locked on the inside.

MRS RUMMEL. Yes, that's just what I'm saying; he found the door locked. And, just imagine, the man who was inside had to jump out of the window.

MRS HOLT. From right up in the attic!

MRS LYNGE. And it was Mrs Bernick's brother?

MRS RUMMEL. Of course it was.

MRS LYNGE. And that was why he ran away to America?

MRS HOLT. Well, you can quite see that he had to.

MRS RUMMEL. Because afterwards something came to light that was nearly as bad. Just fancy, he had made free with the firm's money –

MRS HOLT. But we don't know that for certain, Mrs Rummel; it may have been only a rumour.

MRS RUMMEL. Well now, I must say – ! Wasn't it known all over the town? Didn't old Mrs Bernick nearly go bankrupt just because of that? I have it from my husband himself. But far be it from me to ...

MRS HOLT. Well, at any rate, the money didn't go to Mrs Dorf, because she –

MRS LYNGE. Yes, how were things between Dina's parents after that?

MRS RUMMEL. Well, Dorf went off and left his wife and child. But the lady herself was brazen enough to stay on here for a whole year. She didn't dare show herself in the theatre any more, but she kept herself by washing and sewing –

MRS HOLT. And then she tried to get a dancing-school going.

MRS RUMMEL. Naturally that didn't succeed. What parents would trust their children to a person like that? But she didn't hold out very long; our fine lady wasn't used to work, you see; she developed chest trouble and died.

MRS LYNGE. Well! That really is a dreadful story.

MRS RUMMEL. Yes, you can well believe it's been very hard on the Bernicks. It's the dark spot in the sun of their happiness, as my husband once put it. So don't ever speak of those things in this house, Mrs Lynge.

MRS HOLT. And, for heaven's sake, not about the half-sister either!

MRS LYNGE. Yes, hasn't Mrs Bernick a half-sister, too?

MRS RUMMEL. *Did* have – fortunately. Relations are broken off between them now. Oh yes, she was utterly eccentric! Just imagine, she cut her hair short and went about in men's boots in wet weather.

MRS HOLT. And when the half-brother – the ne'er-do-well – had run away, and the whole town, naturally, was feeling outraged over him, what do you suppose she does? She goes over and joins him!

MRS RUMMEL. Yes, but the scandal she caused before she went, Mrs Holt!

MRS HOLT. Sh! Don't talk about it.

MRS LYNGE. Heavens, did she make a scandal, too?

MRS RUMMEL. Yes, indeed. Now, I'll tell you, Mrs Lynge, Karsten Bernick had just got engaged to Betty Tönnesen and when he came in, arm in arm with her, to see her aunt and announce it –

MRS HOLT. – Because the Tönnesens were orphans, you know –

MRS RUMMEL. – Lona Hessel got up from the chair she was sitting in and gave Karsten Bernick – the charming, exquisite Karsten Bernick – a ringing box on the ear.

MRS LYNGE. Well, I never!

MRS HOLT. Yes, it's absolutely true.

MRS RUMMEL. And then she packed her trunk and went to America.

MRS LYNGE. Oh, she must have had her eye on him herself.

MRS RUMMEL. Exactly! Just what she had. She fancied they were going to make a match of it when he came home from Paris.

MRS HOLT. Just think of her believing a thing like that! Bernick, a man of the world, young and charming, an exquisite gentleman – all the women adoring him –

MRS RUMMEL. – Yet at the same time so correct, Mrs Holt; so steady in his morals –

MRS LYNGE. But what has become of this Miss Hessel in America?

MRS RUMMEL. Well, you see, over that there hangs, as my husband once put it, a veil which is better not lifted.

MRS LYNGE. What does that mean?

MRS RUMMEL. She has no connexion with the family any longer, as you can imagine; but the whole town knows this much, that she has sung for money in cafés over there –

MRS HOLT. – And that she has given public lectures –

MRS RUMMEL. – And that she has published a preposterous book.

MRS LYNGE. Just think.

MRS RUMMEL. Ah yes; Lona Hessel, too, is undoubtedly one of the dark spots in the Bernicks' happiness. So now you know all about it, Mrs Lynge. God knows, I only mentioned it to put you on your guard.

MRS LYNGE. Oh, you can trust me absolutely. But that poor Dina Dorf! I'm really sorry for her.

MRS RUMMEL. Oh, for her it was sheer good luck. Supposing she had remained in her parents' hands? We took charge of her, naturally, and advised her as best we could. Later on Miss Bernick arranged for her to come and live in the house here.

MRS HOLT. But she has always been a difficult child. You can imagine – all those bad examples. A girl like that is not like one of our own; she can be led, but she can't be driven, Mrs Lynge.

MRS RUMMEL. Sh! Here she comes. [*Aloud.*] Yes, Dina really is a capable girl. Oh, are you there, Dina? Here we are, sitting and neglecting our sewing!

MRS HOLT. Ah, how good your coffee smells, Dina dear. A cup of coffee like this in the middle of the morning –

MRS BERNICK [*out on the steps*]. The coffee is all ready.

[*Miss Bernick and Dina have, in the meantime, helped the maid to bring out the coffee things. The women all go and sit outside, talking with excessive kindliness to Dina. After a little while she comes into the room and looks for her needlework.*]

MRS BERNICK [*outside at the coffee-table*]. Dina, don't you want some, too?

DINA. No, thank you; I won't have any.

[*She sits down to her sewing. Mrs Bernick and Rörlund exchange a few words; a moment later he comes into the room.*]

RÖRLUND [*making an excuse to go across to the table, and speaking in a low voice*]. Dina.

DINA. Yes?

RÖRLUND. Why won't you come outside?

DINA. When I came in with the coffee I could see, from the look of the strange lady, that they'd been talking about me.

RÖRLUND. And didn't you see, too, how kind she was to you when you came out?

DINA. But that's what I can't stand!

RÖRLUND. You have an obstinate temperament, Dina.

DINA. Yes.

RÖRLUND. But why have you?

DINA. It's the way I'm made.

RÖRLUND. Couldn't you try to be different?

DINA. No.

RÖRLUND. Why not?

DINA [*looking at him*]. Because I'm like the 'Fallen Sisters'.

RÖRLUND. Why, Dina!

DINA. Mother was one of them, too.

RÖRLUND. Who has been talking to you about things like that?

DINA. No one; they never talk. Why don't they? They all handle me so gently – as though I should fall to pieces if – Ah, how I hate all this kindliness!

RÖRLUND. My dear Dina, I quite understand that you feel restricted here, but –

DINA. Yes, if only I could get right away! I could make my way all right, once I was living among people who weren't ... so ... so ...

RÖRLUND. So what?

DINA. So respectable and moral.

RÖRLUND. Now, Dina, you don't mean that.

DINA. Oh, you know quite well what I mean. Hilda and Netta come here every day so that I can take them as examples. I can never be perfect like them. And I don't mean to be. Ah, if only I were right away, I should be good, too!

RÖRLUND. But Dina, my dear, you are good.

DINA. What use it is to me here?

RÖRLUND. Going away. ... Are you thinking of it seriously?

DINA. I wouldn't stay a day longer if it weren't for you.

RÖRLUND. Tell me, Dina, why do you specially like being with me?

DINA. Because you teach me so much that's fine.

RÖRLUND. Fine? Do you call what I am able to teach you fine?

DINA. Yes. Or, rather ... you don't teach me anything, but when I hear you talk, it makes me see so much that is fine.

RÖRLUND. What exactly do you understand by a fine thing?

DINA. I've never thought about it.

RÖRLUND. Then think about it now. What do you understand by a fine thing?

DINA. A fine thing is something that is great – and far away.

RÖRLUND. Hm. My dear Dina, I am deeply concerned about you.

DINA. Only that?

RÖRLUND. You know quite well how indescribably dear you are to me.

DINA. If I were Hilda or Netta, you wouldn't be afraid of letting people see it.

RÖRLUND. Ah, Dina, you've no idea of the thousand considerations – When it's one's function to be a moral pillar of the community one lives in, why – one can't be too careful. If I were sure that people would put the right interpretation on my motives ... But that must take care of itself; you must and you shall be helped to rise. Dina, is it agreed that when I come – when circumstances allow me to come – and say, 'Here is my hand', that you will take it and be my wife? Do you promise me that, Dina?

DINA. Yes.

RÖRLUND. Thank you! Thank you. Because, for me, too – ... Ah, Dina, I'm so fond of you – sh! There's someone coming. Dina, for my sake, go out to the others.

[*She goes out to the coffee-table. At the same moment, Rummel, Sandstad and Vigeland come out from the farthest room on the left, followed by Bernick, who has a bundle of papers in his hand.*]

BERNICK. Well, then, the matter's settled.

VIGELAND. Yes, the Lord be praised. Let it stand.

RUMMEL. It *is* settled, Bernick! A Norseman's word stands fast as the rocks of the Dovrefjeld. You know that.

BERNICK. And no retreating, no weakening, whatever opposition we meet.

RUMMEL. We stand or go under together, Bernick.

HILMAR TÖNNESEN [who has come to the garden door]. Go under? With all due deference, isn't it the railway scheme that's going under?

BERNICK. No, on the contrary; that's to go ahead –

RUMMEL. – Full steam, Mr Tönnesen.

HILMAR TÖNNESEN [coming forward]. Really?

RÖRLUND. What?

MRS BERNICK [at the garden door]. But, my dear Karsten, what is all this – ?

BERNICK. My dear Betty! Now, how can that interest you? [To the three men.] But now we must get the lists drawn up. The sooner the better. As a matter of course, we four put our names down first. The position we occupy in the community makes it our duty to do everything we can.

SANDSTAD. That goes without saying, Mr Bernick.

RUMMEL. We'll bring it off, Bernick. We're pledged to that.

BERNICK. Oh yes. I've no fear about the result. We must get to work, each one in his own circle, and if we can once point to genuine, active sympathy in every section of the community, it follows automatically that the municipality will have to contribute its share.

MRS BERNICK. But, Karsten, you really must come and tell us –

BERNICK. Oh, my dear Betty, women can't grasp this kind of thing.

HILMAR TÖNNESEN. So you are really going to back the railway after all?

BERNICK. Yes, naturally.

RÖRLUND. But last year, sir – ?

BERNICK. Last year it was quite a different matter. Then they were talking of a coast-line –

VIGELAND. – Which would have been quite superfluous, Mr Rörlund, because we already have the steamship –

SANDSTAD. – And would have been disproportionately expensive –

RUMMEL. – Yes, and would have actually damaged vested interests here in town.

BERNICK. The main point was that it would have done no good to our community as a whole. Therefore I opposed it and so the inland route was adopted.

HILMAR TÖNNESEN. Yes, but that isn't going to touch the towns around here.

BERNICK. It's going to touch our town, my dear Hilmar. Because we're going to run a branch line down here.

HILMAR TÖNNESEN. Aha! Quite a new idea, then?

RUMMEL. Yes, a first-rate idea, isn't it?

RÖRLUND. Hm.

VIGELAND. It cannot be denied that Providence seems to have designed the terrain especially for a branch line.

RÖRLUND. Do you really say so, Mr Vigeland?

BERNICK. Yes, I must confess that I too consider I was specially guided. I made a journey up there on business this spring, and so by chance came into a valley where I'd never been before. It struck me like a flash of lightning that this was the place to lay a branch-line to town. I've had an engineer to survey the region: I have the preliminary calculations here, and the estimate: there is nothing to prevent it.

MRS BERNICK [*still at the garden door with the other women*]. But, my dear Karsten, fancy your keeping all this a secret!

BERNICK. Oh, my dear Betty, you wouldn't have been able to grasp the real nature of the business. Besides, I haven't spoken about it to a living person till today. But now the decisive moment's come; we must work openly and with all our strength. Yes, even if I have to risk everything I have, I'll put this business through.

RUMMEL. The same with us, Bernick; you can count on us.

RÖRLUND. Do you really expect so much, then, gentlemen, from this undertaking?

BERNICK. I should think we do! What a lift it will give to our whole community! Just think of the huge tracts of forest it will open up; think of all the rich deposits of ore that can be worked; think of the river, with one waterfall above another! The possibilities for industrial development there!

RÖRLUND. And you are not afraid that a more frequent intercourse with a corrupt world outside –

BERNICK. Oh no, make your mind easy, Mr Rörlund. Our industrious little town rests nowadays, thank God, on a sound moral foundation; we have all helped to drain it, if I may put it so; and we shall continue to do so, each in his own way. You, Mr Rörlund, continue your benefi-cent activity in our schools and homes. We, the prac-tical men of affairs, support society by spreading pros-perity in as wide a circle as possible. And our women – yes, come in, ladies; you are welcome to hear this – our women, I say, our wives and daughters – you must go on working undisturbed, ladies, at your benevolent tasks, and be, at the same time, a help and comfort to those nearest you, as my dear Betty and Marta are for me and Olaf – [*Looking round.*] Why, where's Olaf gone today?

MRS BERNICK. Oh, now it's the holidays, it's impossible to keep him at home.

BERNICK. Then he's sure to be down by the water again. You'll see; he'll come to grief before he's finished.

HILMAR TÖNNESEN. Pooh! A little sport with the forces of nature –

MRS RUMMEL. How nice of you to be such a real family man, Mr Bernick.

BERNICK. Ah well, the family, you know, is the kernel of the community. A good home, honourable and faithful friends, a small, close circle where no disturbing elements throw their shadows –

[*Krap, the head clerk, comes in from the right with letters and newspapers.*]

KRAP. The foreign mail, Mr Bernick. And a telegram from New York.

BERNICK [*taking it*]. Ah, from the owners of the *Indian Girl*.

RUMMEL. Ah, the post's come. Then I must ask you to excuse me.

SANDSTAD. Good-bye, Mr Bernick.

BERNICK. Good-bye, gentlemen, good-bye. And remember, now, we have a meeting this afternoon at five o'clock.

THE THREE MEN. Yes. Oh yes. Quite all right. [*They go out to the right.*]

BERNICK [*who has read the telegram*]. Well, this really is typically American! Absolutely outrageous!

MRS BERNICK. Goodness, Karsten, what is it?

BERNICK. Look here, Krap! Read it!

KRAP [*reading*]. 'Least possible repairs. Send *Indian Girl* soon as floatable. Good season. At worst, cargo keep her afloat.' Well, I must say –

BERNICK. 'Cargo keep her afloat'! These gentlemen know perfectly well that, with that cargo, she'll go to the bottom like a stone if anything happens.

RÖRLUND. Yes, this shows what things are like in these big communities that are praised so highly.

BERNICK. You're right there. No consideration, even for human life, once profit comes into the story. [*To Krap.*] Can the *Indian Girl* put to sea in four or five days?

KRAP. Yes, if Mr Vigeland will agree to our stopping work on the *Palm Tree* in the meantime.

BERNICK. Hm. He won't do that. Well, will you go through the mail, please? By the way, did you see Olaf down on the quay?

KRAP. No, Mr Bernick. [*He goes to the farthest room on the left.*]

BERNICK [*looking at the telegram again*]. These gentlemen think nothing of risking the lives of eighteen men –

HILMAR TÖNNESEN. Well, it's a seaman's calling to brave the elements. There must be something stimulating in being there, so to speak, with a slender plank between you and the depths –

BERNICK. I'd like to see the ship-owner here who could bring himself to do a thing like that! Not one. Not a single one. [*Catches sight of Olaf.*] Ah, thank goodness, there he is, all right.

[*Olaf, with a fishing-line in his hand, has come running up the street and in through the garden gate.*]

OLAF [*still in the garden*]. Uncle Hilmar, I've been down looking at the steamer.

BERNICK. Have you been on the wharf again?

OLAF. No, I was only out in a boat. Just think, Uncle Hilmar, there's a whole circus company come ashore with horses and wild animals; and there were such a lot of passengers, too!

MRS RUMMEL. Well! Are we really to see – circus-riders?

RÖRLUND. We? I trust not.

MRS RUMMEL. No, not *we*, of course, but –

DINA. I should like to see a circus.

OLAF. So should I.

HILMAR TÖNNESEN. You are a little idiot! Is that worth looking at? It's simply a matter of training. Now it's a different thing to see the gaucho racing over the pampas on his snorting mustang. But, good heavens! Here in these little places – !

OLAF [*taking hold of Miss Bernick*]. Aunt Marta, look, look! There they come!

MRS HOLT. Yes, good gracious! There they are.

MRS LYNGE. Oh! *Dreadful* people!

[*Several passengers and a crowd of townsfolk come along the street.*]

MRS RUMMEL. Oh yes, they're a regular lot of mountebanks. *Do* look at that woman in the grey dress, Mrs Holt; she's got a carpet-bag on her back.

MRS HOLT. Yes, look! She's carrying it on the handle of her sunshade. That will be the manager's wife, I suppose.

MRS RUMMEL. And there no doubt we have the manager himself; the man with the beard. Well, he looks exactly like a gangster. Don't look at him, Hilda.

MRS HOLT. Nor you either, Netta.

OLAF. Mother, the manager's waving to us.

BERNICK. What?

MRS BERNICK. What do you say, child?

MRS RUMMEL. Good heavens, yes! The woman's waving, too!

BERNICK. Now, that's too insolent.

MISS BERNICK [*with an involuntary cry*]. Ah!

MRS BERNICK. What is it, Marta?

MISS BERNICK. Oh no; nothing ... I only thought –

OLAF [*shouting with delight*]. Look, look! There come the others with the horses and the wild animals! And there are the Americans, too! All the sailors from the *Indian Girl*.

['*Yankee Doodle*' *can be heard, accompanied by clarinet and drum.*]

HILMAR TÖNNESEN [*stopping his ears*]. Ugh! Ugh!

RÖRLUND. I think we should withdraw a little, ladies; this

kind of thing is not for us. Let us go back to our work again.

MRS BERNICK. Should we pull the curtains, perhaps?

RÖRLUND. Yes, that was just what I was thinking.

[*The women take their places at the table. Rörlund shuts the garden door and pulls the curtains across it and the windows; the room becomes half-dark.*]

OLAF [*who is peeping out*]. Mother, the manager's wife is standing by the pump, washing her face.

MRS BERNICK. What! In the middle of the market-place?

MRS RUMMEL. And in broad daylight!

HILMAR TÖNNESEN. Well, if I happened to be on a desert journey and was standing by a spring, I shouldn't consider – Ugh! That appalling clarinet!

RÖRLUND. Really, the police would be quite justified in intervening.

BERNICK. Oh, come. One mustn't be too particular with foreigners; those people haven't got that deep-rooted sense of decency that keeps us within proper bounds. Let them go their own way. What does it matter to us? All this disorderliness – setting oneself up against tradition and good manners – fortunately for us it's quite alien to our community, if I may say so. What's this?

[*The strange woman comes briskly in through the door on the right.*]

THE WOMEN [*in shocked and low voices*]. The circus woman! The manager's wife!

MRS BERNICK. Heavens! What does this mean?

MISS BERNICK [*jumping up*]. Ah –

THE WOMEN. Good morning, Betty dear! Good morning, Marta! Good morning, my dear brother-in-law!

MRS BERNICK [*with a cry*]. Lona!

BERNICK [*falling back a step*]. As sure as I'm alive – !

MRS HOLT. But, goodness gracious – !

MRS RUMMEL. It can't be possible – !

HILMAR TÖNNESEN. *Well!* Ugh!

MRS BERNICK. Lona! Is it really – ?

MISS HESSEL. Really me? Why, of course it is! You can fall on my neck, if that's what you want to know.

HILMAR TÖNNESEN. Ugh! Ugh!

MRS BERNICK. And now you come here as – ?

BERNICK. – And are you really going to perform – ?

MISS HESSEL. Perform? Perform how?

BERNICK. Well, I mean – in the circus.

MISS HESSEL. Hahaha! My dear man, are you crazy? Do you think I belong to the circus? Well, it's true I've turned my hand to a good many trades and made a fool of myself in a good many ways –

MRS RUMMEL. H'm.

MISS HESSEL. But I never took up trick riding.

BERNICK. Then you're not –

MRS BERNICK. Ah, thank goodness!

MISS HESSEL. No, no; we came like other respectable people. Second class, it's true. But we're used to that.

MRS BERNICK. 'We', you say?

BERNICK [*a step nearer*]. Who are the 'we'?

MISS HESSEL. My boy and I, of course.

THE WOMEN [*with a cry*]. Your boy!

HILMAR TÖNNESEN. What!

RÖRLUND. Well, I must say – !

MRS BERNICK. But what do you mean, Lona?

MISS HESSEL. I mean John, of course. I haven't any other boy but John, so far as I know – or 'Johan', as you used to call him.

MRS BERNICK. Johan!

MRS RUMMEL [*aside to Mrs Lynge*]. The ne'er-do-well brother!

BERNICK [*hesitating*]. Is Johan with you?

MISS HESSEL. Of course, of course. I don't travel without him. But you all look so sad. And you're sitting in this half-light, sewing something white. There hasn't been a death in the family, has there?

RÖRLUND. My dear lady, you find yourself in the Society for Fallen Sisters.

MISS HESSEL [*lowering her voice*]. What do you say? Do you mean that these nice, quiet-looking women are –

MRS RUMMEL. Well! Now, I must say – !

MISS HESSEL. Oh, I see, I see! Bless me, if that isn't Mrs Rummel! And there's Mrs Holt, too! Well, we three haven't got younger since we last met. But look here, my good friends; let the Fallen Sisters wait for one day – they won't be any the worse for it. A happy occasion like this –

RÖRLUND. A home-coming is not always a happy occasion.

MISS HESSEL. Is that so? How do you read your Bible, Parson?

RÖRLUND. I am not a parson.

MISS HESSEL. Oh well, you will be some day. But my, oh my! These charity garments here smell of mortality; just as if they were shrouds. I'm used to the air of the prairies, let me tell you.

BERNICK [*mopping his forehead*]. Yes, it certainly is a little oppressive in here.

MISS HESSEL. You just wait; we'll soon get up out of the vault. [*Pulling the curtains aside.*] We must have broad daylight when my boy comes in. My yes! then you'll see a boy worth looking at –

HILMAR TÖNNESEN. Ugh! Ugh!

MISS HESSEL [*opening the doors and the windows*]. Well, that is to say, when he's managed to get a wash, up at the hotel. He got as grubby as a pig on the steamer.

HILMAR TÖNNESEN. Ugh! Ugh!

MISS HESSEL. 'Ugh'? Why, surely it's never – ! [*Pointing to Hilmar and asking the others*] Is *he* still loafing about here, saying 'Ugh' all the time?

HILMAR TÖNNESEN. I don't 'loaf'; I'm staying here for the sake of my health.

MISS HESSEL [*who has caught sight of Olaf*]. Is he yours, Betty? Give us your hand, boy. Or perhaps you're afraid of your ugly old aunt?

RÖRLUND [*as he puts his book under his arm*]. Ladies, I don't think we are in the mood for any more work today. But we meet again tomorrow, do we not?

MISS HESSEL [*as the visitors get up to say good-bye*]. Yes, let's do that. I shall be there.

RÖRLUND. *You?* May I ask, Miss Hessel, what you are going to do in our community?

MISS HESSEL. I am going to let in some fresh air, Mr Parson.

ACT TWO

——————— * ———————

[*The garden room in the Bernicks' house. Mrs Bernick is sitting alone at the work-table with her sewing. A little later Bernick comes in from the right with his hat on and carrying his gloves and stick.*]

MRS BERNICK. You home already, Karsten?

BERNICK. Yes. I've got a man coming.

MRS BERNICK [*with a sigh*]. Ah yes. Johan will be down here again, I expect.

BERNICK. I tell you, it's one of my men I'm seeing. [*Putting down his hat.*] Where are all the ladies gone today?

MRS BERNICK. Mrs Rummel and Hilda hadn't time to come.

BERNICK. Ah yes. Sent an excuse?

MRS BERNICK. Yes. They had so much to see to at home.

BERNICK. Only to be expected. And the others aren't coming either, of course?

MRS BERNICK. No; they were prevented, too, today.

BERNICK. I could have told you that beforehand. Where's Olaf gone?

MRS BERNICK. I let him go out for a little while with Dina.

BERNICK. Hm; Dina. Giddy little minx! Making all that fuss of Johan as soon as she saw him yesterday.

MRS BERNICK. But, Karsten dear, Dina hasn't the least idea—

BERNICK. Well, Johan, anyway, should have had the tact not to pay special attention to her. I saw the expression on Vigeland's face.

MRS BERNICK [*dropping her sewing in her lap*]. Karsten, can you imagine what they've come home for?

BERNICK. Hm. Well, he has a farm over there which presumably isn't going very well. And she mentioned yesterday that they had to travel second class –

MRS BERNICK. Yes. I'm afraid it may well be something of that sort. But her coming with him! She! After the unpardonable way she insulted you!

BERNICK. Oh, don't think about those old stories.

MRS BERNICK. How can I think of anything else just now? After all, he is my brother. Though it's not on his account ... but all the unpleasantness it will make for you, Karsten, I'm so dreadfully afraid that –

BERNICK. What are you afraid about?

MRS BERNICK. Might they not want to imprison him for that missing money of your mother's?

BERNICK. What nonsense! How can they prove that there was any money missing?

MRS BERNICK. Good gracious, the whole town knows that, unfortunately! And you yourself said –

BERNICK. I've never said anything. The town knows nothing about the business. Those were all unfounded rumours.

MRS BERNICK. Oh, how magnanimous you are, Karsten!

BERNICK. Don't let's have any more of these reminiscences, I tell you. You don't know how you're tormenting me, raking up all this. [*He paces up and down the room and then flings his stick away.*] That they should come home just now – now, when I need perfect goodwill both from the town and the Press! There will be letters to the newspapers all over the district. Whether I'm friendly to them or unfriendly, there will be gossip and insinuations. ... They'll rake up all this ancient history – just as you do. In a community like ours – [*Throwing his gloves on the table.*] And not a single person here I can talk to, or get any support from.

MRS BERNICK. No one at all, Karsten?

BERNICK. No, who *could* there be? That they should come down on me just at this moment! There's no question about it: they'll make a scandal, one way or another – she especially. It's a downright calamity to have people like that in one's family.

MRS BERNICK. Well, I really can't help –

BERNICK. What can't you help? Their being relations? No, that's perfectly true.

MRS BERNICK. And I didn't ask them to come home, either.

BERNICK. There we are! 'I didn't ask them to come home. I didn't write for them. I didn't drag them home by the hair of their heads.' Oh, I know the whole thing off by heart!

MRS BERNICK [*bursting into tears*]. But you're so unkind –

BERNICK. Yes, that's right! Start crying, so that the town can have that to talk about as well. Stop that nonsense, Betty. Go and sit outside; somebody might come in. Do you want them to see Mrs Bernick with red eyes? Yes, that would be fine, if it came out everywhere that – Tsh! I hear somebody in the hall. [*There is a knock.*] Come in!

[*Mrs Bernick goes out to the garden steps with her sewing. Aune comes in from the right.*]

AUNE. Good morning, sir.

BERNICK. Good morning. Well, you can guess what I want you for?

AUNE. The head clerk said something yesterday, sir, about your not being satisfied with –

BERNICK. I am dissatisfied with the whole state of affairs at the yard, Aune. You have made no progress with the wreck. The *Palm Tree* ought to have been under sail long ago. Mr Vigeland comes here bothering me every day. He's a difficult man to have for a partner.

AUNE. The *Palm Tree* can go to sea the day after tomorrow.

BERNICK. At last! But the American, the *Indian Girl*; she's been lying here five weeks and –

AUNE. The American? I understood that we were to make every effort to finish your own boat first.

BERNICK. I have given you no reason to think that. You should have got on as fast as possible with the American, too. But you haven't.

AUNE. The hull of the vessel's absolutely rotten, sir; the more we patch it the worse it gets.

BERNICK. That's not the real source of the trouble. Krap has told me the whole truth. You don't understand how to work with the new machines I've installed – or rather, you won't work with them.

AUNE. Mr Bernick, sir, I'm getting on for sixty; right from boyhood, I've been used to the old way of working –

BERNICK. We can't use it nowadays. You mustn't think, Aune, that it's for the sake of the profit; I don't need that, luckily. But I have to consider the community in which I live and the business I direct. Progress must come from me, or it won't come at all.

AUNE. I want progress too, sir.

BERNICK. Yes. For your own limited circle – for the working class. Oh, I know all about your political agitations. You make speeches, you stir the people up. But when a chance of tangible progress turns up – as now, with our machines – you won't collaborate; you're afraid.

AUNE. Yes, I certainly am afraid, Mr Bernick; I am afraid for all the people the machines rob of their bread. You often speak, sir, of considering the community; but I think the community has its duties, too. How dare science and capital set these new inventions to work before the community has educated a generation that can use them?

BERNICK. You read and think too much, Aune. You get no good from it. It's that that makes you discontented with your position.

AUNE. It isn't that, sir. But I can't bear to see one good workman after another discharged and losing his livelihood because of these machines.

BERNICK. Hm. When printing was discovered, a good many scribes lost their livelihood.

AUNE. Would you have been so pleased with that invention, sir, if you'd been a scribe in those days?

BERNICK. I didn't fetch you here to argue. I sent for you to tell you that the damaged vessel, the *Indian Girl*, must be ready to sail the day after tomorrow.

AUNE. But, sir –

BERNICK. You hear me: the day after tomorrow. At the same time as our own boat. Not an hour later. I have my own good reasons for pressing the matter. Have you read this morning's paper? Well, then you know that the Americans have been making trouble again. This rowdy gang is upsetting the whole town; not a night goes by without fighting in the public-houses and in the streets. Their abominable behaviour in other ways I won't talk about.

AUNE. Yes, it's true enough; they're a bad lot.

BERNICK. And who gets the blame for this nuisance? I do! Yes, it all falls on *me*. These newspaper men are blaming us in their indirect way for using all our resources on the *Palm Tree*. And I, whose purpose in life is to influence my fellow-citizens by my example, I have to let things like that be cast in my teeth. I can't stand it. I can't have my name besmirched like that.

AUNE. Oh, your name is good enough to bear that, sir, and more.

BERNICK. Not at the moment. Just now I need all the respect and goodwill my fellow-citizens can give me. I have a big undertaking on hand, as you will have heard. But if ill-disposed people succeed in shaking the absolute confidence I command, it may involve me in serious difficulties. So I intend to silence these newspaper men and their malicious criticism at all costs. That's why I have set the limit at the day after tomorrow.

AUNE. You might just as well set the limit at this afternoon, sir.

BERNICK. You mean I'm asking for impossibilities?

AUNE. Yes, with the workmen we have now.

BERNICK. Very well. Then we must look somewhere else.

AUNE. Are you really going to lay off still more of the old hands?

BERNICK. No, I'm not thinking of that.

AUNE. Because I think it would make bad blood, both in the town and in the Press, if you did that.

BERNICK. Quite possibly. So we won't do that. But if the *Indian Girl* isn't cleared the day after tomorrow, I shall discharge *you*.

AUNE [*with a start*]. Me? [*Laughing.*] Now you're joking, sir.

BERNICK. You had better not rely on that.

AUNE. You couldn't think of discharging *me*? Me, whose father and grandfather worked at the shipyard all their lives, and I myself, too –

BERNICK. Who's forcing me to it?

AUNE. You're asking impossibilities, sir.

BERNICK. Oh? 'Where there's a will there's a way.' Yes or no; answer me definitely, or you're discharged on the spot.

AUNE [*a step nearer*]. Have you really thought, sir, what it means, to discharge an old workman? You expect him to look for another job? Well, of course, he can do that; but is that all there is to it? You ought to be in the home of a workman discharged like that, the evening he comes back and puts down his tool-chest.

BERNICK. Do you think I am discharging you without regret? Haven't I always been a considerate employer?

AUNE. So much the worse, sir. For that very reason they won't blame you, at home. They won't say anything to me, because they daren't. But they'll look at me when I'm not noticing, and sort of think 'He must have asked for it'. You see, it's that – it's that I can't bear. I may be poor, but I'm looked on as the head of my own family. My little home – it's a little community too, sir. And I've been able to support it and keep it up because my wife believed in me and my children believed in me. Now, that will all go to pieces.

BERNICK. Well, if nothing else can be done, the lesser must give way to the greater; when all is said, the individual must be sacrificed to the majority. That's the only answer I can give you, and that's the way things work in this world. But you're a stiff-necked man, Aune! You're opposing me, not because you can't do anything else, but because you don't want to prove the superiority of machines over hand-work.

AUNE. And you're insisting on this, sir, because you know that if you turn me off you'll at least show the Press your good intentions.

BERNICK. Well, what if I am? You hear what it involves for me – on the one hand to have the whole Press attacking me, and on the other to get it well-disposed towards me at the moment when I'm working for a great cause and the public benefit. Well, what can I do? Can I deal with it any way but as I am doing? I tell you the question here is whether I should keep up your home, as you put it, and so perhaps keep down hundreds of new homes – hundreds of homes that will never be set up, will never have a fire lit, if I don't succeed in putting through what I'm working for now. That's why I have given you the choice.

AUNE. Well, if that's how it is, then I've nothing more to say.

BERNICK. Hm. My dear Aune, I'm very sorry we have to part.

AUNE. We're *not* parting, sir.

BERNICK. What?

AUNE. Even a working man has something to stand up for in this world.

BERNICK. Very true; very true. And you think, then, you can promise – ?

AUNE. The *Indian Girl* can be cleared the day after to-morrow. [*He bows and goes out to the right.*]

BERNICK. Aha! I made that stiff-necked fellow give way at last. I take that as a good omen.

[*Hilmar Tönnesen, with a cigar in his mouth, comes through the garden gate.*]

HILMAR TÖNNESEN [*on the steps*]. Good morning, Betty! Good morning, Bernick!

MRS BERNICK. Good morning.

HILMAR TÖNNESEN. Why, you've been crying, I see. You know about it, then?

MRS BERNICK. About what?

HILMAR TÖNNESEN. That the scandal is in full swing? Ugh!

BERNICK. What do you mean?

HILMAR TÖNNESEN [*coming in*]. Why, the two Americans are going about the streets, showing themselves off with Dina Dorf.

MRS BERNICK [*following him*]. But, Hilmar, can they possibly – ?

HILMAR TÖNNESEN. Yes, unfortunately; it's perfectly true. Lona was even so tactless as to call after me; but of course I pretended not to hear.

BERNICK. And it certainly won't have gone unnoticed.

HILMAR TÖNNESEN. No, you may be sure it won't. People stopped and stared after them. It seemed to spread over the town like wildfire – like a fire on the western prairies. People were standing in the windows of all the houses, waiting for the procession to come by; cheek by jowl behind the venetian blinds. Ugh! Oh, I beg your pardon, Betty; I say 'Ugh' because all this gets on my nerves. If it goes on, I shall have to think of going farther afield.

MRS BERNICK. But you should have spoken to him and pointed out –

HILMAR TÖNNESEN. In the open street? No, thank you – really! This fellow, on top of everything, daring to show himself here in town! Well, we'll see if the papers won't put a stopper on him. Yes, I'm sorry, Betty, but –

BERNICK. The papers, do you say? Have you heard any hint of that?

HILMAR TÖNNESEN. Well, I have. ... When I left you yesterday evening I strolled up to the club, because I didn't feel very well. I saw all right, by the sudden silence, that the two Americans were being discussed. Then in comes that impudent fellow Hammer, the editor, and congratulates me loudly on the return of my rich cousin.

BERNICK. Rich – ?

HILMAR TÖNNESEN. Yes, that's how he put it. I looked him up and down, of course, with a well-deserved stare and gave him to understand that I knew nothing about

Johan Tönnesen's wealth. 'Really,' says he, 'that's odd. In America people generally get on if they've something to start with, and, after all, your cousin didn't go over there with empty hands.'

BERNICK. Well, please don't –

MRS BERNICK [*in distress*]. There, you see, Karsten –

HILMAR TÖNNESEN. Well, at any rate, I've had a sleepless night on account of that fellow. And there he is going about the streets looking as if there was nothing against him. Why on earth didn't he disappear for good? It's intolerable, how some people hang on to life.

MRS BERNICK. Good heavens, Hilmar! What are you saying?

HILMAR TÖNNESEN. Oh, I'm not saying anything. But there he goes and escapes with a whole skin from railway accidents and attacks of Californian bears and Black-foot Indians ... Never even scalped! Ugh! Here they are.

BERNICK [*looking up the street*]. Olaf's with them, too.

HILMAR TÖNNESEN. Oh, of course. They want to remind people that they belong to the first family in town. Look, look! There come all the idlers out of the drug-store, staring after them and making remarks. This really is too much for my nerves. How on earth a man is to keep the flag of idealism flying under these conditions – !

BERNICK. They're coming straight here. Listen now, Betty; it's my specific wish that you should treat them with all possible friendliness.

MRS BERNICK. Will you really let me, Karsten?

BERNICK. Certainly, certainly. And you too, Hilmar. They won't be here very long, let us hope, and when we are alone with them – no hints. We mustn't do anything to hurt their feelings.

MRS BERNICK. Oh, Karsten, how magnanimous you are!

BERNICK. Oh, well; never mind that.

MRS BERNICK. No, let me thank you. And forgive me for being so cross before. You had every reason for –

BERNICK. Now, that's enough, I tell you!

HILMAR TÖNNESEN. Ugh!

[*Johan Tönnesen and Dina, and after them Miss Hessel and Olaf, come in through the garden.*]

MISS HESSEL. Good morning, good morning, my dear people.

JOHAN TÖNNESEN. We've been out looking at all the old places, Karsten.

BERNICK. Yes, so I hear. A good many changes, aren't there?

MISS HESSEL. The great and good works of Mr Karsten Bernick everywhere. We have been up in the public gardens you presented to the town –

BERNICK. Oh, there?

MISS HESSEL. 'The gift of Karsten Bernick', as it says over the entrance. Oh, yes, you're the man who does everything here.

JOHAN TÖNNESEN. And you've got some fine ships, too. I met my old school-fellow, the captain of the *Palm Tree*.

MISS HESSEL. Oh yes, and you've built a new schoolhouse, too; and I hear it's you who've laid on the town's gas and water.

BERNICK. Oh well, one must work for the community one lives in.

MISS HESSEL. Very decent of you. But it's a pleasure, too, to see how people value you. I don't think I'm vain, but I couldn't help reminding one or two people we talked to that we belonged to the family.

HILMAR TÖNNESEN. Ugh!

MISS HESSEL. Are you saying 'ugh' to that?

HILMAR TÖNNESEN. No, I said 'hm'.

MISS HESSEL. Oh well; do, if you want to, poor fellow. But you're quite alone today?

MRS BERNICK. Yes, we're alone today.

MISS HESSEL. Oh, by the way, we met one or two of the Virtuous Sisters up at the market-place; they seemed to be very busy. But *we* haven't managed to have a proper talk yet. Yesterday, those three railway pioneers were here, and then we had that parson –

HILMAR TÖNNESEN. – Schoolmaster –

MISS HESSEL. *I* call him the parson. But what do you think of *my* work now, these fifteen years? Hasn't he grown a fine fellow? Who would recognize the madcap who ran away from home?

HILMAR TÖNNESEN. Hm –

JOHAN TÖNNESEN. Ah, Lona, don't boast too much.

MISS HESSEL. No, I'm really proud of it. Heaven knows, it's the only thing I have done in the world, but it gives me a kind of right to be here. Yes, Johan, when I think how we two started over there, with only our four paws –

HILMAR TÖNNESEN. Hands.

MISS HESSEL. I say paws. They were grubby enough –

HILMAR TÖNNESEN. Ugh!

MISS HESSEL. – And empty, at that.

HILMAR TÖNNESEN. Empty! Well, I must say – !

MISS HESSEL. What must you say?

HILMAR TÖNNESEN. I must say – ugh!

[*He goes out on the garden steps.*]

MISS HESSEL. What's the matter with the man?

BERNICK. Oh, don't worry about him; he is rather nervous nowadays. But wouldn't you like to see round the garden a little? You haven't been down there yet and I have an hour free just now.

MISS HESSEL. Oh yes, I should. You can well believe I've been here in this garden with you often enough in my thoughts.

MRS BERNICK. You'll find that there have been great changes there, too.

[*Bernick, his wife and Miss Hessel go down into the garden, where they can be seen, off and on, during the following dialogue.*]

OLAF [*at the garden door*]. Uncle Hilmar, do you know what Uncle Johan asked me? He asked if I'd like to go to America with him.

HILMAR TÖNNESEN. You, you little idiot – you who go about tied to your mother's apron-strings!

OLAF. Yes, but I won't any longer. You'll see, when I'm grown up –

HILMAR TÖNNESEN. Oh, stuff and nonsense! You've no real craving for the stimulating effects of –

[*They go down together into the garden.*]

JOHAN TÖNNESEN [*to Dina, who has taken off her hat and stands in the doorway on the right, shaking the dust off her dress*]. You've got really warm with your walk.

DINA. Yes, it was a lovely walk. I've never had such a lovely walk before.

JOHAN TÖNNESEN. Perhaps you don't often go for walks in the morning?

DINA. Oh yes; but only with Olaf.

JOHAN TÖNNESEN. I see. Perhaps you'd rather go down the garden than stay here?

DINA. No, I'd rather stay here.

JOHAN TÖNNESEN. So would I. And so it's agreed, that we go for a walk like that every morning.

DINA. No, Mr Tönnesen, you mustn't do that.

JOHAN TÖNNESEN. What mustn't I do? You promised, you know.

DINA. Yes, but now I think it over, I – You can't go out with me.

JOHAN TÖNNESEN. But why not?

DINA. Of course, you're a stranger; you can't understand it. But I'll tell you –

JOHAN TÖNNESEN. Well?

DINA. No, I'd rather not talk about it.

JOHAN TÖNNESEN. Oh yes, do. You can talk to me about anything.

DINA. Well, I must explain. ... I am not like the other girls. There is something – something about me. That's why you can't.

JOHAN TÖNNESEN. But I can't make head or tail of all this. You haven't done anything wrong?

DINA. No, I haven't myself, but – no, now I won't talk about it any more. You'll get to know it all right from the others.

JOHAN TÖNNESEN. Hm.

DINA. But there was something else I wanted to ask you about.

JOHAN TÖNNESEN. And what was that?

DINA. Is it really so easy to – get to be something worth while over there in America?

JOHAN TÖNNESEN. Well, it isn't always exactly easy. One often has to suffer a good deal and work hard at first.

DINA. Yes, I'd willingly do that.

JOHAN TÖNNESEN. You?

DINA. I can work all right. I am strong and healthy and Aunt Marta has taught me a lot.

JOHAN TÖNNESEN. Well, why the dickens don't you come along with us, then?

DINA. Ah, now you're only joking; you said that to Olaf, too. But this was what I wanted to know, whether the people over there are very ... very sort of virtuous?

JOHAN TÖNNESEN. Virtuous?

DINA. Yes. I mean, are they sort of ... proper and respectable, as they are here?

JOHAN TÖNNESEN. Well, at any rate they're not so bad as people here think they are. There's no need for you to be afraid of that.

DINA. You don't understand me. What I want is that they *shouldn't* be so proper and virtuous.

JOHAN TÖNNESEN. No? What do you want them to be then?

DINA. I should like them to be natural.

JOHAN TÖNNESEN. Why, yes; that's maybe just what they are.

DINA. Why, then, it would be a grand thing for me if I could get over there.

JOHAN TÖNNESEN. Yes, it surely would. So you must come with us.

DINA. No, I wouldn't go with you; I'd have to go alone. Oh, I should make something of it; I should soon be all right.

BERNICK [*standing at the bottom of the garden steps with the two women*]. Stay there, stay there; I'll get it, Betty dear. You might easily catch cold. [*He comes into the room and looks for his wife's shawl.*]

MRS BERNICK [*outside in the garden*]. You must come too, Johan; we're just going down to the grotto.

BERNICK. No, Johan must stay here for the moment. Here, Dina; take my wife's shawl and go with them. Johan's going to stay here with me, Betty dear. I want to hear how things are going over there.

MRS BERNICK. Very well. You come and join us, then. You know where to find us.

[*Mrs Bernick, Miss Hessel and Dina go down through the garden to the left. Bernick watches them for a moment, goes across and shuts the farther door on the left, then goes up to Johan and seizes both his hands, clasping and shaking them.*]

BERNICK. Johan, now we are alone; you must let me thank you.

JOHAN TÖNNESEN. Oh, nonsense!

BERNICK. My house and home, the happiness of my family life, my whole position as a citizen of this community – I owe it all to you.

JOHAN TÖNNESEN. Well, I'm glad of it, my dear Karsten. So some good came of that silly business, after all.

BERNICK [grasping his hands again]. Thank you, thank you, all the same! Not one man in ten thousand would have done what you did for me then.

JOHAN TÖNNESEN. It's not worth talking about! Weren't we both young and irresponsible? After all, one of us had to take the blame.

BERNICK. But whose business was that, if not the guilty one's?

JOHAN TÖNNESEN. Ah, no! On that occasion it was the business of the innocent one. I was free and independent and had no relations; it was an absolute blessing to me to get away from that grind in the office. You, on the other hand, had your old mother still alive; and, besides, you'd just become secretly engaged to Betty, and she was so fond of you. What would have become of her if she had come to know – ?

BERNICK. True; true. But –

JOHAN TÖNNESEN. And wasn't it purely for Betty's sake that you broke off that affair with Madame Dorf? After all, it was simply in order to make a clean break that you were up at her place that evening –

BERNICK. Yes, that accursed evening when that drunken fellow came home! Yes, Johan, it was for Betty's sake; but still ... to think that you could be so magnanimous, turn appearances against yourself and go away –

JOHAN TÖNNESEN. Don't be so full of scruples, my dear Karsten! We agreed it should be that way. You had to be saved and you were my friend. Oh, I was mighty proud

of that friendship! Here was I, drudging along like a poor
stay-at-home; and there were you, coming back from
your grand foreign tour, a distinguished gentleman.
You'd been in London and Paris. And then you chose me
for your friend, although I was four years younger than
you. Oh yes, it was because you were making love to
Betty; I realize that now, all right. But how proud I was
of it! And who wouldn't have been? Who wouldn't have
willingly sacrificed himself for you? Especially as it only
meant a month's gossip – and with it a chance to escape
into the wide world.

BERNICK. Hm. My dear Johan, I will tell you frankly that
the episode isn't quite forgotten yet.

JOHAN TÖNNESEN. Isn't it? Well, what does it matter to
me, once I'm settled over there again on my farm –

BERNICK. You're going back, then?

JOHAN TÖNNESEN. Of course.

BERNICK. But not too soon, I hope?

JOHAN TÖNNESEN. As soon as possible. It was only to
please Lona that I came over with her.

BERNICK. Oh? How was that?

JOHAN TÖNNESEN. Well, you see, Lona isn't young any
longer, and a kind of homesickness has come over her
lately – only she wouldn't ever admit it. [Smiling.] How
could she dare leave an irresponsible creature like me
alone behind her? – me, who at only nineteen had been
mixed up in –

BERNICK. And then?

JOHAN TÖNNESEN. Well, Karsten, now I'm going to
make a confession I'm ashamed of.

BERNICK. You haven't told her the real story, have you?

JOHAN TÖNNESEN. Yes, I have. It was wrong of me, but
I couldn't do anything else. You've no idea what Lona
has been to me. You've never been able to stand her, but

to me she's been like a mother. In those first years, when we had such a tough time over there – my, how she worked! And when I was ill for a long time and couldn't earn anything, and couldn't prevent her, she took to singing in the cafés; she gave a course of lectures that people made fun of, and wrote a book that she laughed and cried over afterwards – all to keep my body and soul together. Could I watch her, last winter, going about pining for home, when she had struggled so for me? No, I couldn't do that, Karsten. And so I said, 'You go, Lona. You needn't be anxious about me; I'm not so irresponsible as you think.' And so – she came to know.

BERNICK. And how did she take it?

JOHAN TÖNNESEN. Well, she took the view (and quite true, too) that since I knew I was innocent, I needn't mind making a trip over here myself. But make your mind easy; Lona won't give anything away and I'll keep a better hold on my tongue another time.

BERNICK. Yes, yes. I'll count on that.

JOHAN TÖNNESEN. Here is my hand. And now don't let's talk about that old business any more. Fortunately, it's the only piece of folly either of us has been mixed up in, I fancy. Now I'm really going to enjoy the few days I shall have here. You can't think what a jolly walk we had this morning. Who would have thought that little monkey who ran around and played angels in the theatre – ! But, tell me, old man, what happened to her parents afterwards?

BERNICK. Why, my dear Johan, I don't know anything to tell you, except what I wrote you directly after you'd gone. You got the two letters all right?

JOHAN TÖNNESEN. Oh yes, I did. I've got them both. That drunken swine ran away from her, didn't he?

BERNICK. And broke his neck later on when he was drunk.

JOHAN TÖNNESEN. And she died soon after, too? But of course you did all you could for her, without attracting attention?

BERNICK. She was proud. She didn't betray anything and she wouldn't accept anything.

JOHAN TÖNNESEN. Well, in any case, you did the right thing in taking Dina into your house.

BERNICK. Yes, that's true. But, as a matter of fact, it was really Marta who was responsible for that.

JOHAN TÖNNESEN. So it was Marta? Yes, that reminds me – where's Marta today?

BERNICK. Oh, *she?* When she hasn't her school to go to, she has her sick people.

JOHAN TÖNNESEN. It was Marta, then, who looked after her?

BERNICK. Marta has always had a certain weakness for education. That's why she took a post in the Council School. It was very silly of her.

JOHAN TÖNNESEN. Yes, she looked fagged out yesterday. I'm rather afraid her health isn't good enough for it.

BERNICK. Oh, as far as her health goes, I expect she could manage it. But it is awkward for me. It looks as though I – her brother – wasn't willing to support her.

JOHAN TÖNNESEN. Support her? I thought she had enough to live on of her own –

BERNICK. Not a penny. You remember what a difficult time that was for my mother when you went away. She carried on for a time with my help. But naturally I couldn't go on like that indefinitely, so I had myself taken into the firm. But it didn't work very well that way either, so I had to take control of the whole concern. And when we made up our balance-sheet it came out that there was practically nothing left of mother's share.

And as mother died soon afterwards, of course Marta was left with nothing.

JOHAN TÖNNESEN. Poor Marta!

BERNICK. Poor? Why? Surely you don't think I let her want for anything? Oh no; that I can say – I'm a good brother. She lives with us, of course, and eats at our table. She can easily clothe herself on her teacher's salary, and a single woman – what more does she need?

JOHAN TÖNNESEN. Hm. We don't think that way in America.

BERNICK. No, I can well believe it, in a revolutionary society like America. But here in our little world, where, thank God, corruption has made no inroads – not so far, at any rate – here, women are content to take a seemly even if retiring, position. Beside, it's Marta's own fault. She might have been provided for long ago if she had chosen.

JOHAN TÖNNESEN. You mean she could have married?

BERNICK. Yes. She could have been very comfortably settled indeed. She's had several good offers, oddly enough. A woman with no private means, no longer young and quite undistinguished.

JOHAN TÖNNESEN. Undistinguished?

BERNICK. Oh I don't hold that against her. I don't in the least want her to be any different. You know, in a big house like ours, it is always convenient to have an ordinary sort of person like that who can be turned on to anything that comes along.

JOHAN TÖNNESEN. Yes, but she herself?

BERNICK. She? How do you mean? Why, of course, she has plenty to interest herself in; she has me and Betty and Olaf and – and *me*. People shouldn't think primarily of themselves, especially not women. We all have a community, greater or smaller, to support and work for. I certainly have, at any rate. [*Indicating Krap, who has come in from the right.*] There you have an instance on the spot. Do you think it is my own affairs that take up my time? Not a bit of it. [*Quickly, to Krap.*] Well?

KRAP [*softly, showing him a pile of papers*]. All the purchase contracts in order.

BERNICK. Excellent! Capital! Now, my dear fellow, I'm afraid you'll have to excuse me for the moment. [*Quietly and with a shake of the hand.*] Thank you, thank you, Johan. And be sure that anything I can do to be of service to you – well, you understand. Come along, Mr Krap. [*They go into Bernick's room.*]

JOHAN TÖNNESEN [*looking after him for a time*]. Hm.
[*He is about to go into the garden. At that moment Miss Bernick comes in from the right with a little basket on her arm.*]

JOHAN TÖNNESEN. Ah, hullo, Marta!

MISS BERNICK. Oh, Johan! Is it you?

JOHAN TÖNNESEN. You out so early, too?

MISS BERNICK. Yes. If you wait a moment, the others will be here quite soon.
[*About to go out on the left.*]

JOHAN TÖNNESEN. Look here, Marta, are you always in such a hurry?

MISS BERNICK. I?

JOHAN TÖNNESEN. Yesterday you kept out of the way, so that I couldn't get a word with you, and today –

MISS BERNICK. Yes, but –

JOHAN TÖNNESEN. We were always together before, we two old playfellows.

MISS BERNICK. Ah, Johan, that is a great many years ago.

JOHAN TÖNNESEN. Oh, well, it's fifteen years ago; neither more nor less. Do you think I've changed so much, then?

MISS BERNICK. You? Why yes, you too, though –

JOHAN TÖNNESEN. What do you mean?

MISS BERNICK. Oh, nothing. ...

JOHAN TÖNNESEN. It doesn't exactly seem to have cheered you up to see me again!

MISS BERNICK. I have waited so long, Johan – too long.

JOHAN TÖNNESEN. Waited? For me to come?

MISS BERNICK. Yes.

JOHAN TÖNNESEN. And why did you think I would come?

MISS BERNICK. To put right the injury you had done.

JOHAN TÖNNESEN. I?

MISS BERNICK. Have you forgotten that a woman died in need and shame on your account? Have you forgotten that on your account the best years of a growing child's life were embittered?

JOHAN TÖNNESEN. And must I hear this from you? Marta, hasn't your brother ever –

MISS BERNICK. Hasn't he what ?

JOHAN TÖNNESEN. Hasn't he ever – well, I mean, hasn't he ever said a word to excuse me?

MISS BERNICK. Oh, well, Johan, you know Karsten's strict principles.

JOHAN TÖNNESEN. Hm. Oh, quite so. I know my old friend Karsten's strict principles. But this is really – ! Oh, well. I've just been talking to him. I think he has altered rather.

MISS BERNICK. How can you say that? Karsten has always been an exceptional man.

JOHAN TÖNNESEN. Well, I didn't mean it quite like that. But never mind. Hm. Now I realize the light you've seen me in. It's the ne'er-do-well's homecoming you have been waiting for.

MISS BERNICK. Listen, Johan. I will tell you what light I've seen you in. [Pointing down into the garden.] Do you see the girl playing down there in the grass with Olaf?

That's Dina. You remember the confused letter you wrote me when you went away? You wrote that I was to believe in you. I have believed in you, Johan. All the wicked things we heard of after you'd gone – they must have been the wildness of youth, done without thought, on the impulse of the moment.

JOHAN TÖNNESEN. What do you mean?

MISS BERNICK. Oh, you understand well enough. Don't let's talk about it any more. But of course you had to go away and begin again, a new life. Do you see, Johan, I have been your deputy here at home – I, your old play-fellow. The duties you forgot to discharge here, or could not – I have discharged them for you. I am telling you this so that you shall not have that too to reproach yourself with. The child that was wronged, I have been a mother to, have brought her up as best I could –

JOHAN TÖNNESEN. And wasted the whole of your life in doing it –

MISS BERNICK. It's not been wasted. But you're late in coming, Johan.

JOHAN TÖNNESEN. Marta – if only I could tell you. ... Well, let me at any rate thank you for your faithful friendship.

MISS BERNICK [smiling sadly]. Hm. Well, so now we have talked it out, Johan. Hush; someone's coming. Good-bye. I can't ... now –

[She goes out through the farthest door at the left back. Miss Hessel comes in from the garden, followed by Mrs Bernick.]

MRS BERNICK [still in the garden]. But, good heavens, Lona, what are you thinking of?

MISS HESSEL. Leave me alone, I tell you. I must talk to him and I'm going to.

MRS BERNICK. But there would be the most dreadful scandal! Ah, Johan, are you still here?

MISS HESSEL. Out you go, my boy. Don't hang about indoors in the stuffy air. Go down the garden and talk to Dina.

JOHAN TÖNNESEN. Yes, that's what I was just going to do.

MRS BERNICK. But –

MISS HESSEL. Look here, John, have you looked at Dina properly?

JOHAN TÖNNESEN. Yes, I think I have.

MISS HESSEL. Well, you should look at her to some purpose, my boy. She would be the very thing for you.

MRS BERNICK. But, Lona!

JOHAN TÖNNESEN. For me?

MISS HESSEL. Yes; to look at, I mean. Go along!

JOHAN TÖNNESEN. All right. I'm only too pleased to. [He goes down into the garden.]

MRS BERNICK. Lona, you absolutely astound me. You can't mean this seriously?

MISS HESSEL. Yes. Upon my soul! Isn't she sound and healthy and honest? That's just the wife for John. It's someone like that he needs over there; it'll be rather different from an old half-sister.

MRS BERNICK. Dina! Dina Dorf! But think –

MISS HESSEL. I'm thinking first and foremost of the boy's happiness. I must give him a hand, that's certain; he's not very good at this sort of thing himself. He's never really taken much interest in women.

MRS BERNICK. He? Johan? Well, it seems to me we've had some unfortunate proofs that –

MISS HESSEL. Oh, bother that stupid story! Where's Karsten gone? I want to speak to him.

MRS BERNICK. You're not to, Lona, I tell you!

MISS HESSEL. I'm going to. If the boy takes to her – and she to him – then they shall have each other. Karsten's such a shrewd man; he must find a way out –

MRS BERNICK. And do you imagine that this unseemly American behaviour will be tolerated here?

MISS HESSEL. Nonsense, Betty!

MRS BERNICK. – That a man like Karsten, with his strict, moral views –

MISS HESSEL. Oh, come! They're not so excessively strict, are they?

MRS BERNICK. What are you daring to say?

MISS HESSEL. I'm daring to say that I don't think Karsten is much more moral than other men.

MRS BERNICK. So your hate for him is still as deep as that! But what are you doing here, if you've never been able to forget? I can't understand how you could dare to look him in the face, after offending him as you did then.

MISS HESSEL. Yes, Betty, I lost control of myself pretty badly that time.

MRS BERNICK. And how magnanimously he's forgiven you – he, who had never done anything wrong! Because *he* couldn't help your going about building up hopes. But since that time you've hated me, too. [*Bursting into tears.*] You've always begrudged me my happiness. And now you've come here to bring all this down on me – to show the town what kind of family I've brought Karsten into. Oh yes, it's me it comes back on, and that's what you want. Oh, it's wicked of you! [*She goes out crying, through the farthest door on the left.*]

MISS HESSEL [*looking after her*]. Poor Betty!

[*Bernick comes in from his room.*]

BERNICK [*still at the door*]. Yes, yes, that's right, Krap; that's excellent. Send twenty pounds for the famine relief. [*Turning.*] Lona! [*Coming nearer.*] Are you alone? Isn't Betty coming?

MISS HESSEL. No. Shall I fetch her?

BERNICK. Oh no, no. Let it be! Oh Lona, you don't know

how I've longed to talk freely to you – to be able to beg your forgiveness.

MISS HESSEL. Now look here, Karsten. Don't let's be sentimental. It doesn't suit us.

BERNICK. You must listen to me, Lona. I know how much appearances are against me, now you've heard all this about Dina's mother. But I swear to you it was only a passing infatuation. I did really love you once; truly and honestly.

MISS HESSEL. Why do you think I've come home?

BERNICK. Whatever you have in mind, I beseech you not to do anything before I've cleared myself. I can do that, Lona; at any rate, I can explain myself.

MISS HESSEL. Now you're frightened. You used to love me once, you say. Yes, you assured me of that, often enough, in your letters. And perhaps it was true, too, in a way – so long as you were living out there in a great, free world that gave you courage to think freely and greatly yourself. Maybe you found more character and will and independence in me than in most people at home here. And then, of course, it was a secret between us two; there was no one who could make merry over your bad taste.

BERNICK. But, Lona, how can you think –

MISS HESSEL. But when you came back, when you heard the scorn that poured down on me, met the laughter at what were called my eccentricities –

BERNICK. You *were* indiscreet in those days.

MISS HESSEL. Mostly to annoy those prudes of both sexes who infested the town. And then when you met that fascinating young actress –

BERNICK. That was just a piece of showing off; nothing more. I swear to you, not a tithe of the rumours and slanders that circulated were true.

MISS HESSEL. Maybe. But then when Betty came home, blooming and lovely and worshipped by everybody, and when it became known that she'd get all Aunt's money and I shouldn't get anything –

BERNICK. Now, there we have it, Lona. And now you shall hear the plain truth. I didn't love Betty at that time; I didn't break with you because of any new attachment. It was simply for the sake of the money. I was driven to it. I had to make sure of the money.

MISS HESSEL. And you tell me that to my face?

BERNICK. Yes, I do. Listen to me, Lona –

MISS HESSEL. And yet you wrote to me that you had been overcome by an irresistible love for Betty, appealed to my generosity, implored me for Betty's sake to say nothing about what had been between us –

BERNICK. I had to, I tell you.

MISS HESSEL. Then, by God, I'm not sorry I lost control of myself as I did that day!

BERNICK. Let me explain, coolly and quietly, what the position was at that moment. My mother, as you remember, was the head of the firm. But she had absolutely no business-sense. I was fetched back from Paris in a hurry. The times were critical. I was expected to pull things straight. What did I find? I found – what had to be kept absolutely secret – a business practically ruined. Yes, practically ruined, that old, respected house, that had stood for three generations. What could I do, the son, the only son, but look about me for some way of saving it?

MISS HESSEL. So you saved the House of Bernick at a woman's expense.

BERNICK. You know quite well that Betty loved me.

MISS HESSEL. But what about me?

BERNICK. Believe me, Lona – you would never have been happy with me.

MISS HESSEL. Was it out of consideration for my happiness that you threw me over?

BERNICK. Do you think I acted as I did from selfish motives? If I had been alone at that time, I would have begun over again cheerfully and fearlessly. But you have no idea how the head of a big business grows, under the pressure of his immense responsibilities, to be himself a part of that heritage. Do you know that the welfare or misery of hundreds, even of thousands, depends on him? Don't you realize that the whole of that community – what you and I regard as our home – would have been heavily involved if the House of Bernick had fallen?

MISS HESSEL. Is it also for the sake of the community that, for fifteen years, you have been living on a lie?

BERNICK. On a lie?

MISS HESSEL. What does Betty know of all this that's behind her marriage with you – that happened before it?

BERNICK. Can you imagine that I would wound her to no purpose by laying those things bare?

MISS HESSEL. To no purpose, you say? Ah well; you're a business man; of course you should understand what is to your purpose. But now listen, Karsten. Now I too am going to speak coolly and quietly. Tell me, are you really happy after all?

BERNICK. In my family, do you mean?

MISS HESSEL. Yes, of course.

BERNICK. Yes, I am, Lona. Ah, it has not been in vain, your self-sacrificing friendship for me. I can truly say that I have become happier year by year. Betty is so good and docile. And the way she has learnt, with the passage of years, to adapt her personality to what is characteristic in mine ...

MISS HESSEL. Hm.

BERNICK. At the beginning she had a lot of high-flown

notions about love; she couldn't reconcile herself to the idea that bit by bit it must turn into the mild warmth of friendship.

MISS HESSEL. But now she quite accepts that?

BERNICK. Absolutely. You can realize that daily contact with me has not been without its mellowing influence upon her. People must learn to reduce their mutual claims, if they are to give a good account of themselves in the community in which they are placed. Betty has gradually learnt to see that, so that our household is now an example to our fellow-citizens.

MISS HESSEL. But these fellow-citizens know nothing about the lie?

BERNICK. About the lie?

MISS HESSEL. Yes, the lie that you've been living on these fifteen years.

BERNICK. You call that – ?

MISS HESSEL. I call it the lie. The threefold lie. First the lie to me, then the lie to Betty and then the lie to Johan.

BERNICK. Betty has never asked me to speak.

MISS HESSEL. Because she hasn't known anything.

BERNICK. And you won't ask it – out of consideration for her, you won't ask it?

MISS HESSEL. Oh no. I dare say I shall know how to bear the peals of laughter; I have a broad back.

BERNICK. And Johan won't ask me either; he has promised me that.

MISS HESSEL. But you yourself, Karsten? Isn't there anything in yourself that wants to be free of the lie?

BERNICK. You suggest that I should sacrifice, of my own accord, my family happiness and my position in the community?

MISS HESSEL. What right have you to stand where you stand?

BERNICK. In fifteen years, day by day, I have purchased some small right – by the conduct of my life and by what I have worked for and achieved.

MISS HESSEL. Yes, you have worked and achieved a great deal, both for yourself and for others. You are the richest and most powerful man in the town. They daren't do anything but bow to your will, any of them, because you pass for a man without a spot or flaw. Your home passes for a model home, your life for a model life. But all this magnificence, and you yourself with it, stands on a quaking bog. A moment may come, a word may be spoken, and you and all your glory will go to the bottom, unless you save yourself in time.

BERNICK. Lona, what did you come here for?

MISS HESSEL. To help you get solid ground under your feet, Karsten.

BERNICK. Revenge! You want to revenge yourself? I guessed as much. But you won't succeed. There is only one person who can speak with authority, and he is silent.

MISS HESSEL. Johan?

BERNICK. Yes, Johan. If anyone else accuses me, I shall deny the whole thing. If they try to break me, I shall fight for my life. But you will never succeed, I tell you. He, who could destroy me, is silent – and he is going away again.

[*Rummel and Vigeland come in from the right.*]

RUMMEL. Good morning, good morning, my dear Bernick. You must come up to the Chamber of Commerce with us. We have a meeting about the railway business, you know.

BERNICK. I can't. It's impossible at the moment.

VIGELAND. You really must, Mr Bernick.

RUMMEL. You must, Bernick. There are people working against us. Hammer, the newspaper man, and the others who backed the coast line insist that there are private interests behind this new proposal.

BERNICK. Well, explain to them, then –

VIGELAND. It's no use our explaining to them, Mr Bernick.

RUMMEL. No, no, you must come yourself; of course nobody will dare to suspect you of that sort of thing.

MISS HESSEL. No, I should think not.

BERNICK. I can't, I tell you. I'm not well. Or, anyway, wait – let me collect myself.

[*Rörlund comes in from the right.*]

RÖRLUND. You must excuse me, Mr Bernick. I am very greatly perturbed –

BERNICK. Well, what's the matter with you?

RÖRLUND. Allow me to ask you a question, Mr Bernick. Is it with your consent that the young girl who has found shelter under your roof shows herself in the open street with a man who –

MISS HESSEL. What man, Mr Parson?

RÖRLUND. With the man from whom, of all men on earth, she should be kept farthest away.

MISS HESSEL. Oh, indeed?

RÖRLUND. Is it with your consent, Mr Bernick?

BERNICK [*who is looking for his hat and his gloves*]. I know nothing about it. Excuse me, I am in a hurry. I'm off to the Chamber of Commerce.

HILMAR TÖNNESEN [*coming from the garden and going across to the farthest door at the left*]. Betty, Betty! Listen! Here!

MRS BERNICK [*at the door*]. What is it?

HILMAR TÖNNESEN. You must go down the garden and put an end to the flirtation that a certain friend of ours is carrying on with Miss Dina Dorf. It has quite upset my nerves to hear it.

MISS HESSEL. Really! Why, what did this friend of ours say?

HILMAR TÖNNESEN. Oh, only that he wants her to go to America with him. Ugh!

RÖRLUND. Can such things be possible? ⎱ [together]
MRS BERNICK. What do you say? ⎰

MISS HESSEL. But that would be a grand idea!

BERNICK. Impossible! You can't have heard right.

HILMAR TÖNNESEN. Ask him himself, then. There come the two of them. Only leave me out of it.

BERNICK [to Rummel and Vigeland]. I'll follow you – in a moment –

[Rummel and Vigeland go out to the right. Johan Tönnesen and Dina come in from the garden.]

JOHAN TÖNNESEN. Hurrah, Lona, she's coming with us!

MRS BERNICK. But, Johan – what an irresponsible – !

RÖRLUND. Is this true? What a shocking scandal! What arts of seduction have you – ?

JOHAN TÖNNESEN. Come, come, man! What are you talking about?

RÖRLUND. Answer me, Dina. Is this your intention? Is it your full and free decision?

DINA. I must get away from here.

RÖRLUND. But with him – with him!

DINA. Show me anyone else who would have had the courage to take me.

RÖRLUND. Well then, you shall know who he is.

JOHAN TÖNNESEN. Be quiet!

BERNICK. Not another word!

RÖRLUND. That would be an ill service to the community of whose morals I am appointed guardian. And I should behave unpardonably to this young girl in whose upbringing I too have had a considerable share, and who is for me –

JOHAN TÖNNESEN. Be careful what you are doing!

RÖRLUND. She *shall* know it! Dina, it is this man who caused all your mother's unhappiness and shame.

BERNICK. Mr Rörlund!

DINA. He! [*To Johan.*] Is this true?

JOHAN TÖNNESEN. Karsten, you answer.

BERNICK. Not another word. Let that be enough for today.

DINA. Then it's true.

RÖRLUND. True, true. And more than that. This man you put your trust in did not run away from home empty-handed. The widow Bernick's money – Mr Bernick can bear witness –

MISS HESSEL. Liar!

BERNICK. Ah!

MRS BERNICK. Oh, my God!

JOHAN TÖNNESEN [*going towards Rörlund with his arm uplifted*]. You dare to – !

MISS HESSEL [*checking him*]. Don't hit him, Johan.

RÖRLUND. Oh yes, you can assault me if you want to. But the truth shall out; and that is the truth. Mr Bernick has said so himself and the whole town knows it. Now, Dina, now you know him.

[*A short pause.*]

JOHAN TÖNNESEN [*in a low voice, seizing Bernick's arm*]. Karsten. Karsten, what have you done?

MRS BERNICK [*softly and in tears*]. Oh, Karsten, to think that I should bring all this shame on you!

SANDSTAD [*coming quickly in from the right and calling, with his hand on the door-handle*]. You simply must come now, Mr Bernick. The whole railway's hanging by a thread.

BERNICK [*beside himself*]. What is it? What must I – ?

MISS HESSEL [*seriously and with emphasis*]. You must come to the rescue of the community, Karsten.

SANDSTAD. Yes, come, come. We need all the weight of your moral credit.

JOHAN TÖNNESEN [*close to him*]. Bernick, we two will have a talk tomorrow.

[*He goes out through the garden. Bernick goes out to the right with Sandstad, like an automaton.*]

ACT THREE

————————— * —————————

[*The garden room in the Bernicks' house. Bernick, with a cane in his hand, comes in very angry, from the farthest room to the left back, and leaves the door half open behind him.*]

BERNICK. That's right. At last the thing's been taken seriously. I don't think he'll forget that thrashing. [*To someone inside the room.*] What do you say? And *I* say you're a foolish mother! You make excuses for him and encourage him in all his naughtiness. Not naughtiness? What do you call it, then? To slip out of the house in the night and go to sea in a fishing smack! Stay away till far on in the day and give me all that terrible anxiety – I've quite enough already without that. And now the young devil dares to threaten he'll run away. Well, let him try it. You? No, I quite believe it; you don't worry yourself much whether he comes to grief or not. I believe if he were to get killed –! Really? Yes, but I have work to be carried on after me in this world; I can't afford to lose my child. No arguing, Betty. It's to be as I say; he's to stay in the house. [*Listening.*] Hush! Don't let anyone notice anything.

[*Krap comes in from the right.*]

KRAP. Have you a moment to spare, Mr Bernick?

BERNICK [*throwing down the cane*]. Certainly, certainly. Have you come from the shipyard?

KRAP. Just this moment. Hm. ...

BERNICK. Well? There isn't anything wrong with the *Palm Tree*, is there?

KRAP. The *Palm Tree* can sail tomorrow, but –

BERNICK. The *Indian Girl*, then? Didn't I guess that that stiff-necked –

KRAP. The *Indian Girl* can sail tomorrow, too. But I don't think she'll get very far.

BERNICK. What do you mean?

KRAP. Excuse me, Mr Bernick, but that door's ajar and I think there's someone in there.

BERNICK [*shutting the door*]. There we are. But what is this business that nobody must hear?

KRAP. It's this, that your foreman Aune has made up his mind to let the *Indian Girl* go to the bottom with all hands.

BERNICK. But, goodness gracious, how can you think –?

KRAP. I can't explain it to myself any other way, Mr Bernick.

BERNICK. Well, tell me then, in as few words as –

KRAP. I will. You know yourself how slowly things have gone at the yard since we got the new machines and these new, inexperienced men.

BERNICK. Yes, yes.

KRAP. But this morning when I got down there I noticed that the repairs on the American ship had gone ahead at an extraordinary rate. The large patch in the hull – you know, the rotten part –

BERNICK. Yes, yes; what about it?

KRAP. Completely repaired – to all appearances. Sheathed over. Looked like new. Heard that Aune himself had been working there by lamp-light all night.

BERNICK. Yes, yes – and then?

KRAP. I went and examined it. The men had just laid off for breakfast. So I took the opportunity of looking round, both outside and on board, without anybody noticing. Rather difficult, getting down into that boat with her cargo shipped, but I got what I wanted. There are underhand goings-on, Mr Bernick.

BERNICK. I can't believe you, Krap. I can't – I won't believe a thing like that of Aune.

KRAP. I'm sorry about it, but it's the plain truth. There are underhand doings, I tell you. No new timber put in, so far as I could tell. Only plugged and caulked and patched over the plating and tarpaulin and that sort of thing. Fair scamped! The *Indian Girl* will never get to New York; she'll go to the bottom like a cracked pot.

BERNICK. This is terrible! But what do you think he means by it?

KRAP. Obviously wants to discredit the machines. Wants to revenge himself. Wants to get the old work-people taken back again.

BERNICK. And so he's sacrificing all those lives. ...

KRAP. He said the other day there weren't any men aboard the *Indian Girl* – only beasts.

BERNICK. Yes, yes, may be – but doesn't he consider the huge capital that will be lost?

KRAP. Aune doesn't look on huge capital with a very kindly eye, Mr Bernick.

BERNICK. True enough. He is a mischief-maker, always stirring up trouble. But such unprincipled behaviour! Listen, Krap; we must think twice about this. Not a word about it to anyone. Our yard will be thought badly of, if people get to know a thing like this.

KRAP. Of course, but –

BERNICK. You must manage to get down there again in the dinner-hour; I must have absolute certainty.

KRAP. You shall, Mr Bernick. But, excuse me asking, what are you going to do then?

BERNICK. Report the case, naturally. We can't make ourselves parties to a crime. I can't have anything on my conscience. Besides, it will make a good impression on the Press, and the general public too, when they see that I put all personal considerations aside and let justice take its course.

KRAP. Very true, Mr Bernick.

BERNICK. But first and foremost, complete certainty. And until then, silence –

KRAP. Not a word, Mr Bernick. And you shall have your certainty.

[*He goes out through the garden and down the street.*]

BERNICK [*half aloud*]. Shocking! But no. It's impossible. Unthinkable!

[*As he is about to go into his room, Hilmar Tönnesen comes in from the right.*]

HILMAR TÖNNESEN. Good morning, Bernick. Well, I congratulate you on your victory in the Chamber of Commerce yesterday.

BERNICK. Oh, thanks.

HILMAR TÖNNESEN. It was a glorious victory, I hear. The victory of intelligent public spirit over self-interest and prejudice. Almost like a punitive raid. Wonderful that you could do it – after that disagreeable scene here –

BERNICK. Oh, well, never mind that.

HILMAR TÖNNESEN. But the main battle hasn't been fought yet.

BERNICK. In the matter of the railway, you mean?

HILMAR TÖNNESEN. Yes. You know, of course, what Hammer, the editor, is hatching?

BERNICK [*anxiously*]. No! What's that?

HILMAR TÖNNESEN. He's got hold of the rumour that's going round and is going to make an article of it.

BERNICK. What rumour?

HILMAR TÖNNESEN. Why, about the big purchase of property along the branch line, of course.

BERNICK. What do you mean? Is there a rumour of that?

HILMAR TÖNNESEN. Yes, it's all over the town. I heard it in the club when I dropped in. They say one of our lawyers has been secretly commissioned to buy up all the forests, all the ore deposits, all the water power –

BERNICK. And isn't it known for whom?

HILMAR TÖNNESEN. At the club they thought it must be for an outside company that had got news of your plans and cut in before the prices rose. Isn't it a mean trick? Ugh!

BERNICK. Mean?

HILMAR TÖNNESEN. Yes; outsiders poaching on our preserves like that. And that one of our own lawyers should lend himself to such a thing! Now it'll be outsiders who'll take all the profits.

BERNICK. But surely this is only an empty rumour?

HILMAR TÖNNESEN. It's believed, anyhow. And tomorrow or the day after, Hammer, of course, will nail it down as a fact. Already there was a general feeling of indignation up there. I heard several people saying that if this rumour's confirmed, they'll take their names off the list.

BERNICK. Impossible!

HILMAR TÖNNESEN. Is it? Why do you suppose these creatures, with their shopkeepers' souls, are so ready to join in your undertaking? Don't you think they've smelt out something themselves?

BERNICK. Impossible, I tell you. There's that much public spirit in our little community, at any rate –

HILMAR TÖNNESEN. Here? Oh well, you're an optimist and you judge others by yourself. But I, who am a fairly shrewd observer. ... There's not one here – of course, with the exception of ourselves – not one, I tell you, who keeps the flag of idealism flying. [*Going towards the background.*] Ugh! There they are!

BERNICK. Who?

HILMAR TÖNNESEN. The two Americans. [*Looking out to-wards the right.*] And who is it they're with? Why, good Lord, if it isn't the captain of the *Indian Girl*!

BERNICK. What can they want with him?

HILMAR TÖNNESEN. Oh, it's very suitable company. They say he's been a slave-trader or a pirate; and who knows what those two have been up to all these years.

BERNICK. It isn't right, I tell you, to think like that of them.

HILMAR TÖNNESEN. Yes, but you're an optimist. Well, here they are, of course, on top of us again, so I'll get away while I can. [*Going up towards the door on the left.*] [*Miss Hessel comes in from the right.*]

MISS HESSEL. Hello, Hilmar! Is it I who's driving you away?

HILMAR TÖNNESEN. Not at all. I was in a hurry. I was go-ing to have a word with Betty. [*Going in to the farthest room on the left.*]

BERNICK [*after a short silence*]. Well, Lona?

MISS HESSEL. Well?

BERNICK. How do I stand with you today?

MISS HESSEL. As you did yesterday. One lie more or less –

BERNICK. I must explain this. Where has Johan gone?

MISS HESSEL. He's coming. He had to speak to somebody about something.

BERNICK. After what you heard yesterday, you will realize that my whole position is ruined if the truth comes to light.

MISS HESSEL. I realize that.

BERNICK. It's obvious, of course, that I had nothing to do with the crime there was all that talk about.

MISS HESSEL. That can be taken for granted. But who was the thief?

BERNICK. There was no thief. No money was stolen; not a shilling was missing.

MISS HESSEL. What?

BERNICK. Not a shilling, I said.

MISS HESSEL. But the rumour? How did that shameful rumour get about, that Johan – ?

BERNICK. Lona, I seem to be able to talk to you in a way I can't with anyone else. I won't hide anything from you. I had my share in the spreading of the rumour.

MISS HESSEL. You? And you could do that to him, when, for your sake, he'd –

BERNICK. You mustn't condemn me without remembering how things stood at that time. I explained it to you yesterday. I came home and found my mother involved in a whole lot of rash undertakings; failures of various kinds added to the trouble and it seemed as though misfortune of every sort rained down on us; our house was on the brink of ruin. I was half heedless and half desperate. You know, Lona, I think it was mostly to take the edge off my thoughts that I drifted into that entanglement that led to Johan's going away.

MISS HESSEL. I see.

BERNICK. You can well imagine all kinds of rumours got about when you and he were gone. This wasn't his first piece of giddiness, they said. Some said Dorf had had a large sum of money from him for holding his tongue and going away. Others insisted that *she* had had it. At the same time, it was no secret that our house had difficulty in meeting its commitments. What was more natural than that the tattlers should find a connexion between these two rumours? When she stayed on here, living in poverty, then they declared that he had taken the money with him to America, and rumours made the sum bigger and bigger every day.

MISS HESSEL. And you, Karsten?

BERNICK. I seized upon that rumour as a drowning man on a plank.

MISS HESSEL. You helped it to spread?

BERNICK. I did not contradict it. Our creditors had begun to threaten us; I *had* to pacify them. It was essential that no one should suspect the solidarity of our business. A temporary misfortune had hit us – all that was needed was that they should not press us, only give us time, and everyone would get his due.

MISS HESSEL. And everyone did get it, then?

BERNICK. Yes, Lona, that rumour saved our house and made me the man I am now.

MISS HESSEL. A lie, then, has made you the man you are now.

BERNICK. Whom did it hurt – then? Johan intended never to come back.

MISS HESSEL. You ask whom it hurt. Look into yourself and tell me whether you have not been hurt.

BERNICK. Look into any man you choose, and you will find, in every single man, at least one black spot that he has to cover.

MISS HESSEL. And you call yourselves the pillars of the community.

BERNICK. The community has nothing better to support it.

MISS HESSEL. Then what does it matter whether such a community is supported or not? What is it that counts here? The sham and the lie, nothing else. Here are you, the first man in the town, living in splendour and happiness, in power and honour – you, who have branded an innocent man a criminal.

BERNICK. Don't you think I feel the injury I have done him deeply enough? And don't you think I am prepared to make it good again?

MISS HESSEL. How? By speaking out?

BERNICK. Can you ask that?

MISS HESSEL. What else can make good an injury like this?

BERNICK. I am rich, Lona. Johan can ask what he likes –

MISS HESSEL. Yes! You offer him money, and hear what he'll answer!

BERNICK. Do you know what his plans are?

MISS HESSEL. No. He has turned silent since yesterday. It's as though this business had suddenly made him a full-grown man.

BERNICK. I must speak to him.

MISS HESSEL. Here he is.

[*Johan Tönnesen comes in from the right.*]

BERNICK [*going towards him*]. Johan!

JOHAN TÖNNESEN [*avoiding him*]. No. Let me – ! Yesterday morning I gave you my word not to speak.

BERNICK. You did.

JOHAN TÖNNESEN. But I didn't know then –

BERNICK. Johan, just let me have two words, to explain the situation –

JOHAN TÖNNESEN. No need; I can grasp the situation quite all right. The business was in a tight place and so, as I was away, and you had my unprotected name and reputation in your hands ... Well, I don't blame you overmuch; we were young and irresponsible in those days. But now I need the truth and now you must speak.

BERNICK. And just now I need all my moral credit and so I cannot speak.

JOHAN TÖNNESEN. I don't mind much about the fictions you have set going about me; it is the other thing you must take the blame for. Dina shall be my wife, and here, here in this town, I mean to live and build up a life with her.

MISS HESSEL. You mean to do that?

BERNICK. With Dina? As your wife? Here, in town!

JOHAN TÖNNESEN. Yes, right here. I shall stay here to defy all those liars and back-biters. But for me to win her, you must set me free.

BERNICK. Have you considered that, if I admit the one thing, it will mean admitting the other too? You will say that I can prove, from our books, that there never was any dishonesty? But I can't. Our books were not kept very accurately at that time. And even if I could, what would be gained by it? Shouldn't I, in any case, be exposed as the man who had once saved himself by an untruth, and who, for fifteen years, had let that untruth and all that followed establish itself without lifting a finger to stop it? You don't know our society any longer, or you'd know that this would smash me to pieces.

JOHAN TÖNNESEN. I can only say that I will take Mrs Dorf's daughter as my wife and live with her here in this town.

BERNICK [wiping the sweat off his forehead]. Listen to me, Johan – and you too, Lona. It's no ordinary position I am in just at the moment. I am so situated that if you strike this blow you will ruin me, and not only me, but also a great and happy future for the community – which, after all, is your childhood's home.

JOHAN TÖNNESEN. And if I don't strike, I shall ruin my own future happiness.

MISS HESSEL. Go on, Karsten.

BERNICK. Well now, listen. It's all connected with the business of the railway; and that business isn't quite so simple as you think. You've heard, of course, that last year there was a question of a coast line. It had a good deal of powerful support here in the town and in the neighbourhood, and especially in the newspapers. But I prevented it because it would have damaged our steamboat trade along the coast.

MISS HESSEL. Have you interests in the steam-boat trade yourself?

BERNICK. Yes. But no one dared to suspect me on that account; I had my good name to cover and safeguard me. In any case, I could have stood the loss. But the town could not have stood it. Then the inland line was decided on. When that was done, I unobtrusively assured myself that a branch line could be run down here to the town.

MISS HESSEL. Why 'unobtrusively', Karsten?

BERNICK. Have you heard of the extensive buying-up of forests, mines and water-power?

JOHAN TÖNNESEN. Yes, it's presumably an outside company –

BERNICK. As these properties lie now, they are practically worthless to their scattered occupants; they have therefore been sold comparatively cheap. If one had waited till the branch line had been discussed, the owners would have demanded extortionate prices.

MISS HESSEL. Quite. But what about it?

BERNICK. Now comes something that can be interpreted in different ways; a thing that, in our community, a man can only attempt if he can rely upon a spotless and honourable name.

MISS HESSEL. Well?

BERNICK. It is I who have bought it all.

MISS HESSEL. You?

JOHAN TÖNNESEN. On your own account?

BERNICK. On my own account. If the branch line comes off, I am a millionaire; if it doesn't, I am ruined.

MISS HESSEL. That's risky, Karsten.

BERNICK. I've staked everything I have on it.

MISS HESSEL. I'm not thinking of your money; but when it comes out that –

BERNICK. Yes, that's the crux. With the unsullied name I

have borne up till now, I can take the whole transaction on myself, carry it through and say to my fellow-citizens, 'See, I have risked this for the good of the community.'

MISS HESSEL. Of the community?

BERNICK. Yes. And not one of them will doubt my intention.

MISS HESSEL. Nevertheless, there are men here who have acted more openly than you; without ulterior motives, without reservations.

BERNICK. Who?

MISS HESSEL. Why, Rummel and Sandstad and Vigeland, of course.

BERNICK. To win them over, I had to let them in on the business.

MISS HESSEL. And then?

BERNICK. They have stipulated for a fifth part of the profits between them.

MISS HESSEL. Oh, these pillars of the community!

BERNICK. And isn't it the community itself that forces us into crooked ways? What would have happened here if I hadn't dealt secretly? They would all have thrown themselves into the concern, divided it, scattered it, mismanaged and bungled the whole thing. There isn't a single man in this town, except me, who understands how to conduct an undertaking on such a big scale as this will be. In this country it's only we men of foreign stock who have any capacity for big business. That's why my conscience absolves me in this particular case. It's only in my hands that these properties can become of permanent benefit to the many people they will provide with a living.

MISS HESSEL. I believe you're right there, Karsten.

JOHAN TÖNNESEN. But I don't know these 'many people', and my life's happiness is at stake.

BERNICK. The welfare of the place where you were born is also at stake. If anything comes out which casts a shadow on my former conduct, then all my opponents will join forces and fall upon me. A youthful indiscretion is never wiped out in our community. People will go over the whole of my subsequent life, bring up a thousand little incidents, read and interpret them in the light of what has been discovered; they will crush me under a load of rumours and slanders. I shall have to withdraw from the railway affair. If I take my hand off it, it will go to pieces. And there I lose, at one stroke, my fortune and my standing as a citizen.

MISS HESSEL. Johan, after what you have just heard, you must go away and say nothing.

BERNICK. Yes, yes, Johan, you must!

JOHAN TÖNNESEN. Very well, I will go away and I will say nothing. But I shall come back and then I shall speak.

BERNICK. Stay over there, Johan. Don't say anything, and I will gladly share with you –

JOHAN TÖNNESEN. Keep your money and give me back my name and reputation!

BERNICK. And sacrifice my own!

JOHAN TÖNNESEN. That's for you and your community to settle. I must and shall and will win Dina for myself. So I shall leave tomorrow on the *Indian Girl*.

BERNICK. On the *Indian Girl*?

JOHAN TÖNNESEN. Yes, the captain has promised to take me. I'm crossing, I tell you, selling my farm and putting my affairs in order. In two months I shall be back again.

BERNICK. And then you will speak?

JOHAN TÖNNESEN. Then the man who is to blame shall take the blame.

BERNICK. Are you forgetting that then I shall have to take the blame for something I am not to blame for?

JOHAN TÖNNESEN. Who was it, fifteen years ago, who got the benefit of that shameful rumour?

BERNICK. You're making me desperate! But if you speak, I shall deny it all! I shall say it's a plot against me. Revenge. That you've come over here to get money out of me!

MISS HESSEL. For shame, Karsten!

BERNICK. I'm desperate, I tell you. And it's my life I'm fighting for. I shall deny it all, all!

JOHAN TÖNNESEN. I have your two letters. I found them in my box among my other papers. I read them through this morning. They are plain enough.

BERNICK. And you will make them public?

JOHAN TÖNNESEN. If necessary.

BERNICK. And in two months you will be here again?

JOHAN TÖNNESEN. I hope so. The wind is good. In three weeks I shall be in New York – if the *Indian Girl* doesn't go down.

BERNICK [*starting*]. Go down? Why should the *Indian Girl* go down?

JOHAN TÖNNESEN. I don't see why either.

BERNICK [*almost inaudibly*]. Go down?

JOHAN TÖNNESEN. Well, Bernick, now you know what to expect; you must think it over in the meantime. Good-bye! Say good-bye to Betty for me, though she hasn't treated me very like a sister. But I'll see Marta myself. She must tell Dina – she must promise me – [*He goes out by the farthest door on the left.*]

BERNICK [*looking in front of him*]. The *Indian Girl* – ? [*Quickly.*] Lona, you must prevent this.

MISS HESSEL. You see yourself, Karsten: I've no power over him any longer. [*She goes after Johan into the room on the left.*]

BERNICK [*perturbed*]. Go down – ?

[*Aune comes in from the right.*]

AUNE. Beg pardon, sir, have you a minute?

BERNICK [*turning angrily*]. What do you want?

AUNE. If you'll allow me, sir, to ask you a question?

BERNICK. Very well, hurry up. What do you want to ask about?

AUNE. I wanted to ask if it's settled, finally settled, that I shall be discharged from the yard if the *Indian Girl* can't sail tomorrow?

BERNICK. What's the matter now? The boat *will* be ready to sail.

AUNE. Yes, she will. But suppose she wasn't, should I be discharged then?

BERNICK. What is the point of this senseless question?

AUNE. I very much wanted to know, sir. Please answer me: should I be discharged?

BERNICK. Do I usually keep my word or not?

AUNE. Then tomorrow I should have lost the position I hold in my home and with the people who belong to me – lost my influence among the workmen – lost all chance of doing good among the poor and lowly in this community.

BERNICK. Aune, we've settled that point.

AUNE. Yes. Then the *Indian Girl* must sail. [*Short silence.*]

BERNICK. Listen to me. I can't have my eye on everything – can't be answerable for everything. You are prepared to assure me that the repairs are satisfactorily carried out?

AUNE. You gave me very short time, sir.

BERNICK. But the repairs are all right, you say?

AUNE. The weather is good, and it is summer. [*Another silence.*]

BERNICK. Have you anything more to say to me?

AUNE: I don't know of anything else, sir.

BERNICK. Well, then – the *Indian Girl* sails –

AUNE. Tomorrow?

BERNICK. Yes.

AUNE. Very good. [*He bows and goes out.*]

[*Bernick stands a moment in doubt; then he goes quickly over towards the door as if to call Aune back, but stops uncertainly with his hand on the door-knob. At that moment the door is opened from outside and Krap comes in.*]

KRAP [*softly*]. Ah, he was here. Has he confessed?

BERNICK. Hm. Have you discovered anything?

KRAP. Is there any need to? Didn't you see his bad conscience looking out of his eyes, Mr Bernick?

BERNICK. Oh, nonsense. Those things don't show. I'm asking you whether you have discovered anything?

KRAP. Couldn't get there. It was too late. They were already hauling the ship out of the dock. But this hurry itself shows plainly that –

BERNICK. It doesn't show anything. The inspection has taken place, then?

KRAP. Of course it has, but –

BERNICK. There you are, then. And naturally they've found nothing to complain of.

KRAP. Mr Bernick, you know well enough how that kind of inspection is conducted, especially in a yard that has such a good name as ours.

BERNICK. All the same, we're covered.

KRAP. Mr Bernick, couldn't you really see by Aune's look – ?

BERNICK. Aune has completely reassured me, I tell you.

KRAP. And I tell you that I am morally certain that –

BERNICK. What's all this about, Krap? I know you've got a grudge against the man, but if you want to pick a quarrel with him you should find another opportunity. You know how important it is for me – or rather for the company – that the *Indian Girl* should be under sail tomorrow.

KRAP. Very good, then. Let it go at that. But when we hear from *that* ship next – hm!

[*Vigeland comes in from the right.*]

VIGELAND. Good morning to you, Consul. Have you a moment to spare?

BERNICK. At your service, Mr Vigeland.

VIGELAND. Well, I only wanted to know whether you don't agree that the *Palm Tree* should sail tomorrow.

BERNICK. Why, yes; it's a settled thing.

VIGELAND. But the captain's just come to me and told me the storm signals are up.

KRAP. The barometer has fallen a good deal since this morning.

BERNICK. Has it? Is there a storm coming?

VIGELAND. A stiff breeze at any rate. But it isn't a headwind. On the contrary –

BERNICK. Hm. Well, what do you say?

VIGELAND. I say, as I said to the captain, that the *Palm Tree* is in the hands of Providence. And besides, she's only crossing the North Sea to begin with. And freights are standing tolerably high just now in England, so that –

BERNICK. Yes. It would probably mean a loss for us if we waited.

VIGELAND. The vessel's sound enough; and besides, she's fully insured. But it's a much more risky business with the *Indian Girl*.

BERNICK. What do you mean?

VIGELAND. Well, she's sailing tomorrow, too.

BERNICK. Yes, the owners hurried things on – and besides –

VIGELAND. Well, if that old hulk can venture out – and with such a crew into the bargain – it would be a disgrace if we didn't –

BERNICK. Very well, then. You've got her ship's papers with you, I suppose?

VIGELAND. Yes, here they are.

BERNICK. Good. Then go in with Mr Krap will you?

KRAP. If you'll just come this way. That's soon dealt with.

VIGELAND. Thank you. And we leave the issue in the hands of the Almighty, Mr Bernick.

[*He goes with Krap into the nearest room on the left. Rörlund comes in through the garden.*]

RÖRLUND. Ah, do I really find you at home at this time of day, Mr Bernick?

BERNICK [*absently*]. As you see.

RÖRLUND. Well, I really came in to see your wife. I rather thought she might need a word of consolation.

BERNICK. I dare say she does. But I would like to speak to you for a moment, too.

RÖRLUND. With pleasure, Mr Bernick. But what is the matter? You look quite pale and disturbed.

BERNICK. Really? Do I? Well, what else can one expect? All the things that are piling up round me at the moment! All my business concerns – and this railway project. Listen, Mr Rörlund; tell me something – let me ask you a question.

RÖRLUND. Most willingly, Mr Bernick.

BERNICK. There's an idea that has struck me. When one is on the threshold of a far-reaching enterprise, which promises to further the welfare of thousands ... if it should demand the sacrifice of an individual – ?

RÖRLUND. How do you mean?

BERNICK. Take, for example, a man who is thinking of setting up a large factory. He knows for certain because all his experience has taught him that – that sooner or later, in the running of that factory, there will be loss of life.

RÖRLUND. Yes, that is only too probable.

BERNICK. Or a man undertakes mining operations. He takes on fathers of families and young men in the flower of their youth. Can't it be said with certainty that some of these will not come through alive?

RÖRLUND. Yes, unfortunately, that's probably so.

BERNICK. Very well, then. A man like that knows beforehand that the enterprise he is starting will undoubtedly at some point cost human life. But that enterprise is for the general good; for every life it costs it will just as certainly further the welfare of many hundreds.

RÖRLUND. Ah, you're thinking of the railway, of all these dangerous excavations and the blasting and that.

BERNICK. Yes. You're right. I'm thinking of the railway. And besides ... the railway will lead to both factories and mines. But don't you think, all the same – ?

RÖRLUND. My dear Consul, you are almost too conscientious. I think if you put the matter into the hands of Providence –

BERNICK. Yes. Yes, of course. Providence ...

RÖRLUND. – Then you need have no compunction. You can build your railway with an easy mind.

BERNICK. Yes, but now I will put you a special case. Suppose there's a charge to be fired in a dangerous place, and unless it is fired the railway can't be built. Suppose the engineer knows it will cost the life of any workman who lights the fuse, and yet it must be fired and it is the engineer's duty to send a workman to do it ...

RÖRLUND. Hm –

BERNICK. I know what you're going to say. It would be heroic for the engineer to take the match and go and light the charge himself. But people don't do that kind of thing. And so he must sacrifice a workman.

RÖRLUND. That's a thing none of our engineers would ever do.

BERNICK. No engineer in the big countries would hesitate to do it.

RÖRLUND. In the big countries? No, that I can believe. In those corrupt and unprincipled communities –

BERNICK. Oh, there's something to be said for those communities.

RÖRLUND. Can you say that? You, who yourself – ?

BERNICK. In the big communities they have plenty of elbow-room, they can forge ahead with a useful project; they have the courage to sacrifice something for a great object. But here they are tied down by all kinds of petty scruples and considerations.

RÖRLUND. Is human life a petty consideration?

BERNICK. When that life constitutes a threat to the welfare of thousands. ...

RÖRLUND. But you're putting up quite impossible cases, my dear Mr Bernick. I don't understand you at all today. And then you point to the big communities. Yes, out there – what is a human life worth there? They don't reckon in terms of life, but in terms of capital. But I think we look at things from a rather different moral standpoint. Look at all our fine ship-owners. Name me a single one of them who, for mere gain, would sacrifice a human life. And then think of those scoundrels in the big countries who, just to make money, send out one unseaworthy ship after another.

BERNICK. I'm not talking about unseaworthy ships.

RÖRLUND. No. But I am, Mr Bernick.

BERNICK. Yes, but what's the point of it? It doesn't touch the case. Ah, these petty, timid considerations. If one of our generals were to lead his men under fire and get them shot down, he would have sleepless nights after it. It isn't like that in other places. You should hear what that fellow in there has to say –

RÖRLUND. That fellow? Who? The American?

BERNICK. Yes, of course. You should hear how people in America –

RÖRLUND. Is he in there? And you didn't tell me? I shall go at once –

BERNICK. It won't be any use; you won't get anywhere with him.

RÖRLUND. We shall see about that. Oh, here he is.

[*Johan Tönnesen comes in from the room on the left.*]

JOHAN TÖNNESEN [*speaking back through the open door*]. All right, Dina; we'll leave it at that. But I'm not going to let you go, all the same. I shall come back, and things will come right between us then.

RÖRLUND. With your permission, sir, what are you referring to? What do you want?

JOHAN TÖNNESEN. I want that girl to be my wife. The girl to whom you blackened my character yesterday.

RÖRLUND. You – ? You can imagine that – ?

JOHAN TÖNNESEN. I mean to have her for my wife.

RÖRLUND. Well, in that case, you shall hear – [*Goes across to the half-open door.*] Mrs Bernick, will you be so good as to be a witness. ... And you too, Miss Marta. And let Dina come in. [*Sees Miss Hessel.*] Ah, are you here too?

MISS HESSEL [*at the door*]. Shall I come too?

RÖRLUND. As many of you as like: the more the better.

BERNICK. What are you going to do?

[*Miss Hessel, Mrs Bernick, Miss Bernick, Dina and Hilmar Tönnesen come out from the room.*]

MRS BERNICK. Mr Rörlund, with the best will in the world I can't prevent him –

RÖRLUND. I shall prevent him, Mrs Bernick. Dina, you are a thoughtless girl. But I don't blame you too much. You have been here too long without the moral support that you needed to steady you. I blame myself for not having given you this support sooner.

DINA. You mustn't say anything now!

MRS BERNICK. But what is it?

RÖRLUND. It is precisely now that I must speak, Dina, although your behaviour today and yesterday has made it ten times more difficult for me. But to save you, all other considerations must give way. You remember the word I gave you. You remember what you promised to answer, when I found the time had come. Now I must not hesitate any longer, and therefore – [*To Johan Tönnesen.*] This young girl that you are pursuing, is my promised wife.

MRS BERNICK. What do you say?

BERNICK. *Dina!*

JOHAN TÖNNESEN. She! Your – ?

MISS BERNICK. No, no, Dina!

MISS HESSEL. It's a lie!

JOHAN TÖNNESEN. Dina, is this man speaking the truth?

DINA [*after a short pause*]. Yes.

RÖRLUND. This, we may hope, has defeated all your arts of seduction. The step I have decided on for Dina's good can be revealed to the whole of our community. I cherish the hope – I am *sure* – that it will not be misinterpreted. But now, Mrs Bernick, I think we had better take her away from here and try to restore her mind to peace and equilibrium.

MRS BERNICK. Yes, come along. Oh, Dina, what a wonderful thing for you!

[*She takes Dina out to the left; Rörlund goes with them.*]

MISS BERNICK. Good-bye, Johan. [*She goes out.*]

HILMAR TÖNNESEN [*at the garden door*]. Hm – I really must say –

MISS HESSEL [*who has followed Dina with her eyes*]. Don't

lose heart, my boy! I shall be here keeping an eye on the parson. [*She goes out to the right.*]

BERNICK. Now you won't sail on the *Indian Girl*, Johan.

JOHAN TÖNNESEN. More than ever.

BERNICK. But aren't you coming back, then?

JOHAN TÖNNESEN. I'm coming back.

BERNICK. After this? What do you propose to do after this?

JOHAN TÖNNESEN. Revenge myself on the whole pack of you. Crush as many of you as I can.

[*He goes out to the right. Vigeland and Krap come in from Bernick's room.*]

VIGELAND. There you are. The papers are in order now, Mr Bernick.

BERNICK. Good. Good.

KRAP [*in a low voice*]. It's settled, then, that the *Indian Girl*'s to sail tomorrow?

BERNICK. She's to sail.

[*He goes into his room. Vigeland and Krap go out to the right. Hilmar Tönnesen is going to follow them, but at that moment Olaf puts his head cautiously out round the door on the left.*]

OLAF. Uncle! Uncle Hilmar!

HILMAR TÖNNESEN. Ugh! Is that you? Why aren't you staying upstairs? You're supposed to be in your room.

OLAF [*a few steps nearer*]. Hush! Uncle Hilmar, do you know the news?

HILMAR TÖNNESEN. Yes, I know you got a thrashing to-day.

OLAF [*looking threateningly towards his father's room*]. He shan't hit me again. But do you know that Uncle Johan is sailing tomorrow with the Americans?

HILMAR TÖNNESEN. What's that got to do with you? Get along upstairs again.

OLAF. I may go on a buffalo hunt yet, Uncle.

HILMAR TÖNNESEN. Rot! A coward like you –

OLAF. Well, you just wait; you'll find out something in the morning.

HILMAR TÖNNESEN. Little idiot!

[*He goes out through the garden. Olaf runs back into the room and shuts the door when he sees Krap, who comes in from the right.*]

KRAP [*going across to Bernick's door and half opening it*]. Excuse me coming again, Mr Bernick, but it's blowing up for a regular storm. [*Waits a moment; there is no answer.*] Is the *Indian Girl* to sail just the same?

[*After a short pause, Bernick answers from inside the room.*]

BERNICK. The *Indian Girl* is to sail just the same.

[*Krap closes the door and goes out again to the right.*]

ACT FOUR

———— * ————

[*The garden room at the Bernicks'. The work-table has been moved away. It is a stormy afternoon and already dark. The darkness increases during the following scene.*

A servant lights the chandelier; two maids bring in pots of flowers, lamps and lights, which they put on the table and on stands along the walls. Rummel, in evening dress, with gloves and a white tie, is standing in the room giving instructions.]

RUMMEL [*to the servant*]. Only every other light, Jacob. It mustn't look too festive; it's to come as a surprise. And all these flowers? Oh well, let them stay. It will just look as though they had them there every day.

[*Bernick comes out from his room.*]

BERNICK [*at the door*]. What does all this mean?

RUMMEL. Dear me, are you there? [*To the servants.*] Yes, you can go now, for the moment.

[*The footman and the maids go out by the farthest door on the left.*]

BERNICK [*coming farther in*]. But, Rummel, what does all this mean?

RUMMEL. It means that your proudest moment is at hand. This evening the town is coming in procession to honour its leading citizen.

BERNICK. *What* do you say?

RUMMEL. A procession, banners and music! We should have had torches, too, but we didn't like to risk it in this stormy weather. Of course, there will be illuminations. And that will look rather well, too, when it gets into the papers.

BERNICK. Listen, Rummel; I won't have any of this!

RUMMEL. Oh, it's too late now. We shall have them here in half an hour.

BERNICK. But why didn't you tell me about it before?

RUMMEL. Just because I was afraid you'd raise objections. But I consulted your wife. She allowed me to make a few arrangements, and she's going to see about refreshments.

BERNICK [listening]. What's that? Are they coming already? I think I hear singing.

RUMMEL [at the garden door]. Singing? Oh, that's only the Americans. It's the *Indian Girl* that's hauling out to the buoy.

BERNICK. Hauling out! Yes ... No! I can't this evening, Rummel; I'm not well.

RUMMEL. Why yes, you do look pretty bad. But you must pull yourself together. Gracious heavens! You simply must pull yourself together. Sandstad and Vigeland and I all attach the greatest importance to carrying out this scheme. Our opponents must be crushed under the weight of as strong an expression of opinion as possible. There are rumours getting about the town. A statement about the purchase of those properties can't be put off any longer. It is imperative that you should tell them, this very evening, amid the songs and speeches and the ringing of glasses – when, in fact, they are in an expansive and festive mood – the risk you have taken for the good of the community. In that expansive and festive mood, as I just expressed it, one can do a surprising amount with our people.

BERNICK. Yes, yes, yes –

RUMMEL. And especially when such a ticklish and delicate matter is to be brought up. Well, thank heavens, you have a name that can carry it off, Bernick. But listen now, we must arrange things a little. Hilmar Tönnesen has written a song to you. It begins most charmingly with the words, 'Hoist the Ideal's flag on high'. And Rörlund has been deputed to make the Festival Oration. Naturally, you must reply to that.

BERNICK. I can't do it this evening, Rummel. Couldn't you – ?

RUMMEL. Impossible – however much I might like to. The speech, you realize, will be mainly addressed to you. There may, of course, be a few words directed to the rest of us. I have spoken to Vigeland and Sandstad about it. We thought you could answer with a toast to the prosperity of the community, Sandstad speak a few words about concord between the different classes of the community, Vigeland express the hope that the new enterprise will not disturb the moral foundation on which we now stand, while I think of saying a few well-chosen words in recognition of woman, whose humbler activities are by no means without significance. But you're not listening –

BERNICK. Yes – yes, I am. But tell me, do you think there's a very heavy sea outside?

RUMMEL. Ah, you're worried about the *Palm Tree*? But she's well enough insured.

BERNICK. Yes, insured ... but –

RUMMEL. And in good repair. And that's the main thing.

BERNICK. Hm. And if anything does happen to a ship, it doesn't necessarily follow that there is loss of life. The ship and the cargo may be lost – and people may lose baggage and papers –

RUMMEL. What the devil – ? Baggage and papers don't matter much.

BERNICK. Don't they? No, no, I only meant – Hush! They're singing again.

RUMMEL. That's aboard the *Palm Tree*.

[*Vigeland comes in from the right.*]

VIGELAND. Well, the *Palm Tree*'s hauling out. Good evening, Consul.

BERNICK. And you, as a man who knows the sea, still hold fast to – ?

VIGELAND. I hold fast to Providence, for my part, Mr Bernick. Besides I have been aboard and distributed some little tracts that will, I hope, work to good effect.

[*Sandstad and Krap come in from the right.*]

SANDSTAD [*still in the doorway*]. Well, if they bring *that* off, they can bring off anything. Ah, there we are! Good evening, good evening.

BERNICK. Anything the matter, Krap?

KRAP. I've nothing to report, Mr Bernick.

SANDSTAD. The whole crew of the *Indian Girl*'s drunk. If those brutes get over alive, I'll be – !

[*Miss Hessel comes in from the right.*]

MISS HESSEL [*to Bernick*]. Well, he asked me to say good-bye to you.

BERNICK. On board already?

MISS HESSEL. Soon, at any rate. We parted outside the hotel.

BERNICK. And he still holds to his purpose?

MISS HESSEL. Firm as a rock.

RUMMEL [*up by the window*]. The deuce take these new-fangled contrivances! I can't get the blinds down.

MISS HESSEL. Are they to be down? I rather thought –

RUMMEL. Down at first, Miss Hessel. Of course you know what's afoot?

MISS HESSEL. Oh yes. Let me help. [*She takes hold of the cord.*] I'll let the blind down on my brother-in-law, though I'd much rather pull it up.

RUMMEL. You can do that later on. When the garden is filled with the singing throng, then the blinds go up and the people look in on a surprised and happy family. A citizen's home should be as transparent as glass.

[*Bernick seems as if he is going to say something, but turns quickly and goes into his room.*]

RUMMEL. Well, let us hold our last council. You come too, Mr Krap? We want you to help us get one or two facts clear.

[*The men all go into Bernick's room. Miss Hessel has pulled down the window blinds and is just going to do the same with those before the open glass door when Olaf jumps down on to the garden step from above. He has a travelling rug over his shoulder and a bundle in his hand.*]

MISS HESSEL. God forgive you, boy, what a fright you gave me!

OLAF [*hiding the bundle*]. Hush, Aunt Lona!

MISS HESSEL. Why are you jumping out of the window? Where are you going?

OLAF. Hush! Don't say anything. I am going to Uncle Johan. Only down to the quay, you know. Just to say good-bye to him. Good night, Aunt Lona! [*He runs out through the garden.*]

MISS HESSEL. No, stay here. Olaf! Olaf!

[*Johan Tönnesen, dressed for a journey, with a haversack on his shoulders, comes cautiously through the door on the right.*]

JOHAN TÖNNESEN. Lona!

MISS HESSEL [*turning*]. What! Have you come back?

JOHAN TÖNNESEN. There are still a few minutes to spare. I must see her once more. We can't part like this.

[*Miss Bernick and Dina, both with outdoor coats on, and the latter with a small carpet bag in her hand, come in from the farther door on the left.*]

DINA. I must go to him! I must!

MISS BERNICK. Yes, you shall go to him, Dina.

DINA. There he is!

JOHAN TÖNNESEN. Dina!

DINA. Take me with you!

JOHAN TÖNNESEN. What!

MISS HESSEL. You want to?

DINA. Yes, take me with you! *He* has written to me and said that this evening it's to be made public to everyone –

JOHAN TÖNNESEN. Dina, you don't love him?

DINA. I've never loved the man. I shall throw myself into the fjord if I have to be engaged to him! Didn't he force me down on my knees last night with his patronizing words! Didn't he make me feel he was raising something inferior up to himself! I won't be despised any longer. I'll go away. May I come with you?

JOHAN TÖNNESEN. Yes, yes – a thousand times yes!

DINA. I shan't be a burden to you for long. Just help me across. Help me to get on my feet just at first –

JOHAN TÖNNESEN. Hurrah! That'll be all right, Dina!

MISS HESSEL [*pointing towards Bernick's door*]. Hush! Quietly, quietly!

JOHAN TÖNNESEN. I'll take good care of you, Dina.

DINA. I won't let you do that. I want to make my own way and I can do it all right over there. Once I get away from here. Oh, these women – you don't know what it is! They've written to me today. They've exhorted me to think of my good fortune, pointed out to me how generously he has behaved. Tomorrow and every day they'll be watching me to see whether I am making myself worthy of it all. I've a horror of all this respectability!

JOHAN TÖNNESEN. Tell me, Dina, is that the only reason why you are going? Am I nothing to you?

DINA. Oh yes, Johan. You are more to me than everybody else.

JOHAN TÖNNESEN. Oh, Dina – !

DINA. They all say here that I must hate and detest you.

That it's my duty. But I don't understand all this about duty. I never can understand it.

MISS HESSEL. And you shan't either, my child!

MISS BERNICK. No, you shan't. And that's why you shall go with him as his wife.

JOHAN TÖNNESEN. Yes, yes!

MISS HESSEL. What? Now I must kiss you, Marta! I never expected that of you.

MISS BERNICK. No, I can well believe it; I didn't expect it of myself. But it was bound to come to the breaking-point some time. Oh, what we suffer here under the tyranny of custom and convention! Rebel against it, Dina. Be his wife. Let there be *something* to defy all this tradition and habit!

JOHAN TÖNNESEN. What is your answer, Dina?

DINA. Yes, I will be your wife.

JOHAN TÖNNESEN. Dina!

DINA. But I will work first and become something myself, just as you are. I won't be just a thing that is taken.

MISS HESSEL. Quite right. That's the spirit!

JOHAN TÖNNESEN. Good. I shall wait and hope –

MISS HESSEL. – And win, my boy! But now, on board!

JOHAN TÖNNESEN. Yes, on board! Ah, Lona, my dear sister, just a word. Listen –

[*He leads her up to the background and talks rapidly to her.*]

MISS BERNICK. Dina, you lucky girl – let me look at you and kiss you once more – for the last time.

DINA. Not the last time. No, my dear Aunt Marta; we shall see each other again.

MISS BERNICK. Never! Promise me that, Dina: Don't ever come back. [*Taking both her hands and looking at her.*] Now go to your happiness, my precious child – over the sea. Oh, how often have I sat in the school-room and longed to be over there! It must be beautiful there; the skies are wider; the clouds move higher than here; a freer wind blows overhead –

DINA. Oh, Aunt Marta, you'll follow us some day.

MISS BERNICK. I? Never. Never. I have my little work in life here, and now I think I can be fully and wholly what I am to be.

DINA. I don't know how I'm to part with you.

MISS BERNICK. Ah! One can part with a great deal, Dina. [*Kissing her.*] But you will never experience that, my precious child. Promise to make him happy.

DINA. I won't promise anything. I hate this promising. Things must take their course.

MISS BERNICK. Yes, yes. They must. You must just be what you are, honest and true to yourself.

DINA. I will be that, Aunt Marta.

MISS HESSEL [*putting into her pocket some papers that Johan has given her*]. Good, good, my dear boy. But off with you now!

JOHAN TÖNNESEN. Yes, there's no time to lose now. Good-bye, Lona. Thanks for all your love. Good-bye, Marta, and thank you, too, for your faithful friendship.

MISS BERNICK. Good-bye, Johan! Good-bye, Dina! And happiness to you all your days!

[*She and Miss Hessel hurry them towards the door at the back. Johan Tönnesen and Dina go quickly down through the garden. Miss Hessel shuts the door and draws the blind down.*]

MISS HESSEL. Now we're alone, Marta. You have lost her and I him.

MISS BERNICK. You – him?

MISS HESSEL. Oh, I had half lost him already over there. The boy was longing to stand on his own feet. That's why I made him think I wanted to come home.

MISS BERNICK. Was that it? Now I understand why you came. But he'll want you back, Lona.

MISS HESSEL. An old half-sister – what will he want with her now? Men tear their way through a great many ties to get to their happiness.

MISS BERNICK. Yes. That does happen, sometimes. ...

MISS HESSEL. But we will hold together, Marta.

MISS BERNICK. Can I be anything to you?

MISS HESSEL. Who more so? We two foster-mothers, haven't we both lost our children? Now we're alone.

MISS BERNICK. Yes, alone. And so, I will tell you ... I loved him more than anything in the world.

MISS HESSEL. Marta! [*Seizing her arm.*] Is this the truth?

MISS BERNICK. My whole life is in those words. I loved him and waited for him. Every summer I expected him to come. And then he came ... but he did not see me.

MISS HESSEL. Loved him! Yet it was you who put his happiness into his hands ...

MISS BERNICK. Shouldn't I give him happiness, since I loved him? Yes, I have loved him. My life has been lived for him, ever since he went. What grounds had I for hope, you wonder? Well, I think I had some grounds. But when he came back again ... then it seemed as if everything was wiped out of his memory. He didn't see me.

MISS HESSEL. It was Dina who overshadowed you, Marta.

MISS BERNICK. It was right that she did. When he went away we were the same age. When I saw him again – oh, that terrible moment! – I felt that I was ten years older than he. He had lived out there in the pure, radiant sunshine and drawn in youth and health with every breath, while I was sitting indoors here, spinning and spinning –

MISS HESSEL. – The thread of his happiness, Marta.

MISS BERNICK. Yes, it was gold I spun. No bitterness! It's true, Lona, isn't it, we have been two good sisters to him?

MISS HESSEL [*throwing her arms around her*]. Marta!
[*Bernick comes out from his room.*]

BERNICK [*to the men inside*]. Yes, yes. Manage the whole thing as you like. When the time comes, I will – [*Shuts the door.*] Oh, is anyone there? Listen, Marta, you must change your dress. And tell Betty to do the same. I don't want anything elaborate, of course. Just a quiet, indoor dress. But you must be quick.

MISS HESSEL. And a happy, contented look, Marta. Put on a cheerful expression.

BERNICK. Olaf must come down too; I will have him beside me.

MISS HESSEL. Hm. Olaf –

MISS BERNICK. I'll tell Betty. [*She goes out by the farthest door to the left.*]

MISS HESSEL. Well, so now the great and solemn hour has come.

BERNICK [*pacing uneasily to and fro*]. Yes, it has.

MISS HESSEL. A man must feel proud and happy, I should think, at a moment like this.

BERNICK [*looking at her*]. Hm!

MISS HESSEL. The whole town will be illuminated, I hear.

BERNICK. Yes, they've got some such plan.

MISS HESSEL. All the Leagues and Societies are going to turn out with their banners. Your name will shine in letters of fire. Tonight telegrams will go to all parts of the country: 'Surrounded by his happy family, Mr Karsten Bernick received the homage of his fellow-citizens as one of the pillars of the community.'

BERNICK. They will. And they will shout 'Hurrah!' outside and the crowd will call me out by that door and I shall have to bow and thank them.

MISS HESSEL. Why '*have*' to ... ?

BERNICK. Do you think I feel happy at this moment?

MISS HESSEL. No, I don't think you can feel entirely happy.

BERNICK. Lona, you despise me.

MISS HESSEL. Not yet.

BERNICK. And you have no right to. Not to despise me. Lona, you have no idea how indescribably lonely I am here, in this narrow, stunted community; how each year I have had to relinquish more and more of my right to a full and satisfying life. What have I achieved, however much it may seem? Scraps and futile patchwork! But nothing else, nothing greater, is tolerated here. If I tried to go one step ahead of the temper and outlook of the moment, it would be all up with my authority. Do you know what we are, we who are counted the pillars of a community? We are the tools of that community, neither more nor less.

MISS HESSEL. Why are you seeing this now for the first time?

BERNICK. Because I have been thinking a good deal lately – since you came back – and especially this evening. Ah, Lona, why didn't I know you, your real self, then – in the old days.

MISS HESSEL. And what if you had?

BERNICK. I would never have given you up. And if I had had you, I should never have stood where I stand now.

MISS HESSEL. And do you never think what she might have been to you ... she, whom you chose instead?

BERNICK. I know at any rate that she has been nothing to me – nothing that I needed.

MISS HESSEL. Because you have never shared your life-work with her. Because you have never let her be on a free and honest footing with you. Because you have left her to be weighed down by the disgrace and shame you fastened on those nearest to her.

BERNICK. Yes, yes, yes. The whole thing comes from the lies and pretences.

MISS HESSEL. Then why don't you break with all these pretences and lies?

BERNICK. Now? It's too late now, Lona.

MISS HESSEL. Karsten, tell me – what satisfaction does this pretence and imposture give you?

BERNICK. It gives me none. I must go under like all the rest of this social system, rotten and wrecked as it is. But a generation is growing up after us. It is my son I am working for; it is for him that I am building up a life's work. There will come a time when truth becomes a settled habit in the life of the people, and on that he shall base a happier life than his father's.

MISS HESSEL. With a lie as the groundwork? Think what it is you are giving your son as a heritage.

BERNICK [*repressing his despair*]. I am giving him a thousand times worse heritage than you know of. But some day the curse must be lifted. And yet – and yet – [*Breaking out.*] How could you bring all this down on me! But it's done now. Now, I must go on. You shan't have the satisfaction of breaking me!

[*Hilmar Tönnesen, with an open letter in his hand, comes in from the right, hurried and distracted.*]

HILMAR TÖNNESEN. But this is really – Betty, Betty!

BERNICK. What is it? Are they coming already?

HILMAR TÖNNESEN. No, no. But I absolutely must speak to somebody – [*He goes out by the farthest door to the left.*]

MISS HESSEL. Karsten, you talk of us coming here to break you. So now let me tell you what stuff he's made of, this prodigal son that your moral community shuns as if he had the plague. He can do without you. for he's gone now.

BERNICK. But he'll come back –

MISS HESSEL. Johan will never come back. He's gone for good, and Dina has gone with him.

BERNICK. Not coming back? And Dina gone with him?

MISS HESSEL. Yes, to be his wife. That's how those two have slapped the face of your virtuous society, just as I did once. ... Well!

BERNICK. Gone. She too. On the *Indian Girl* ...

MISS HESSEL. No. He didn't dare trust such a precious cargo to that abandoned lot. Johan and Dina have sailed on the *Palm Tree*.

BERNICK. Ah! So ... to no purpose ... [*Goes quickly across, tears open the door of his room and calls in.*] Krap, stop the *Indian Girl*. She mustn't sail tonight.

KRAP [*from inside*]. The *Indian Girl*'s already standing out to sea, Mr Bernick.

BERNICK [*shuts the door and says dully*]. Too late ... and to no purpose. ...

MISS HESSEL. What do you mean?

BERNICK. Nothing. Nothing. Go away!

MISS HESSEL. Hm. Look here, Karsten. Johan told me to tell you that he leaves in my hands the name and reputation he once lent you, and likewise the one you stole from him while he was gone. Johan will say nothing and I can act or not, as I like, in the matter. Look, here I have your two letters in my hand.

BERNICK. You have them! And now, now you're going to – this very evening – perhaps when the procession –

MISS HESSEL. I did not come here to expose you, but to rouse you to speak of your own free will. I haven't succeeded. So stay rooted in the lie. Look here: I am tearing your two letters to pieces. ... Take the pieces: there they are. Now there is nothing to bear witness against you, Karsten. You are safe now. Be happy too – if you can.

BERNICK [*deeply moved*]. Lona, why didn't you do this

before? Now it is too late. Life is ruined for me now. I can't go on with my life after today.

MISS HESSEL. What has happened?

BERNICK. Don't ask me. But yet I must live. I *will* live, for Olaf's sake. He shall put everything right, atone for everything –

MISS HESSEL. Karsten!

[*Hilmar Tönnesen comes hurriedly in again.*]

HILMAR TÖNNESEN. No one to be found. All out. Not even Betty.

BERNICK. What's the matter with you?

HILMAR TÖNNESEN. I daren't tell you.

BERNICK. What is it? You must tell me, you shall!

HILMAR TÖNNESEN. Well, then, Olaf has run away on the *Indian Girl.*

BERNICK [*staggering back*]. Olaf – on the *Indian Girl!* No, no!

MISS HESSEL. He has, has he? Now I understand. I saw him jump out of the window.

BERNICK [*at the door of his room, calling in despair*]. Krap, stop the *Indian Girl* at any price!

KRAP [*coming out*]. Impossible, Mr Bernick. How can you think – ?

BERNICK. We *must* stop her. Olaf is on board!

KRAP. What do you say?

RUMMEL [*coming out*]. Olaf run away? It's not possible!

SANDSTAD [*entering*]. He'll be sent back with the pilot, of course.

HILMAR TÖNNESEN. No, no; he has written to me. [*Showing the letter.*] He says he's going to hide in the cargo till they are in the open sea.

BERNICK. I shall never see him again!

RUMMEL. Oh, nonsense. A good, strong ship, newly repaired –

VIGELAND [*who has also come out*]. – Out of your own yard, Mr Bernick.

BERNICK. I shall never see him again, I tell you. I have lost him, Lona, and – I see it now – he has never really belonged to me. [*Listening.*] What is that?

RUMMEL. Music. The procession is coming.

BERNICK. I can't, I won't meet anyone.

RUMMEL. What are you thinking of? This will never do.

SANDSTAD. Impossible. Mr Bernick. Think what you have at stake.

BERNICK. What does all that matter to me now? Whom have I now to work for?

RUMMEL. Can you ask such a question? You have us and the community.

VIGELAND. Yes; that's a true word.

SANDSTAD. And surely you're not forgetting, Consul, that we –

[*Miss Bernick comes in by the farthest door at the left back. Music is heard, softly, far away down the street.*]

MISS BERNICK. The procession's coming now. But Betty isn't at home. I can't understand where she –

BERNICK. Not at home! There, you see, Lona. No support either in joy or in sorrow.

RUMMEL. Up with the blinds! Come and help me, Mr Krap. You too, Sandstad. A dreadful pity the family should be so scattered, just at this moment! Dead against the programme.

[*The blinds are pulled up from the windows and the door. The whole street is seen to be illuminated. On the opposite house is a large transparency with the inscription, 'Long live Karsten Bernick, the Pillar of our Community'.*]

BERNICK [*shrinking back*]. Take away all that! I don't want to see it! Put it out! Put it out!

RUMMEL. With all due respect, are you out of your mind?

MISS BERNICK. What's the matter with him, Lona?

MISS HESSEL. Hush! [*Speaks to her in a low voice.*]

BERNICK. Take away that inscription! It's a mockery, I tell you! Don't you see that all these lights – they're flames, putting out their tongues at us.

RUMMEL. Well, I must admit –

BERNICK. Ah, what do you know about it! But I, I – ! These lights are funeral tapers!

KRAP. Hm –

RUMMEL. Now look here, old man, you're taking all this too hard.

SANDSTAD. The lad will get a trip across the Atlantic and then you'll have him back again.

VIGELAND. Only trust to the hand of the Almighty, Mr Bernick.

RUMMEL. And to the ship, Bernick. It's not going to sink, *that* I know.

KRAP. Hm.

RUMMEL. Now, if it was one of these floating coffins one hears of in the big countries –

BERNICK. I feel my hair turning grey in this hour.

[*Mrs Bernick, with a large shawl over her head, comes in by the garden door.*]

MRS BERNICK. Karsten, Karsten, do you know – ?

BERNICK. Yes, I know. But you, who see nothing, you who can't keep a mother's eye on him – !

MRS BERNICK. But listen – !

BERNICK. Why didn't you watch him? Now I've lost him. Give him back to me, if you can!

MRS BERNICK. But I *can*. I've got him!

BERNICK. You've got him!

THE MEN. Ah!

HILMAR TÖNNESEN. Yes, I thought as much.

MISS BERNICK. You've got him back, Karsten!

MISS HESSEL. Yes. And now win him, too.

BERNICK. You've got him! Is that true, what you're saying? Where is he?

MRS BERNICK. You're not to know that till you've forgiven him.

BERNICK. Forgiven! Good Lord! But how did you find out – ?

MRS BERNICK. Do you think a mother doesn't notice? I was desperately afraid you'd find out something. A word or two that he let slip yesterday. ... And his room was empty and his rucksack and his clothes were gone. ...

BERNICK. Yes, well – ?

MRS BERNICK. I ran and got hold of Aune, and we went out in his sailing-boat. The American ship was just getting under way. But, thank God, we got there in time. We went aboard, had the hold searched and found him. Oh, Karsten, you mustn't punish him!

BERNICK. Betty!

MRS BERNICK. Nor Aune.

BERNICK. Aune? What do you know about him? Is the *Indian Girl* under sail again?

MRS BERNICK. No, that's just it –

BERNICK. Tell me! Go on!

MRS BERNICK. Aune was just as upset as I was. The search took some time, it was getting dark and the pilot made difficulties. And so Aune ventured – in your name –

BERNICK. Well?

MRS BERNICK. To stop the ship till tomorrow.

KRAP. Hm –

BERNICK. Oh, what an unspeakable mercy!

MRS BERNICK. You're not angry?

BERNICK. Oh, what a supreme mercy, Betty!

RUMMEL. You really are too conscientious.

HILMAR TÖNNESEN. Yes, directly there's a prospect of a little battle with the elements, then – ugh!

KRAP [up by the window]. The procession is just coming through the garden gate, Mr Bernick.

BERNICK. Yes, they can come now.

RUMMEL. The whole garden is filling with people.

SANDSTAD. The whole street is crammed.

RUMMEL. The whole town is out, Bernick. This is a really inspiring moment.

VIGELAND. Let us take it in a humble spirit, Mr Rummel.

RUMMEL. All the banners are out. What a procession! There's our committee with Mr Rörlund at its head.

BERNICK. All right. Let them come.

RUMMEL. But, look here, the state of mind you're in –

BERNICK. Well, what about it?

RUMMEL. I should be quite willing to speak on your behalf.

BERNICK. No, thanks. Tonight I will speak for myself.

RUMMEL. But do you know what you're to say?

BERNICK. Make your mind easy, Rummel; I know what I'm to say – now.

[The music has ceased in the meantime. The garden door is thrown open. Rörlund enters at the head of the committee, accompanied by a couple of servants who carry a covered basket. After them come townsfolk of all classes, as many as the room can hold. An immense crowd, with banners and flags, can just be seen outside in the garden and along the street.]

RÖRLUND. Our congratulations to you, sir! I see, by the astonishment depicted on your face, that we are forcing ourselves upon you as unexpected guests, here in your happy family circle, by your peaceful hearth, surrounded by distinguished and public-spirited friends and fellow-citizens. But in response to the impulse of our hearts, we bring you our salutation. It is not the first time such a thing has happened, but it is the first time it has happened on so vast a scale. Many times we have rendered thanks to you for the broad moral foundation on which, so to speak, you have built up our community. This time we hail in you, above all, the clear-sighted, tireless, selfless, nay, self-sacrificing fellow-citizen, who has taken the initiative in an enterprise which, in the opinion of all who know, will give a tremendous impulse to the temporal prosperity and well-being of this community.

VOICES IN THE CROWD. Bravo! Bravo!

RÖRLUND. You, sir, have led our town for many years by your shining example. I am not speaking now of your exemplary domestic life, nor yet of the untarnished virtue of your conduct. Let such things be reserved for private speech. They are not for public celebration. No, I speak of your public service, done openly in the sight of all men. Well-found ships go out from your yards and fly our flag in the farthest seas. A large and happy body of workmen look up to you as to a father. By calling into being new industrial developments you have laid the foundations of prosperity for hundreds of families. In other words, you are, in a special sense, the chief pillar of this community.

VOICES. Hear! Hear! Bravo!

RÖRLUND. And it is precisely this selflessness, shedding its radiance upon all your doings, whose influence is so beneficent, particularly in these times. You are now about to procure for us a – yes, I will not hesitate to call it by its prosaic, everyday name – a railway.

MANY VOICES. Bravo! Bravo!

RÖRLUND. But it would appear that this undertaking is meeting with difficulties, largely set up by narrow, selfish interests.

VOICES. Hear! Hear!

RÖRLUND. It is no longer a secret that certain individuals

who do not belong to our community, have forestalled the hard-working and thrifty citizens of this place and got possession of certain advantages that should by rights have accrued to our own township.

VOICES. Yes, yes! Hear hear!

RÖRLUND. This deplorable fact naturally came to your notice, Mr Bernick. But, nevertheless, you pursued your purpose unswervingly, well knowing that a patriotic citizen must not keep before him only the interests of his own parish.

VARIOUS VOICES. What? No! No! Yes! Yes!

RÖRLUND. It is such a man, loyal to both town and State – such as a man must be and ought to be – that we salute tonight, in your person. May your undertaking be a source of real and enduring prosperity to this community. The railway can, admittedly, be a means of laying us open to corrupting influences from the outer world, but it can also be a means of rapidly ridding us of them. And even as it is, we cannot altogether avoid evil elements from without. But the fact is that, on this festive night itself, we have, as I hear, happily (and more rapidly than we expected), got rid of certain elements of that very kind –

VOICES. Hush! Hush!

RÖRLUND. – *That* I regard as a happy omen for the enterprise. The fact that I touch upon this matter *here* shows that we are in a house where the claims of morality are honoured above the bonds of kinship.

VOICES. Hear! Hear! Bravo!

BERNICK [*simultaneously*]. Permit me –

RÖRLUND. Only a few words more, sir. What you have done for this community you certainly have not done with the idea of any tangible reward for yourself. But you must not refuse a slight token of the appreciation of your grateful fellow-citizens, least of all in this momentous hour, when, as we are assured by men of practical experience, we stand on the threshold of a new era.

MANY VOICES. Bravo! Hear! Hear!

[*He makes a sign to the servants, who bring forward the basket. Members of the committee take out and present, during the following speech, the articles to which he refers.*]

RÖRLUND. Consul Bernick, sir, we have now to present to you a silver coffee-service. Let it grace your board when, in the future as so often in the past, we have the pleasure of meeting together in this hospitable house. And you too, gentlemen, who have so staunchly supported the leader of our community, we beg you each to accept a little souvenir. This silver goblet is for you, Mr Rummel. You have often, to the ring of glasses, championed in eloquent words the civic interests of this community; may you often find worthy occasions to raise and drain this goblet. To you, Mr Sandstad, I present this album with photographs of your fellow-citizens. Your known and acknowledged liberality has placed you in the happy position of possessing friends in all sections of the community. And to you, Mr Vigeland, I have to offer, as an ornament for your study, this volume of family devotions, printed upon vellum and sumptuously bound. Under the mellowing influence of years, you have attained to a view of life that is earnest and grave. Your diligence in your daily duty has, for many years, been sanctified and ennobled by thoughts of higher and holier things. [*Turning to the crowd.*] And now, my friends, long live Consul Bernick and his fellow-workers! Hurrah for the Pillars of our Community!

THE WHOLE CROWD. Long live Consul Bernick! Long live the Pillars of the Community! Hurrah! Hurrah! Hurrah!

MISS HESSEL. Congratulations, Karsten!

[*An expectant silence.*]

BERNICK [*beginning to speak, seriously and slowly*]. Fellow-citizens – your spokesman has said that we stand tonight on the threshold of a new era, and I hope that will turn out to be so. But if it *is* to, we must lay to heart the truth – truth which, until tonight, has been utterly and in every way alien to our community.

[*Surprise among the bystanders.*]

BERNICK. I must begin by rejecting the eulogy with which, as is customary on these occasions, you, Mr Rörlund, have overwhelmed me. I do not deserve it; for, until today, I have not been a disinterested man. Even if I have not always striven for money, nevertheless, as I am well aware now, a craving for power and influence and reputation has been the driving force behind most of my actions.

RUMMEL [*half-aloud*]. What the devil – ?

BERNICK. In the presence of my fellow-citizens I do not reproach myself for this. For I still think I can count myself one of our leading business men.

VOICES. Yes, yes, yes!

BERNICK. But what I do charge myself with is this, that I have often been weak enough to descend to crooked practices because I knew and feared the tendency of our community to suspect dishonest motives behind everything a man undertakes. And now I come to a case in point.

RUMMEL [*uneasily*]. Hm – hm!

BERNICK. There are rumours going about of large purchases of property up inland. This property I have bought – all of it. I alone.

LOW MURMURS. What does he say? Bernick? Consul Bernick?

BERNICK. It is at the moment in my hands. Naturally I have confided in my colleagues, Mr Rummel, Mr Vigeland and Mr Sandstad, and we agree to –

RUMMEL. That's not true! Proof! Proof!

VIGELAND. We agreed to nothing!

SANDSTAD. Well, now I really must say –

BERNICK. That is quite right. We have not yet agreed on the matter I was about to mention. But I am quite sure these three gentlemen will endorse me when I say that I came this evening to an agreement with myself that these properties shall be thrown open to general subscription. Whoever will may take shares in them.

MANY VOICES. Hurrah! Long live Consul Bernick!

RUMMEL [to Bernick in a low voice]. What a vile piece of treachery!

SANDSTAD [similarly]. Fooled us, then!

VIGELAND. Now, may the devil take –! Good heavens, what am I saying?

THE CROWD [from outside]. Hurrah! Hurrah! Hurrah!

BERNICK. Silence, gentlemen. I have no right to this acclamation, for what I have now decided was not my first intention. My intention was to keep the whole myself, and I am still of the opinion that this property can be best administered if it remains entire in one man's hands. But you can choose. If that is what you want, then I am willing to administer it to the best of my ability,

VOICES. Yes, yes, yes!

BERNICK. But first, my fellow-citizens must know me to the core. Then let everyone look into himself, and let it be true, that from tonight we do begin a new era. The old one, with its false colouring, its hypocrisy and its shams, with its pretended respectability and its pitiful calculations, shall remain as a museum, open for instruction. And to this museum we will hand over – will we

not, gentlemen? – the coffee-service and the goblet and
the album and the volume of family devotions printed
upon vellum and sumptuously bound.

RUMMEL. Oh yes, of course.

VIGELAND [*mumbling*]. Since you've taken all the rest,
why –

SANDSTAD. Pray do ...

BERNICK. And now, to the main item in my settlement
with the community. We have been told that certain
'evil elements' have left us tonight. I can add, what is not
known, that the man who was referred to has not gone
alone. With him went, to become his wife –

MISS HESSEL [*loudly*]. – Dina Dorf!

RÖRLUND. What!

MRS BERNICK. What do you say?

[*Great excitement.*]

RÖRLUND. Gone! Run away – with *him*! Impossible!

BERNICK. To become his wife, Mr Rörlund. And I have
more to add. [*Softly.*] Betty, be prepared to hear what's
coming. [*Aloud.*] I say 'All honour to that man', for he
generously took another man's sin upon him. Fellow-
citizens, I will have done with lying; it has come near to
poisoning every fibre of me. You shall know everything.
Fifteen years ago, I was the guilty man.

MRS BERNICK [*in a low and trembling voice*]. Karsten!

MISS BERNICK [*in the same voice*]. Ah, Johan!

[*Speechless amazement among the bystanders.*]

BERNICK. Yes, my fellow-citizens – I was the guilty one
and he went away. The false and wicked rumours which
were spread about afterwards, it is now beyond human
power to refute. But I cannot pity myself for that. Fifteen years ago I raised myself by those rumours; whether
I am to fall by them now, each of you must decide for
himself.

RÖRLUND. What a thunderbolt! The leading man in the town! [*In a low voice to Mrs Bernick.*] Oh, my dear lady, how I grieve for you!

HILMAR TÖNNESEN. Such a confession! Well, I must say –!

BERNICK. But we will make no decision tonight. I ask each one of you to go to his home; to collect himself; to look into himself. When your minds are calm again, it will be seen whether I have lost or gained by speaking. Good-bye. I have still much, very much, to repent of; but that concerns my own conscience alone. Good night. Take away these decorations. We all feel they are out of place here.

RÖRLUND. They certainly are. [*In a low voice, to Mrs Bernick.*] Run away! Then she was completely unworthy of me, after all. [*Half-aloud, to the committee.*] Well, gentlemen, after this I think we had better withdraw in silence.

HILMAR TÖNNESEN. How one is to keep the flag of idealism flying after this – Ugh!

[*The information has in the meantime been whispered from mouth to mouth. All those who were taking part in the procession go away through the garden. Rummel, Sandstad and Vigeland go out in angry but subdued altercation. Hilmar Tönnesen slips out to the right. Bernick, Mrs Bernick, Miss Bernick, Miss Hessel and Krap remain behind in the room in silence.*]

BERNICK. Betty, can you forgive me?

MRS BERNICK [*looking at him and smiling*]. Do you know, Karsten, you have just shown me the happiest prospect I have seen for many a year?

BERNICK. How?

MRS BERNICK. For many years I believed that I had had you once and lost you again. Now I know that I have never had you; but I shall win you.

BERNICK [*putting his arms round her*]. Oh, Betty, you have

won me! I first learnt to know you properly through
Lona. But let Olaf come in now.

MRS BERNICK. Yes, you shall have him now. Mr Krap!

[*She talks quietly to him in the background. He goes out through
the garden door. During the following dialogue the illuminations
and the lights in the houses gradually go out.*]

BERNICK [*softly*]. Thank you, Lona, you have saved the
best in me – and for me.

MISS HESSEL. What else was I trying to do?

BERNICK. Well, was it that? Or wasn't it? I can't quite
make you out.

MISS HESSEL. Hm.

BERNICK. It wasn't hatred, then? Nor revenge? Then why
did you come over?

MISS HESSEL. Old friendship doesn't rust.

BERNICK. Lona!

MISS HESSEL. When Johan told me all this, about the lie,
I swore to myself: The hero of my youth shall stand free
and clear.

BERNICK. Oh, how little have I deserved this of you – a
wretched creature like me!

MISS HESSEL. Well, if we women asked for our deserts,
Karsten –

[*Aune comes in from the garden with Olaf.*]

BERNICK [*going to him*]. Olaf!

OLAF. Father, I promise I won't ever do it again.

BERNICK. Run away?

OLAF. Yes, yes. I promise you, Father.

BERNICK. And I promise you you shan't ever have reason
to. In future you shall be allowed to grow up, not as the
inheritor of my life-work, but as someone who has a
life-work of his own to look forward to.

OLAF. And will you let me be whatever I want to?

BERNICK. Yes, you shall.

OLAF. Thank you. Then I won't be a pillar of the community.

BERNICK. No? Why not?

OLAF. Because I think that must be so dull.

BERNICK. You shall be yourself, Olaf. And the rest must take its course. And you, Aune –

AUNE. I know, sir. I'm discharged.

BERNICK. We're not separating, Aune. And forgive me –

AUNE. What do you mean? The boat isn't sailing tonight.

BERNICK. She's not sailing tomorrow, either. I gave you too little time. The job must be done thoroughly.

AUNE. It shall be, sir. And with the new machines, too!

BERNICK. So it shall. But thoroughly and honestly. There's a good deal here that needs a thorough, honest overhaul. Well, good night, Aune.

AUNE. Good night, sir. And thanks, thanks! [*Goes out to the right.*]

MISS BERNICK. They are all gone now.

BERNICK. And we are alone. My name is not shining in letters of fire any more. All the lights in the windows are out.

MISS HESSEL. Would you want them lit again?

BERNICK. Not for anything in the world. Where have I been? You will be shocked when you know. Now I feel as if I had come to my senses after being poisoned. But what I do feel is that I can be young and strong again. Oh, come nearer, closer round me. Come, Betty! Come, Olaf, my boy! And you, Marta – I don't seem to have seen you all these years.

MISS HESSEL. No, that I well believe. Yours is a community of old bachelors: you don't see women.

BERNICK. True. True. And for that very reason – yes, that's settled, Lona – you are not going to leave Betty and me.

MRS BERNICK. No, Lona, you mustn't!

MISS HESSEL. Why, how could I have the conscience to leave you young people who are just beginning to set up house? I'm a foster-mother, you know. You and I, Marta, we two old aunts – What are you looking at?

MISS BERNICK. How the sky is clearing. It's getting light over the sea. The *Palm Tree* has good luck with her.

MISS HESSEL. And good luck on board.

BERNICK. And we – we have a long, hard day's work ahead of us; I most of all. But let it come. So long as you stand close about me, you faithful, truthful women. I have learnt that, too, these last days; it is women who are the pillars of the community.

MISS HESSEL. Then you have learnt a poor kind of wisdom, my dear man. [*Laying her hands firmly on his shoulders.*] No, my dear: the spirit of truth and the spirit of freedom, they are the pillars of the community.

CHARACTERS

———————— * ————————

WERLE, works owner and wholesale merchant
GREGERS WERLE, his son
OLD EKDAL
HJALMAR EKDAL, his son, a photographer
GINA EKDAL, Hjalmar's wife
HEDVIG, their fourteen-year-old daughter
MRS SÖRBY, housekeeper to Werle senior
RELLING, a doctor
MOLVIK, sometime theological student
GRAABERG, a book-keeper
PETTERSEN, servant to Werle senior.
JENSEN, a hired waiter
A fat guest
A thin-haired guest
A near-sighted guest
Six other guests
Several hired waiters

The first act takes place at Werle senior's house; the four following acts at Hjalmar Ekdal's.

ACT ONE

———————— * ————————

[*At Werle's house. A study expensively and comfortably furnished, with bookcases and upholstered furniture, a writing-table with papers and documents in the middle of the room and lighted lamps with green shades, so that it is softly lit. At the back of the room are open folding-doors with their curtains drawn back, and through them can be seen a fine, spacious room, brilliantly lit with lamps and candelabra. In the study, downstage right, a little private door leads to the offices. Down left is a fireplace with a bright fire, and farther back a double-door to the dining-room.*

Pettersen, Werle's servant, in livery, and Jensen, the hired waiter, in black, are putting the study straight. In the larger room two or three other hired waiters are going round tidying and lighting more candles. From inside the dining-room can be heard the murmur of conversation and the laughter of many voices; someone taps his glass with his knife; there is silence and a health is proposed; then cheers and the murmur of conversation again.]

PETTERSEN [*lighting a lamp on the mantelpiece and putting on the shade*]. Just you listen, Jensen; there's the old man on his feet now, making a long speech – a toast to Mrs Sörby.

JENSEN [*moving an arm-chair forward*]. D'you think it's true, what they say – that there's something between 'em?

PETTERSEN. Lord knows.

JENSEN. Of course, he's been a lad in his time, all right.

PETTERSEN. Maybe.

JENSEN. But they say it's for his son he's giving this luncheon party.

PETTERSEN. Yes. His son came home yesterday.

JENSEN. I never knew before that old Werle so much as had a son.

PETTERSEN. Oh yes, he's got a son. But he just buries himself up there at the Höidal works. He's never been to town all the years I've been in service here.

A HIRED WAITER [at the door of the other room]. I say, Pettersen, there's an old chap here that –

PETTERSEN [muttering]. Oh damn! What's he want to come now for!

[Old Ekdal appears from the right in the inner room. He is dressed in a shabby great-coat with a high collar and woollen gloves. He has a stick and a fur cap in his hand and a brown-paper parcel under his arm. He wears a dirty, reddish-brown wig and a little grey moustache.]

PETTERSEN [going towards him]. Good Lord! What do you want in here?

EKDAL [at the door]. I simply must get into the office, Pettersen.

PETTERSEN. The office shut an hour ago, and –

EKDAL. So I heard at the door, old man. But Graaberg's in there still. Be a good chap, Pettersen, and let me slip in that way. [Points to the private door.] I've gone in that way before.

PETTERSEN. All right; you can, then. [Opens the door.] But remember, now, you're to go out the proper way. We've got visitors.

EKDAL. I know, I know. Thanks, Pettersen, old man. Good old friend! Thanks. [Muttering under his breath.] Old idiot! [He goes into the office. Pettersen shuts the door after him.]

JENSEN. Is he one of the chaps in the office?

PETTERSEN. No. He just does a bit of copying at home, when they're pressed. But for all that, he's been a proper gentleman in his time, has old Ekdal.

JENSEN. Yes, he looked that sort, somehow.

PETTERSEN. He is. You mightn't think it, but he was a lieutenant.

JENSEN. Good lord! Him a lieutenant!

PETTERSEN. Yes he was, all right. But he took to the timber trade or whatever it was. He's supposed to have played old Werle a real, low-down trick one time, so they say. You see, those two, they were running the Höidal works together then. Oh, I know old Ekdal well, I do. Many's the time we've had a glass of bitters or a bottle of beer together at Mother Eriksen's.

JENSEN. Can't have much to treat you with, he can't.

PETTERSEN. Oh Lord, it's me that does the treating! What d'you think! Seems to me one ought to show a bit of respect for gentry that's come down in the world.

JENSEN. Did he go bankrupt, then?

PETTERSEN. No, it was a bit worse than that. He got penal servitude.

JENSEN. Penal servitude!

PETTERSEN. Or maybe it was only first division – [*Listening.*] Sh! They're getting up from table now.

[*The dining-room door is thrown open from inside by two servants. Mrs Sörby comes out talking to two of the guests. The rest of the guests follow by degrees, and among them Werle senior. Last come Hjalmar Ekdal and Gregers Werle.*]

MRS SÖRBY [*in passing, to the servant*]. Pettersen, will you have coffee served in the music-room?

PETTERSEN. Very good, Mrs Sörby.

[*She and the two men go up into the inner room and then out to the right. Pettersen and Jensen go out the same way.*]

A FAT GUEST [*to a thin-haired one*]. Whew! That dinner! That was quite a stiff job of work.

THE THIN-HAIRED GUEST. Oh, it's incredible what one can manage in three hours with a little good-will.

THE FAT GUEST. Yes, but afterwards, my dear fellow, afterwards!

A THIRD GUEST. I gather that coffee and liqueurs are to be served in the music-room.

THE FAT GUEST. Excellent! And perhaps Mrs Sörby will play us something.

THE THIN-HAIRED GUEST [*in an undertone*]. So long as Mrs Sörby doesn't play us a trick, my friend.

THE FAT GUEST. Oh, not a bit of it! Berta wouldn't throw her old friends over. [*They laugh and go into the inner room.*]

WERLE [*in a low, depressed voice*]. I don't think anyone noticed it, Gregers.

GREGERS [*looking at him*]. What?

WERLE. Didn't you notice it either?

GREGERS. What should I have noticed?

WERLE. We were thirteen at table.

GREGERS. Really? Thirteen, were we?

WERLE [*with a glance towards Hjalmar Ekdal*]. In the ordinary way, we are always twelve. [*To the others.*] Will you come in here, gentlemen. [*He and the remaining guests, except Hjalmer and Gregers, go out at the back to the right.*]

HJALMAR [*who has overheard the conversation*]. You shouldn't have sent me that invitation, Gregers.

GREGERS. What! The party is supposed to be for *me*. And if I can't ask my best and only friend –

HJALMAR. But I don't think your father likes it. In the ordinary way, I never come to the house.

GREGERS. No, so I gather. But I had to see you and talk to you, because I expect to be off again directly. Well, my friend, we two old schoolfellows certainly have drifted a long way apart. We haven't seen each other now for sixteen or seventeen years.

HJALMAR. Is it as long as that?

GREGERS. Yes, it's quite that. Well now, how are you getting on? You're looking well. You've put on flesh; you're almost stout.

HJALMAR. Well, you can hardly call it stout; but no doubt I look more of a man than I did.

GREGERS. Yes, you do; your outer man hasn't suffered.

HJALMAR [*in a gloomier voice*]. But the inner man, my friend! It's a different matter there, as you can guess. You know, of course, the terrible catastrophe that has overtaken us all since you and I last met.

GREGERS [*lowering his voice*]. How are things with your father now?

HJALMAR. My dear fellow, don't let's talk about it. My poor, unhappy father makes his home with me, of course. He has no one else in the world to lean on. But it's heartbreaking for me to talk about all this, you know. I'd rather you told me how you have been getting on up there at the works.

GREGERS. I have had a fine, solitary life. A good opportunity to think things over – all sorts of things. Come over here and let's be comfortable. [*He sits down in an arm-chair by the fireplace and pulls Hjalmar down into another beside him.*]

HJALMAR [*with sentiment*]. But I'm grateful to you all the same, Gregers, for asking me here. I know now that you haven't anything against me any more.

GREGERS [*in surprise*]. Whatever made you think I had anything against you?

HJALMAR. Why, you had – for the first few years.

GREGERS. What first few years?

HJALMAR. After our great misfortune came upon us. And it was only natural that you should. After all, your father himself was nearly dragged into this – this dreadful business! It all hung on a hair.

GREGERS. And because of that, I was to have a grudge against you? Whoever put that idea into your head?

HJALMAR. You *did* have, Gregers. I know. It was your father himself who told me.

GREGERS [*a little puzzled*]. My father! I see. Well ... was that the reason you never let me hear from you afterwards? Not a single word?

HJALMAR. Yes.

GREGERS. Not even when you went and took up photography?

HJALMAR. Your father said I'd better not write to you – about anything.

GREGERS [*abstractedly*]. Well, well. Maybe he was right. But tell me, Hjalmar, are you finding things more or less tolerable now?

HJALMAR [*with a slight sigh*]. Oh yes, on the whole. I can't honestly say I don't. At first, as you can imagine, it was rather difficult for me. They were such completely different conditions I had to tackle. But then everything else was quite different too. That great, overwhelming misfortune of father's – the shame and the disgrace, Gregers –

GREGERS [*with a shudder*]. Yes, yes, Quite. Yes.

HJALMAR. I couldn't dream of staying on at the university; there wasn't a shilling left. On the contrary, there were debts. Mostly to your father, I believe –

GREGERS. Oh ...

HJALMAR. Well, anyway, I thought it best to make a clean break, you know, and got right away from the old life and the old connexions. It was your father, more than anyone else, who advised me to. And as he did so much to help me –

GREGERS. My father did?

HJALMAR. Yes, surely you know that? Where was I to get

the money to learn photography and set up a studio and start in business? It mounts up, you know, all that.

GREGERS. And it was my father who paid for it all?

HJALMAR. Yes, my dear fellow, don't you know that? I understood from him that he'd written and told you.

GREGERS. Not a word about its being *he*. He must have forgotten. We've never written each other anything but business letters. So it was my father, was it?

HJALMAR. Yes, it certainly was. He has never wanted anyone to know about it, but it *was* he. And it was he, too, who made it possible for me to get married. But perhaps you don't know about that either?

GREGERS. No, I certainly didn't. [*Taking him by the arm and giving it a little shake.*] But my dear Hjalmar, I can't tell you how glad I am about all this – but a bit bothered too. I may have been unjust to my father, after all, over certain things. Because all this shows a kind heart, doesn't it? It rather suggests the working of conscience –

HJALMAR. Conscience?

GREGERS. Well, well – whatever you like to call it. But I really can't tell you how glad I am to hear this about my father. So you're married, Hjalmar! That's more than I'm ever likely to be. Well, I hope you're happy in your marriage?

HJALMAR. Yes, I certainly am. She's as good and capable a wife as any man could ask for. And she's not altogether without education either.

GREGERS [*a little surprised*]. Why, no; I'm sure she isn't.

HJALMAR. No. Life is an education, you see. Associating with me every day ... and then there are one or two quite intelligent people who come to see us pretty regularly. I assure you, you wouldn't know Gina again.

GREGERS. Gina?

HJALMAR. Yes, my dear man, don't you remember she was called Gina?

GREGERS. Who was called Gina? I haven't the foggiest idea what –

HJALMAR. But don't you remember she was in service here at one time?

GREGERS [looking at him]. Is it Gina Hansen?

HJALMAR. Yes, of course it's Gina Hansen.

GREGERS. – Who kept house for us the last year of Mother's illness?

HJALMAR. Yes, of course. But my dear fellow, I know for certain that your father wrote you I was married.

GREGERS [getting up]. Yes, he did that all right. But not that – [Walking about the room.] Oh, wait a minute. Perhaps, after all, when I come to think of it ... my father always writes me such short letters. [Sitting on the arm of a chair.] Look here. Tell me, Hjalmar – this is rather funny – how did it happen that you got to know Gina ... your wife?

HJALMAR. Oh, it happened quite simply. Gina didn't stay long in the house here. Everything was so upset then, what with your mother's illness. ... Gina couldn't stand it, so she left. That was the year before your mother died – or it may have been the same year.

GREGERS. It was the same year. I was up at the works at the time. But afterwards?

HJALMAR. Well, Gina went home to live with her mother, a Mrs Hansen, a capable, hard-working woman who ran a little restaurant. And she had a room that she let, too; a very nice, comfortable room.

GREGERS. And you, I suppose, were lucky enough to get it?

HJALMAR. Yes. As a matter of fact, it was your father who

gave me the idea. And you see that's where it was, really, that I got to know Gina.

GREGERS. And it ended in your engagement?

HJALMAR. Yes. Young people get attached to each other very easily. Hm. ...

GREGERS [*getting up and walking to and fro*]. Tell me. When you'd got engaged, was it then that my father got you to ... I mean ... was it then that you began to think of taking up photography?

HJALMAR. Yes, it was. Because I did so want to get settled and have a home of my own as soon as possible. And your father and I both thought this idea of photography was the best way. And Gina thought so too. Besides, you see, there was another reason; as luck would have it, Gina'd had some lessons in retouching.

GREGERS. It all worked out extraordinarily well.

HJALMAR [*happily, getting up*]. Yes it did, didn't it? Don't you agree, it all worked out extraordinarily well?

GREGERS. I must admit it did. My father's been almost like a kind of Providence to you.

HJALMAR [*with emotion*]. He did not fail his old friend's son in the days of his distress. He's got a good heart, you know, when all's said.

MRS SÖRBY [*entering on the arm of Werle senior*]. Now, no arguing, my dear Mr Werle. You mustn't stay in there any longer, looking at all those lights. It isn't good for you.

WERLE [*letting go her arm and passing his hand over his eyes*]. Yes, I rather think you are right.

[*Pettersen and Jensen, the waiter, come in with trays.*]

MRS SÖRBY [*to the guests in the other room*]. Now, gentlemen, if you please; if anyone would like a glass of punch, he must come in here.

THE FAT GUEST [*coming over to Mrs Sörby*]. Now, now! Is it true that you've done away with that pleasant privilege of smoking where we liked?

MRS SÖRBY. Yes, my dear sir; it's forbidden here, in Mr Werle's domain.

THE THIN-HAIRED GUEST. And when did you introduce this harsh decree about cigars, Mrs Sörby?

MRS SÖRBY. After our last dinner, Mr Balle. For certain persons who were here then let themselves go beyond all bounds.

THE THIN-HAIRED GUEST. And going beyond all bounds isn't allowed, eh, Mrs Berta? Not the least bit?

MRS SÖRBY. Not in any way, Mr Balle.

[*Most of the guests have collected in Werle's room; the waiters are handing round glasses of punch.*]

WERLE [*to Hjalmar, who is over at a table by himself*]. What's that you're so absorbed in, Ekdal?

HJALMAR. It's only an album, Mr Werle.

THE THIN-HAIRED GUEST [*who is strolling about*]. Ah! Photographs. Yes, that's your line, of course.

THE FAT GUEST [*in an arm-chair*]. Haven't you brought any of your own?

HJALMAR. No, I haven't.

THE FAT GUEST. You should have. It's so good for the digestion to sit still and look at pictures.

THE THIN-HAIRED GUEST. And it's adding your mite to the entertainment, you know.

A NEAR-SIGHTED GUEST. And all contributions are gratefully received.

MRS SÖRBY. What these good gentlemen mean is that if one is asked out to dinner one should do some work in return, Mr Ekdal.

THE FAT GUEST. Pure pleasure, in a household that gives you a good dinner.

THE THIN-HAIRED GUEST. Bless my soul! When it comes to the battle for existence –

MRS SÖRBY. You're right there! [*They go on laughing and joking.*]

GREGERS [*quietly*]. You must talk to them, Hjalmar.

HJALMAR [*with a shrug*]. What am I to talk about?

THE FAT GUEST. Don't you think, Mr Werle, that Tokay may be considered a comparatively wholesome drink?

WERLE [*by the fireplace*]. I can guarantee the Tokay you had today, at any rate; it is one of the very finest years. And you realized that yourself, I'm sure.

THE FAT GUEST. Yes, it had a most remarkable bouquet.

HJALMAR [*diffidently*]. Is there any difference in the years?

THE FAT GUEST [*laughing*]. By jove, that's good!

WERLE [*smiling*]. It certainly isn't worth while offering *you* a noble wine.

THE THIN-HAIRED GUEST. It's the same with Tokays as with photographs, Mr Ekdal. Sunshine is essential. That's true, isn't it?

HJALMAR. Oh yes; the light certainly plays its part.

MRS SÖRBY. Why, then, it's just the same as with you people at Court. You like a place in the sun too, so I've heard.

THE THIN-HAIRED GUEST. Oh, tut, tut! Fancy perpetrating an old joke like that!

THE NEAR-SIGHTED GUEST. Our friend is showing her mettle –

THE HIN-HAIRED GUEST. – And that at our expense! [*Threateningly.*] Mrs Berta! Mrs Berta!

MRS SÖRBY. Well, but it's perfectly true that the vintages can differ enormously. The old vintages are the best.

THE NEAR-SIGHTED GUEST. Do you count me among the old ones?

MRS SÖRBY. Far from it.

THE THIN-HAIRED GUEST. That disposes of you! But what about *me*, now, my dear Mrs Sörby?

THE FAT GUEST. Yes, and me! What vintage do you consider us?

MRS SÖRBY. I count you among the sweet years, gentlemen. [*She takes a sip from her glass of punch; the guests laugh and joke with her.*]

WERLE. Mrs Sörby can always find a way out – if she wants to. Pass up your glasses, gentlemen! Pettersen, fill them up! Gregers, shall we take a glass together? [*Gregers does not move.*] Won't you join us, Ekdal? I had no chance of drinking with you at dinner.

[*Graaberg, the book-keeper, looks in at the private door.*]

GRAABERG. Beg your pardon, sir, but I can't get out.

WERLE. Have you got locked in again?

GRAABERG. Yes, and Flakstad's gone off with the keys.

WERLE. Oh well, just go out this way.

GRAABERG. But there's someone else ...

WERLE. Never mind. Come along, both of you. Come along.

[*Graaberg and old Ekdal come out from the office.*]

WERLE [*involuntarily*]. Ugh!

[*The laughing and joking dies away. Hjalmar starts at the sight of his father, puts down his glass and turns towards the fireplace.*]

EKDAL [*without looking up, but bowing abruptly from side to side as he goes across muttering*]. Excuse me. Came the wrong way. Door locked. Door locked. Excuse me. [*He and Graaberg go out at the back to the right.*]

WERLE [*between his teeth*]. Damn that Graaberg!

GREGERS [*open-mouthed and staring at Hjalmar*]. But surely that was never – !

THE FAT GUEST. What's the matter? Who was it?

GREGERS. Oh, no one. Just the book-keeper and another man.

THE NEAR-SIGHTED GUEST [*to Hjalmar*]. Did *you* know the man?

HJALMAR. I don't know ... I didn't notice. ...

THE FAT GUEST [*getting up*]. What the devil's happening? [*He goes over to some of the others, who are talking under their breath.*]

MRS SÖRBY [*whispering to the servant*]. Give him something outside. Something really good.

PETTERSEN [*nodding*]. I will. [*He goes out.*]

GREGERS [*to Hjalmar in a low, shocked voice*]. So it really *was* he?

HJALMAR. Yes.

GREGERS. And yet you stood here and said you didn't know him!

HJALMAR [*whispering angrily*]. But how could I – ?

GREGERS. – Let your father recognize you?

HJALMAR [*resentfully*]. Oh, if you were in my place, you – [*The conversation among the guests, which has gone on in low voices, now changes to forced vivacity.*]

THE THIN-HAIRED GUEST [*affably approaching Hjalmar and Gregers*]. Aha! You two rubbing up old memories of college days, eh? Won't you smoke, Mr Ekdal? Would you like a light? Oh no; that's true, we mustn't –

HJALMAR. No thanks, I won't.

THE FAT GUEST. Haven't you got some charming little poem to recite to us, Mr Ekdal? You used to recite delightfully once upon a time.

HJALMAR. I'm afraid I can't remember anything.

THE FAT GUEST. Ah, that's a pity. Well, what shall we do then, Balle? [*The two men cross the room and go into the other.*]

HJALMAR [*gloomily*]. Gregers, I must go. You understand. When a man has experienced one of Fate's crushing blows. ... Say good-bye to your father for me.

GREGERS. Yes, of course. Are you going straight home?

HJALMAR. Yes. Why?

GREGERS. Well then, perhaps I'll come over and see you presently.

HJALMAR. No. You mustn't do that. Not to my home. My house is a sad one, Gregers. Especially after a splendid banquet like this. We can always meet outside, somewhere in town.

MRS SÖRBY [coming over to them and speaking quietly]. Are you going, Mr Ekdal?

HJALMAR. Yes.

MRS SÖRBY. Remember me to Gina.

HJALMAR. Thank you.

MRS SÖRBY. And say that I'll look in on her one day soon.

HJALMAR. I will. Thanks. [To Gregers.] Stay here. I'll slip out without their seeing me. [He strolls across the room, then into the other room and out to the right.]

MRS SÖRBY [in a low voice, to the servant, who has come back]. Well, did the old man take something with him?

PETTERSEN. Oh yes. I gave him a bottle of brandy.

MRS SÖRBY. Oh, you might have found something better than that.

PETTERSEN. Not a bit of it, Mrs Sörby. Brandy is the best thing he knows of.

THE FAT GUEST [in the doorway, with a piece of music in his hand]. Do you think we might play something together Mrs Sörby?

MRS SÖRBY. Yes, let us, by all means.

GUESTS. Good! Good!

[She and all the visitors go through the drawing-room and out to the right. Gregers remains standing by the fireplace. Werle looks for something on the writing-table and seems to want Gregers to go; but as he does not move, Werle goes towards the doorway.]

GREGERS. Will you stay a moment, Father?

WERLE [*pausing*]. What is it?

GREGERS. I must have a word with you.

WERLE. Can't it wait till we're alone?

GREGERS. No, it can't; because we may never happen to be alone.

WERLE [*approaching*]. What does that mean?

[*During the following dialogue a piano is heard in the distance from the music-room.*]

GREGERS. How could you people here let that family go so miserably to pieces?

WERLE. You mean the Ekdals, presumably.

GREGERS. Yes, I mean the Ekdals. Lieutenant Ekdal was such a close friend of yours once.

WERLE. Yes, unfortunately; altogether too close. And well I knew it. I suffered for it for many years. It's thanks to him that my own good name and reputation were touched.

GREGERS [*quietly*]. Was *he* actually the only one guilty?

WERLE. Who else are you thinking of?

GREGERS. After all, you and he were both in the big timber deal together.

WERLE. But wasn't it Ekdal who made the survey of the area – that inaccurate survey? It was he who was responsible for all that illegal felling on State property. In fact, he was responsible for the whole concern up there. I knew nothing about what Lieutenant Ekdal was undertaking.

GREGERS. Lieutenant Ekdal seems not to have known himself what he was undertaking.

WERLE. That may be so. But the fact remains that he was condemned and I was acquitted.

GREGERS. Oh yes. I know there were no proofs.

WERLE. Acquittal is acquittal. Why are you raking up this miserable old story – this business that turned my hair grey before my time? Is this the kind of thing you've been brooding over all these years up there? I can assure you, Gregers, here in town those stories were forgotten long ago – as far as *I'm* concerned.

GREGERS. But what about the unfortunate Ekdals?

WERLE. What, precisely, did you want me to do for those people? By the time Ekdal was released he was a broken-down man, past help from anyone. There are people in this world who dive to the bottom the moment they're winged, and never come up again. You can take my word for it, Gregers, I did all I could, short of compromising myself and encouraging all sorts of suspicion and gossip.

GREGERS. Suspicion? Yes. Just so.

WERLE. I've found Ekdal some copying to do for the office and I pay him far, far more for it than his work is worth.

GREGERS [*without looking at him*]. I don't doubt that.

WERLE. You're amused? Perhaps you don't think I'm speaking the truth? Admittedly there's nothing to show for it in my books; I never enter up expenses of that kind.

GREGERS [*smiling coldly*]. Ah, no. There are certain expenses it's better not to enter up.

WERLE [*starting*]. What do you mean by *that*?

GREGERS [*taking a grip on his courage*]. Have you entered what it cost you to have Hjalmar Ekdal taught photography?

WERLE. I? Why should I enter it?

GREGERS. I know now that it was you who paid for it. And I know now, what's more, that it was you who made it possible for him to set up in such a comfortable business.

WERLE. Well, and that's what you call doing nothing for the Ekdals! I can assure you, those people have let me in for quite enough expense.

GREGERS. Have you entered any of those expenses in your books?

WERLE. Why do you ask that?

GREGERS. Oh, there are reasons for it. Look here, tell me – when you begin to feel such affection for your old friend's son, wasn't it just at the moment when he was proposing to get married?

WERLE. Oh, good Lord! How can I – after all these years – ?

GREGERS. You wrote me a letter at that time – a business letter, naturally – and said in a postscript, quite shortly, that Hjalmar Ekdal had married a Miss Hansen.

WERLE. Yes, that was quite true; that was her name.

GREGERS. But you didn't mention that this Miss Hansen was Gina Hansen, who was once our housekeeper.

WERLE [*with an ironical laugh that is nevertheless a little forced*]. Why, no; it never occurred to me that you were so keenly interested in our former housekeeper.

GREGERS. Nor was I. But [*dropping his voice*] there were others in this house who *were* keenly interested in her.

WERLE. What do you mean by that? [*Turning on him in fury.*] You surely don't mean me?

GREGERS. Yes, I do mean you.

WERLE. And you dare – ! You have the insolence – ! How can he, the ungrateful cur, that – that photographer – how dare he presume to make such suggestions!

GREGERS. Hjalmar has never said a single word about it. I don't think he so much as dreams of anything of the kind.

WERLE. But where did you get it from, then? Who could have said such a thing?

GREGERS. It was what my poor, unhappy mother said – and the last time I saw her.

WERLE. Your mother! Yes; I might have known it! You and she, you always stuck together. It was she who turned you against me from the beginning.

GREGERS. No it was all she had to bear and suffer – till she was broken down and went utterly to pieces.

WERLE. Oh, she had nothing whatever to bear and suffer! No more than plenty of other people, at any rate. But there's no getting along with sickly, hysterical people. I know that well enough. And so you go about harbouring suspicions of that kind, raking up all sorts of malicious old rumours about your own father. Look here, Gregers, I really think, at your age, you might employ yourself more usefully.

GREGERS. Yes. It is about time.

WERLE. And then perhaps your mind would be easier than it seems to be now. What's it going to lead to, your going on, year in, year out, up there at the works? Toiling away – at a mere clerk's work – and refusing to take a shilling more than the ordinary monthly wage? It's pure stupidity.

GREGERS. Yes, if only I were as sure about that. ...

WERLE. I understand you all right. You want to be independent; not to owe me anything. Well, now the opportunity for that has occurred – for you to be independent and your own master in everything.

GREGERS. Really? In what way?

WERLE. When I wrote you that it was essential for you to come to town at once ... well ...

GREGERS. Yes, what exactly is it that you want? I've been waiting all day to find out.

WERLE. I want to propose that you should come into partnership in the firm.

GREGERS. I! Into your firm? As a partner?

WERLE. Yes. We shouldn't necessarily have to be together much. You could take over the business here in town and I would move up to the works.

GREGERS. *You* would?

WERLE. Yes. You know, I'm not up to so much work now as I once was. I have to be careful of my eyes, Gregers; they've begun to be rather troublesome.

GREGERS. Well, they've always been that.

WERLE. Not as bad as they are now. And besides ... circumstances might perhaps make it desirable for me to live up there ... at any rate for a time.

GREGERS. I'd never dreamt of such a thing.

WERLE. Look here, Gregers; it's true we differ on any number of matters. But, after all, we are father and son. It seems to me we ought to be able to come to some sort of understanding with each other.

GREGERS. At least outwardly, I suppose you mean?

WERLE. Well, that would be something, at any rate. Think it over, Gregers, Don't you think it ought to be possible? Eh?

GREGERS [*his eyes growing cold as he looks at him*]. There's something behind this.

WERLE. How do you mean?

GREGERS. You must be wanting to make use of me in some way.

WERLE. In a close relationship like ours one person can always be of use to the other.

GREGERS. Yes, so they say.

WERLE. I should like to have you at home for a while. I'm a lonely man, Gregers; I've always felt lonely ... all through my life. But most of all now that I'm getting on, I need to have someone about me ...

GREGERS. Well, you have Mrs Sörby.

WERLE. Yes, I have. And, to tell the truth, she's become almost indispensable to me. She's intelligent, she's even-tempered; she makes the place cheerful. And I need that pretty badly.

GREGERS. Quite so. Then you've already got exactly what you want.

WERLE. Yes, but I'm afraid it can't go on. That kind of
arrangement easily puts a woman in a false position in
the eyes of the world. And I'm not sure that a man is
any the better for it, either.

GREGERS. Oh, when a man gives the dinner-parties you do,
he can take a few risks.

WERLE. Yes, but what about her, Gregers? I'm afraid she
may not stand it much longer. And even if, out of
devotion to me, she did disregard the gossip and the back-
biting and all that. ... Doesn't it seem to you, Gregers –
with your strong and definite views about justice –

GREGERS [interrupting]. Tell me one thing plainly. Are you
thinking of marrying her?

WERLE. And if I were thinking of something of the sort?
What then?

GREGERS. Yes. That's what I am asking too. What then?

WERLE. Would there be any insuperable difficulty on your
side?

GREGERS. No, not at all. Not in any way.

WERLE. Well, I didn't know whether, perhaps, out of regard for the memory of your dead mother –

GREGERS. I am not neurotic.

WERLE. Well, whether you are or not, you've at any rate
lifted a heavy weight from my mind. I'm extremely glad
that I can count on your support in this.

GREGERS [looking unflinchingly at him]. Now I realize how
you want to make use of me.

WERLE. Make use of you! What a way to put it!

GREGERS. Oh, don't let's pick and choose our words. Not
when we are alone, at any rate. [Laughing shortly.] Yes,
that's it! That's why it was that I had to show up in
town at all costs. There must be a show of family life
in this household, for Mrs Sörby's benefit. Tableau, with
father and son! That's something new, isn't it?

WERLE. How dare you take this tone!

GREGERS. When has there been any family life here? Never, so long as I can remember. But now, of course, it would be as well to have a little. For there's no denying it will give just the right impression when it's known that the son flew home – on the wings of filial love – to his aged father's wedding. What will be left, after that, of all the rumours about the miseries and suffering of the poor dead wife? Not a whisper! Her own son strikes them dead.

WERLE. Gregers, I don't believe there's a man in the world you hate as much as me.

GREGERS [*quietly*]. I have seen you at too close quarters.

WERLE. You have seen me with your mother's eyes. [*Dropping his voice a little.*] But you should remember that those eyes were ... clouded, at times.

GREGERS [*trembling*]. I understand what you mean. But who's responsible for my mother's unhappy weakness? It's you, and all those – ! The last of them was this female that Hjalmar Ekdal was fobbed off with when you no longer ... Uh!

WERLE [*shrugging his shoulders*]. Word for word, as if I were listening to your mother. ...

GREGERS [*taking no notice of him*]. And there he is now, with his open, trustful, childlike mind, in the midst of all that deception, living under the same roof with a woman like that and never knowing that what he calls his home is built on a lie. [*Coming a step nearer.*] When I look back on all you've done, it's as if I were looking out over a battle-field with shattered bodies lying everywhere.

WERLE. I almost think the gulf between us is too wide.

GREGERS [*bowing stiffly*]. I have come to that conclusion too. And so I will take my hat and go.

WERLE. *Go?* Out of this house?

GREGERS. Yes. For now at last I see a purpose to live for.

WERLE. What is that purpose?

GREGERS. You would only laugh if you heard it.

WERLE. A lonely man doesn't laugh so easily, Gregers.

GREGERS [*pointing out towards the back*]. Look, Father – your friends are playing Blind Man's Buff with Mrs Sörby. Goodnight and – good-bye.

[*He goes out at the back to the right. Laughter and jokes are heard from the guests, who come into sight in the farther room.*]

WERLE [*muttering scornfully after Gregers*]. Ah, poor fellow! And he says he's not neurotic.

ACT TWO

———————— * ————————

[*Hjalmar Ekdal's studio. The room, which is fairly large, appears to be an attic. On the right is a sloping roof with large panes of glass, half covered by a blue curtain. Up in the right-hand corner is the entrance door; downstage on the same side, a door to the living-room. In the left wall there are again two doors, and between these an iron stove. In the rear wall is a broad double-door, so constructed as to slide back to either side. The studio is cheaply but comfortably furnished and decorated. Between the doors on the right a sofa with a table and some chairs are standing a little out from the wall; on the table is a lighted lamp with a shade; by the fireside an old easy-chair. Various pieces of photographic apparatus and instruments are standing here and there about the room. Against the back wall, to the left of the double-door, is a book case with some books, small boxes, flasks of chemicals, different kinds of instruments, tools and other things. Photographs and some small articles, such as brushes, paper and the like, are lying on the table.*

Gina Ekdal is sitting on a chair by the table, sewing. Hedvig is sitting on the sofa reading a book, with her hands shielding her eyes and her thumbs in her ears.]

GINA [*who has glanced towards her once or twice, as if with suppressed anxiety*]. Hedvig!
[*Hedvig does not hear.*]
GINA [*louder*]. Hedvig!
HEDVIG [*taking her hands away and looking up*]. Yes, Mother?
GINA. Hedvig darling, you mustn't sit and read any longer.

HEDVIG. Oh, but, Mother, can't I read a little more? Just a little?

GINA. No, no. You must put the book away now. Your father doesn't like it; he never reads in the evenings himself.

HEDVIG [*shutting the book*]. No; Father isn't very fond of reading.

GINA [*putting down her sewing and taking a pencil and a little note-book from the table*]. Can you remember how much we paid for the butter today?

HEDVIG. It was one and eight.

GINA. That's right. [*Puts it down.*] It's dreadful, the butter we get through in this house. And then there was the smoked sausage and the cheese – let me see – [*putting it down*] – and then there was the ham – now – [*adding it up*] yes, that by itself comes to –

HEDVIG. And then there's the beer, too.

GINA. Oh yes, of course. [*Puts it down.*] It does mount up. But we can't help it.

HEDVIG. But then you and I didn't need anything hot for dinner, as Daddy was out.

GINA. No, that was a good thing. And then I took eight and six for photographs as well.

HEDVIG. My! Was it as much as that?

GINA. Eight and six exactly.

[*Silence. Gina takes up her sewing again. Hedvig takes paper and pencil and begins to draw, with her left hand shading her eyes.*]

HEDVIG. Isn't it nice to think Daddy's at a big dinner-party at Mr Werle's?

GINA. You can't exactly say he's at Mr Werle's. It was young Mr Werle who asked him. [*After a pause.*] We don't have anything to do with old Mr Werle.

HEDVIG. I'm looking forward awfully to Daddy's coming

home. Because he promised he'd ask Mrs Sörby for something nice for me.

GINA. Yes, you may be sure there's plenty of good things going in that house.

HEDVIG [going on drawing]. And I really think I'm a little bit hungry, too.

[Old Ekdal, with a paper parcel under his arm and another parcel in his coat pocket, comes in from the hall door.]

GINA. How late you are home today, Grandfather.

EKDAL. They'd locked the office. Had to wait in Graaberg's room. And then had to go through ... er ...

HEDVIG. Did they give you any more to copy, Grandfather?

EKDAL. All this lot. Just look.

GINA. That's a good thing.

HEDVIG. And you've got a parcel in your pocket, too.

EKDAL. What? Oh tut! That's nothing. [Puts down his walking-stick in the corner.] There's plenty of work here for a long time, Gina. [Drawing one of the doors in the back wall a little to one side.] Hush! [Peeps into the room for a moment and cautiously slides the door to again.] Ha, ha! They've all gone to sleep together. And she has settled in the basket of her own accord. Ha! Ha!

HEDVIG. Are you certain she isn't cold in the basket, Grandfather?

EKDAL. What an idea! Cold! In all that straw? [Going towards the upper door on the left.] I shall find some matches, shall I?

GINA. There's matches on the chest of drawers.

[Ekdal goes into his room.]

HEDVIG. It was good, wasn't it, Grandfather getting all that copying?

GINA. Yes, poor old Grandfather; he'll make a little pocket-money.

HEDVIG. And besides, he won't be able to sit all the morning down there in that horrid café of Mrs Ericksen's.

GINA. No, nor he will. [*A short silence.*]

HEDVIG. Do you think they're sitting at the dinner-table still?

GINA. Lord knows. They quite likely may be.

HEDVIG. Think of all that lovely food Father's having to eat! I'm certain he'll be happy and pleased when he comes home. Don't you think so, Mother?

GINA. Yes. But think, if we could only tell him we'd got the room let.

HEDVIG. But we don't need that this evening.

GINA. Oh, it would come in very handy, you know. And it's no use as it is.

HEDVIG. No, I mean we don't need it this evening, because Daddy will be in a good temper, anyway. It'll be better for us to have the news about the room for another time.

GINA [*looking across at her*]. Are you glad to have something nice to tell your father when he comes home of an evening?

HEDVIG. Yes, because it's jollier then.

GINA [*thinking this over*]. Well, yes; there's something in that.

[*Old Ekdal comes in again and is going out through the farther door on the left.*]

GINA [*half turning in her chair*]. Do you want anything in the kitchen, Grandfather?

EKDAL. Yes, I do. Don't get up. [*He goes out.*]

GINA. He's never messing about with the fire out there? [*Waiting a moment.*] Hedvig, you go and see what he's up to.

[*Ekdal comes in again with a little mug of steaming water.*]

HEDVIG. Have you been getting some hot water, Grandfather?

EKDAL. Yes, I have. I want it for something. I've got to write, and the ink's got as thick as a pudding. Hm!

GINA. But, Grandfather, you should have your supper first. It's all laid in there.

EKDAL. I can't be bothered with supper, Gina. I'm very busy, I tell you. I don't want anyone coming into my room. Nobody at all – hm! [*He goes into his room. Gina and Hedvig look at each other.*]

GINA [*in a low voice*]. Wherever do you suppose he got the money?

HEDVIG. He must have got it from Graaberg.

GINA. Not a bit of it. Graaberg always sends his money to me.

HEDVIG. Then he must have got a bottle on trust somewhere.

GINA. Poor grandfather, they don't trust him for anything!

[*Hjalmar Ekdal comes in from the right, wearing an overcoat and a grey felt hat.*]

GINA [*throwing down her sewing and getting up*]. Why, Hjalmar, are you back already?

HEDVIG [*at the same time, jumping up*]. Fancy your coming back now, Daddy!

HJALMAR [*putting down his hat*]. Yes, most of them were leaving.

HEDVIG. So early?

HJALMAR. Yes, it was a luncheon party, you know. [*About to take off his overcoat.*]

GINA. Let me help you.

HEDVIG. And me.

[*They help him off with his coat; Gina hangs it up on the back wall.*]

HEDVIG. Were there many people there, Daddy?

HJALMAR. Oh no, not many. We were about twelve or fourteen at table.

GINA. And you had a chance to talk to them all?

HJALMAR. Oh yes, a little. But Gregers monopolized me most of the time.

GINA. Is Gregers as ugly as ever?

HJALMAR. Well, he isn't exactly good-looking. Hasn't the old man come home?

HEDVIG. Yes, Grandfather's in his room writing.

HJALMAR. Did he say anything?

GINA. No. What about?

HJALMAR. He didn't mention that – ? I think I heard he'd been with Graaberg. I'll go in to him for a moment.

GINA. No, no. It's not worth while.

HJALMAR. Why not? Did he say he didn't want me to go in?

GINA. He doesn't want anyone in this evening.

HEDVIG [making signs]. Hm – hm!

GINA [not noticing]. He's been in and got himself some hot water.

HJALMAR. Ah! Then I suppose – ?

GINA. Yes, that's it.

HJALMAR. Ah well! My poor, old, white-haired father! Oh, let him be – let him get what he can out of life.

[Old Ekdal, in dressing-gown and smoking a pipe, comes in from his room.]

EKDAL. You back? Thought it sounded like you talking.

HJALMAR. I've just this minute come in.

EKDAL. I don't believe you saw me there, did you?

HJALMAR. No. But they said you'd gone through – so I thought I'd come after you.

EKDAL. Hm. Nice of you, Hjalmar. Who were they, all those people?

HJALMAR. Oh, various people. There was Flor, he's some-thing at Court, and Balle and Kaspersen and what's-his-name. All people at Court. I don't know who else. ...

EKDAL [*nodding*]. D'you hear that, Gina? He's been mixing with all the people at Court.

GINA. Yes, they keep mighty good company now in that house.

HEDVIG. Did they sing, Daddy, the Court people? Or read aloud?

HJALMAR. No; they just chattered. True, they wanted to make me recite for them; but they couldn't get me to do that.

EKDAL. Couldn't get you to, couldn't they?

GINA. You might just as well have done it.

HJALMAR. No. One can't be at the beck and call of everybody. [*Taking a turn about the room.*] I'm not, at any rate.

EKDAL. No, no. Hjalmar's not that kind. Not he.

HJALMAR. I don't know why I should be the one to provide the entertainment, when I do go out once in a while. Let the rest of them make an effort. Those fellows go from one house to another, eating and drinking, day in day out. Let them have the grace to do something in return for all the good food they get.

GINA. But you didn't say that?

HJALMAR [*humming*]. Hm – hm – hm. Well, they were told a few things. ...

EKDAL. Even though they were people at Court!

HJALMAR. That didn't protect them. [*Casually.*] Later on we had a little dispute about Tokay.

EKDAL. Tokay, did you? That's a grand wine, that is.

HJALMAR [*pausing*]. It *can* be. But then, you know, the vintages are not all equally fine; it depends on how much sunshine the grapes have had.

GINA. Why, Hjalmar, you know absolutely everything.

EKDAL. And was that what they wanted to argue about?

HJALMAR. They tried to. But they were informed that it was just the same with Court officials. All vintages were not equally good in their case either – so they were told.

GINA. Well! The things you do think of!

EKDAL. Ha! Ha! So they had to put that in their pipes and smoke it!

HJALMAR. They had it, straight to their faces.

EKDAL. There you are, Gina! He said it straight to their faces, those people at Court.

GINA. Well, think of that. Straight to their faces.

HJALMAR. Yes, but I don't want it talked about. One doesn't repeat things like that. The whole thing went off quite amicably, of course. They were decent, pleasant fellows – why should I hurt their feelings? Ah, no.

EKDAL. But straight to their faces –

HEDVIG [*ingratiatingly*]. How funny it is to see you in a dinner-jacket. A dinner-jacket suits you, Daddy.

HJALMAR. Yes, don't you think it does? And this one really fits me very well. It sets almost as though it had been made for me. A little tight under the arms, perhaps. Lend a hand, Hedvig. [*He takes the jacket off.*] I'll put on a coat instead. Where have you put my coat, Gina?

GINA. Here it is. [*She fetches the coat and helps him into it.*]

HJALMAR. That's it! Be sure and remember to let Molvik have the jacket back first thing in the morning.

GINA [*putting it aside*]. I'll see to it.

HJALMAR [*stretching himself*]. Ah, I feel more at home in that. And this kind of loose, easy indoor coat suits my style better. Don't you think so, Hedvig?

HEDVIG. Yes, Daddy!

HJALMAR. And if I pull my tie out like this into two flowing ends – you see? Eh?

HEDVIG. Yes, it goes so well with your moustache and your long curly hair.

HJALMAR. I wouldn't exactly call it curly; I would say wavy, rather.

HEDVIG. Oh, but it is; beautifully curly.

HJALMAR. Wavy, actually.

HEDVIG [*after a pause, pulling his coat*]. Daddy!

HJALMAR. Well, what is it?

HEDVIG. Oh, you know perfectly well what it is.

HJALMAR. No, I certainly don't.

HEDVIG [*half-laughing, half-whimpering*]. Oh yes, Daddy! You're not to tease me any longer.

HJALMAR. But what is it?

HEDVIG [*giving him a shake*]. Oh, come along! Give it to me, Daddy! You know. All the good things you promised me.

HJALMAR. There now! Just fancy my forgetting it.

HEDVIG. No, you're only playing a trick with me, Daddy! Oh, it's horrid of you! Where have you hidden it?

HJALMAR. Well, if I didn't go and forget it! But wait a moment. I've got something else for you, Hedvig.

[*Goes across and looks in the pocket of the jacket.*]

HEDVIG [*dancing and clapping her hands*]. Oh, Mother, Mother!

GINA. There you are; if you just give him time –

HJALMAR [*with a sheet of paper*]. Look, here it is.

HEDVIG. That? That's only a piece of paper.

HJALMAR. It's the bill of fare, my dear; the whole bill of fare. Here is the word 'Menu'. That means 'bill of fare'.

HEDVIG. Haven't you got anything else?

HJALMAR. I forgot the rest, I tell you. But you can take my word for it, it's a great treat to have things of that kind. Now go and sit at the table and read the list and I'll tell you afterwards how each dish tastes. There you are, Hedvig.

HEDVIG [*swallowing her tears*]. Thank you.

[*She sits down but does not read it. Gina makes signs to her which Hjalmar notices.*]

HJALMAR [*pacing the floor*]. It's quite incredible, the things the bread-winner of a family has to think of. And if he forgets so much as the least thing – he's met with sour looks at once. Oh well: one gets used even to that. [*Pausing by the stove, near the old man.*] Have you glanced in this evening, Father?

EKDAL. Yes, you may be sure I have. She's gone into the basket.

HJALMAR. Has she now? Gone into the basket! She's beginning to get used to it, then.

EKDAL. Yes, my boy. That was just what I told you. But, you know, there are still one or two little things –

HJALMAR. A few improvements. Yes.

EKDAL. But they must be done, you know.

HJALMAR. Yes, let's talk over those improvements a bit, Father. Come here, and we'll sit on the sofa.

EKDAL. Yes. Good. Hm. ... Think I'll fill my pipe first. Must clean it out, too. Hm. [*He goes into his room.*]

GINA [*smiling to Hjalmar*]. Clean his pipe, indeed!

HJALMAR. Ah well, well, Gina. Let him be. The poor, ship-wrecked old man. Yes, those improvements. We'd better get them off our hands tomorrow.

GINA. You won't have time tomorrow, Hjalmar.

HEDVIG [*interrupting*]. Oh yes, he will, Mother.

GINA. Remember those prints that have to be retouched. They've asked for them so many times.

HJALMAR. Oh, my goodness! Those prints again? They'll be ready all right. Have any new orders come in?

GINA. No, worse luck. I've nothing tomorrow but those two sittings, you remember.

HJALMAR. Nothing else? Oh well, if one doesn't make any effort, of course –

GINA. But what am I to do? I'm advertising all I can, I'm sure.

HJALMAR. Oh, advertising, yes! You see how much use that is. And no one's been to look at the room either, I suppose?

GINA. No, not yet.

HJALMAR. That was only to be expected. If one doesn't keep one's wits about one – One has to pull one's self together, Gina.

HEDVIG [*going over to him*]. Couldn't I bring your flute, Daddy?

HJALMAR. No, thank you. No flute for me. I need no pleasures in this world. [*Pacing about.*] Oh yes, I shall be working all right tomorrow; there won't be any shirking. I shall work just as long as my strength holds out –

GINA. But, my dear Hjalmar, I didn't mean it like that.

HEDVIG. Daddy, shall I bring in a bottle of beer?

HJALMAR. No, certainly not. There is no need to bring anything for me. [*Pausing.*] Beer? Was it beer you said?

HEDVIG [*gaily*]. Yes, Daddy; nice, cool beer.

HJALMAR. Well, if you really want to, you may as well bring in a bottle.

GINA. Yes, do. Then we shall be cosy.

[*Hedvig runs to the kitchen door.*]

HJALMAR [*who is standing by the stove, stops her, looks at her, lays his hand on her head and draws her towards him.*] Hedvig, Hedvig!

HEDVIG [*with tears of joy*]. Oh, Daddy, you dear!

HJALMAR. No, don't call me that. There I sat, enjoying myself at the rich man's table, sat feasting at the groaning board. ... I might at least –

GINA [*sitting down at the table*]. Oh, don't talk nonsense, Hjalmar.

HJALMAR. It's true. But you mustn't call me to account too strictly. You know quite well that I love you, all the same.

HEDVIG [*throwing her arms around him*]. And we love you so awfully much, Daddy!

HJALMAR. And if I'm unreasonable now and again, remember, after all, that I am a man beset by an army of cares. Ah, well. [*Drying his eyes.*] Not beer, at such a moment. Give me my flute.

[*Hedvig runs over to the bookcase and gets it.*]

HJALMAR. Thank you. There we are. With my flute in my hand and you two beside me – ah!

[*Hedvig sits down at the table by Gina. Hjalmar walks to and fro and sets to vigorously on a Bohemian folk-dance, but in a slow, elegiac tempo and with sentimental execution.*]

HJALMAR [*breaks off the tune, stretches out his left hand to Gina and says emotionally*]. Never mind if our roof is low and poor, Gina. It is home, all the same. And this I will say: it is good to be here.

[*He begins to play again. Soon after, there is a knock at the outer door.*]

GINA [*getting up*]. Hush, Hjalmar. I think there's someone there.

HJALMAR [*putting the flute on the shelf*]. There *would* be.

[*Gina goes and opens the door.*]

GREGERS WERLE [*outside in the passage*]. Excuse me –

GINA [*shrinking back a little*]. Oh!

GREGERS. Is it here that Mr Ekdal lives, the photographer?

GINA. Yes, it is.

HJALMAR [*going across to the door*]. Gregers! Is it you, after all? Why, come along in!

GREGERS [*coming in*]. I told you I would come in and see you.

HJALMAR. But this evening – ? Have you left your visitors?

GREGERS. Both the visitors and my father's house. Good evening, Mrs Ekdal. I don't know whether you recognize me.

GINA. Oh yes. You're not very difficult to recognize, Mr Werle.

GREGERS. No; I am like my mother. And no doubt you remember her.

HJALMAR. Have you left the house, did you say?

GREGERS. Yes; I've moved into an hotel.

HJALMAR. I see. ... Well, since you've come, take your coat off and sit down.

GREGERS. Thanks. [*He takes off his overcoat. He is dressed this time in a plain grey tweed suit of a countrified cut.*]

HJALMAR. Here, on the sofa. Make yourself at home.

[*Gregers sits on the sofa, Hjalmar on a chair at the table.*]

GREGERS [*looking round him*]. So it's here that you work, Hjalmar. And you live here too.

HJALMAR. This is the studio, as you can see –

GINA. There's more room here, so we like being out here better.

HJALMAR. We had better living quarters before. But this place has one great advantage; there are such excellent outer rooms.

GINA. And then we have a room on the other side of the passage which we can let.

GREGERS [*to Hjalmar*]. Oh, indeed – you have a lodger, too?

HJALMAR. No, not yet. It can't be done offhand, you know. One has to have one's wits about one. [*To Hedvig.*] What about that beer, my dear? [*Hedvig nods and goes out to the kitchen.*]

GREGERS. So that's your daughter?

HJALMAR. Yes, that's Hedvig.

GREGERS. And she's an only child?

HJALMAR. The only one; yes. She is the brightest joy of our life, and [*lowering his voice*] its darkest sorrow, Gregers.

GREGERS. Why, how do you mean?

HJALMAR. Yes. You see, she's in grave danger of losing her eyesight.

GREGERS. Going blind!

HJALMAR. Yes. There are only the first signs showing as yet; and it may be all right for a time still. But the doctor has warned us. It's bound to come.

GREGERS. That's a terrible misfortune. What's the cause of it?

HJALMAR [sighing]. It's hereditary, it seems.

GREGERS [with a slight start]. Hereditary?

GINA. My husband's mother had weak sight, too.

HJALMAR. Yes, so my father says. I can't remember her myself.

GREGERS. Poor child. And how does she take it?

HJALMAR. Ah, well, you can understand we haven't the heart to tell her a thing like that. She doesn't suspect anything. Gay and light-hearted as she is, singing like a little bird, she is fluttering into a life of everlasting night. [Overcome.] Oh, it's heart-breaking for me, Gregers.

[Hedvig brings in a tray with beer and glasses, which she puts down on the table.]

HJALMAR [stroking her head]. Thank you, Hedvig, thank you.

[Hedvig puts her arm around his neck and whispers in his ear.]

HJALMAR. No. No bread-and-butter. [Looking across.] Unless Gregers would like a piece.

GREGERS [with a gesture of refusal]. No; no, thanks.

HJALMAR [still sadly]. Oh well, you can bring a little, all the same. And if you had a crust, that would be nice. And mind and see there's plenty of butter on it.

[Hedvig nods delightedly and goes out to the kitchen again.]

GREGERS [who has followed her with his eyes]. She strikes me as strong and healthy enough in every other way.

GINA. Yes, thank God, there's nothing else wrong with her.

GREGERS. She's going to be like you in time, Mrs Ekdal. How old would she be now?

GINA. Hedvig's just exactly fourteen; her birthday's the day after tomorrow.

GREGERS. Quite big for her age, then.

GINA. Yes, she's shot up this past year.

GREGERS. Young people growing up make us realize how old we are ourselves. How long have you been married now?

GINA. We've been married now – er – yes, exactly fifteen years.

GREGERS. Why, fancy it's being so long!

GINA [looking at him more attentively]. Yes, that's it, right enough.

HJALMAR. Yes, that's what it is. Fifteen years all but a few months. [Changing the subject.] They must have been long years for you, up there at the works, Gregers.

GREGERS. They were long while I was living through them; but now, looking back, I hardly know how the time went.

[Old Ekdal comes in from his room, without his pipe, but with his old uniform cap on his head; his walk is a little unsteady.]

EKDAL. Now then, Hjalmar, now we can sit down and talk about that business – hm. What was it?

HJALMAR [going towards him]. Father, there's someone here. Gregers Werle – I don't know whether you remember him?

EKDAL [looking at Gregers, who has got up]. Werle? Is that the son? What does he want with me?

HJALMAR. Nothing. It's me he has come to see.

EKDAL. Oh. So there's nothing the matter?

HJALMAR. No, no. Nothing.

EKDAL [*swinging his arms*]. It's not that I'm afraid, but –

GREGERS [*going over to him*]. I just wanted to bring you a greeting from your old hunting-grounds, Lieutenant Ekdal.

EKDAL. Hunting-grounds?

GREGERS. Yes, up there around the Höidal works.

EKDAL. Oh, up there. Yes, I was well known up there once.

GREGERS. You were a mighty hunter in those days.

EKDAL. True enough. I was. You're looking at my uniform. I don't ask anyone's leave to wear it indoors here. So long as I don't go out in the streets in it.

[*Hedvig brings in a plateful of bread-and-butter which she puts on the table.*]

HJALMAR. Sit down, Father, and have a glass of beer. Help yourself, Gregers.

[*Ekdal mutters and stumbles across to the sofa. Gregers sits on the chair nearest to him, Hjalmar on the other side of Gregers. Gina sits a little way from the table and sews. Hedvig stands by her father.*]

GREGERS. Do you remember, Lieutenant Ekdal, when Hjalmar and I used to come up to see you in the summer and at Christmas?

EKDAL. Did you? No, no, no; I don't recollect that. But I can assure you I used to be a first-rate hunter. I've shot bears, too. Shot nine, altogether.

GREGERS [*looking sympathetically at him*]. And now you don't get any more hunting?

EKDAL. Eh, I wouldn't say that, my friend. I get some hunting now and again. Oh, not that kind, of course. For the forest, you know, the forest ... ! [*Drinks.*] Is the forest looking fine up there now?

GREGERS. Not so fine as in your time. A lot's been cut down.

EKDAL. Cut down [*In a low voice, and as if afraid.*] That's a dangerous thing to do, that is. That means trouble. The forest avenges itself.

HJALMAR [*filling his glass*]. A little more, won't you, Father?

GREGERS. How can a man like you – a man who loves the open air – live in the middle of a stuffy city, shut in here by four walls?

EKDAL [*giving a little laugh and glancing at Hjalmar*]. Oh, it's not so bad here. Not at all bad.

GREGERS. But all those things that had come to be a part of your very soul – the cool, sweeping breeze; the free life of forest and heath, with beast and bird – ?

EKDAL [*smiling*]. Hjalmar, shall we show it him?

HJALMAR [*hastily and a little taken aback*]. Oh no, no, Father; not this evening.

GREGERS. What does he want to show me?

HJALMAR. Oh, it's only a kind of – You can see it another time.

GREGERS [*going on talking to the old man*]. Now this is what I thought, Lieutenant Ekdal, that you might come back with me, up to the works. I'm going back quite soon again. I'm sure you could get some copying up there too. And here you've nothing in the world to interest you and liven you up.

EKDAL [*staring at him in amusement*]. Nothing in the world? I, who have –

GREGERS. Oh yes, you have Hjalmar. But he has his own family. And a man like you, who has always felt the pull of a free, open life –

EKDAL [*striking the table*]. Hjalmar, now, he *shall* see it!

HJALMAR. Oh, Father, is it worth while now? It's dark, you know –

EKDAL. Nonsense! It's moonlight. [*Getting up.*] I say he *shall* see it. Let me past. Come and help me now, Hjalmar.

HEDVIG. Oh yes, *do*, Father!

HJALMAR [*getting up*]. Oh well, then.

GREGERS [*to Gina*]. What is it?

GINA. Oh, you mustn't expect anything out of the way.

[*Ekdal and Hjalmar have gone to the back wall and each pushes one of the half-doors aside. Hedvig helps the old man, Gregers remains standing by the sofa and Gina sits on, sewing undisturbed. Through the opening there appears a large, wide, irregular-shaped garret, with recesses and a couple of uncased, straggling chimneys. Bright moonlight falls upon parts of the room from the skylights, while other parts are in deep shadow.*]

EKDAL [*to Gregers*]. You come right over here.

GREGERS [*going over to them*]. But what *is* it I'm to look at?

EKDAL. You look and see. Hm.

HJALMAR [*a little embarrassed*]. All this belongs to Father, you know.

GREGERS [*at the door, looking into the attic*]. Why, you keep poultry, Lieutenant Ekdal.

EKDAL. I should think we do keep poultry! They are roosting now. But you should just see our poultry by daylight, you should.

HEDVIG. And then there's –

EKDAL. Sh! Sh! Don't say anything yet.

GREGERS. And I see you've got pigeons too.

EKDAL. Oh yes, I should think we have got pigeons too! They have their nesting-boxes up there under the eaves, they do. Pigeons like to roost high, you know.

HJALMAR. They're not all the common breed of pigeon, though.

EKDAL. Common! I should think not! We've got tumblers and a pair of pouters, too. But just come here. Can you see that hutch over there by the wall?

GREGERS. Yes. What do you use that for?

EKDAL. That's where the rabbits sleep at night, my dear fellow.

GREGERS. Well, well! So you have rabbits too?

EKDAL. 'Pon my word, I should think we do have rabbits! Hjalmar, my boy, he's asking whether we have rabbits! Hm! But now comes the real thing, you know. Now we come to it! Out of the way, Hedvig! Now, you stand just here. That's it. And now look down there. Don't you see a basket there with straw in it?

GREGERS. Oh yes. And I see there's a bird lying in the basket.

EKDAL. Hm. 'A bird' ...

GREGERS. Isn't it a duck?

EKDAL [a little hurt]. Yes, obviously it's a duck.

HJALMAR. But what kind of duck do you think it is?

HEDVIG. It's not an ordinary kind of duck.

EKDAL. Sh!

GREGERS. And it's not a fancy breed either. ...

EKDAL. No, Mr ... Werle. That's no fancy breed; that's a wild duck.

GREGERS. No, is it really? A wild duck?

EKDAL. Yes. That's what it is. The 'bird', as you called it - it's a wild duck, that is. Our wild duck, my dear fellow.

HEDVIG. My wild duck. Because it belongs to me.

GREGERS. And can it live up here in the loft? It gets on all right here?

EKDAL. Of course, you understand, she has a trough of water to splash about in.

HJALMAR. Fresh water every other day.

GINA [turning round to Hjalmar]. I say, Hjalmar, we're getting absolutely frozen in here.

EKDAL. Hm. Let's shut it up, then. We'd better not disturb them when they're settled for the night, either. You help, Hedvig.

[*Hajlmar and Hedvig push the doors together.*]

EKDAL. Another time you'll be able to see her properly. [*Sits down in the easy-chair by the stove.*] Ah, they're most remarkable birds, I can tell you, wild ducks.

GREGERS. But how did you manage to catch it, Lieutenant Ekdal?

EKDAL. I didn't catch it myself. It's a certain gentleman in town here we have to thank for that.

GREGERS [*reflecting a moment*]. That man ... it's never my father, is it?

EKDAL. Yes; that's it. Your father's the man. Hm.

HJALMAR. That was odd, your guessing that, Gregers.

GREGERS. You explained before that you owed so much to Father, in all sorts of ways. So I thought probably –

GINA. But we didn't get the wild duck from Mr Werle himself –

EKDAL. It's Haakon Werle we have to thank for her, all the same, Gina. [*To Gregers.*] He was out in a boat, you see, and shot her. But he doesn't see very well now, your father. And so she was only wounded.

GREGERS. Ah yes. She was only winged?

HJALMAR. Yes, she got two or three shots.

HEDVIG. She got it in her wing and so she couldn't fly.

GREGERS. Ah. So she dived down to the bottom, then.

EKDAL [*sleepily, with thickened speech*]. May be sure she did. Always do that, wild duck. Stick at the bottom. Deep as they can get, my dear fellow. Bite hold of the weeds and the tangle – and all the rotten stuff down there. And so they never come up again.

GREGERS. But, Lieutenant Ekdal, your wild duck did come up again.

EKDAL. He had such a wonderfully clever dog, your father. And that dog, it dived after the duck and fetched it up again.

GREGERS [*turning to Hjalmar*]. And so you got it?

HJALMAR. Not right away. It was taken to your father's house first. But it didn't thrive there and so Pettersen had instructions to kill it –

EKDAL [*half asleep*]. Hm. Yes, Pettersen. Damned old idiot!

HJALMAR [*lowering his voice*]. That was how we got it, you see; Father knows Pettersen a little, and when he heard this about the wild duck he managed to get hold of it.

GREGERS. And now it is getting on perfectly all right there in the attic.

HJALMAR. Yes, extraordinarily well. It's got quite plump. After all, you see, it's been in there so long that it's forgotten its natural, wild life. And that's what really counts.

GREGERS. You're quite right there, Hjalmar. So long as it never gets a sight of the sky and the sea – But I mustn't stay any longer; I think your father's asleep.

HJALMAR. Never mind about that.

GREGERS. Oh, by the way, you said you had a room to let – an empty room?

HJALMAR. Quite true. Why? Do you know anyone – ?

GREGERS. Can I have the room?

HJALMAR. You?

GINA. What! *You*, Mr Werle?

GREGERS. Can I have the room? If so, I'll move in first thing tomorrow.

HJALMAR. Yes, with the greatest pleasure –

GINA. Oh, but, Mr Werle, that's not a bit the kind of room for you, that isn't.

HJALMAR. Why, Gina, how can you say that?

GINA. Because that room isn't big enough or light enough, and –

GREGERS. That doesn't matter, Mrs Ekdal.

HJALMAR. I think it's quite a pleasant room. And not too badly furnished either.

GINA. But remember those two living down below.

GREGERS. What two are they?

GINA. Oh, there's one of them's been a tutor –

HJALMAR. That's a Mr Molvik, a B.A.

GINA. – And then there's a doctor called Relling.

GREGERS. Relling? I know him a little; he was in practice up at Höidal for a time.

GINA. They're a real rowdy pair. They're generally out on a spree of an evening, and then they come home dreadfully late at night and aren't always quite –

GREGERS. One soon gets used to that sort of thing. I hope I shall be like the wild duck and –

GINA. Well, I think you'd better sleep on it first, all the same.

GREGERS. You're very unwilling to have me in the house, Mrs Ekdal.

GINA. Gracious, no! What ever makes you think that?

HJALMAR. Well, Gina, it really is very odd of you. [*To Gregers.*] But tell me, do you think of staying on in town for the present?

GREGERS [*putting on his overcoat*]. Yes. I mean to stay on now.

HJALMAR. But not at home with your father? What are you thinking of doing, then?

GREGERS. Ah, if I only knew that, my dear fellow, I shouldn't have done so badly after all. But when one is afflicted with a name like Gregers – 'Gregers' – and then 'Werle' after it! Have you ever heard anything so hideous?

HJALMAR. Oh, I don't know ...

GREGERS. Phew. I should feel like spitting at a fellow with a name like that. But once a man *has* the affliction of being Gregers Werle in this world, as I am –

HJALMAR [*laughing*]. Ha, ha! If you weren't Gregers Werle, what would you like to be?

GREGERS. If I could choose, I would like best of all to be a clever dog.

HJALMAR. A dog!

HEDVIG [*involuntarily*]. Oh no!

GREGERS. Yes, a really, extraordinarily clever dog. The kind that goes to the bottom after wild duck when they dive down and bite fast hold of the weeds and the tangle down in the mud.

HJALMAR. Now, look here, Gregers – I don't understand a word of this.

GREGERS. Oh well. There's no great mystery in it, actually. Well then, tomorrow first thing, I'll move in. [*To Gina.*] You mustn't put yourself out for me; I do everything for myself. [*To Hjalmar.*] We'll talk about the other things tomorrow. Good night, Mrs Ekdal. [*Nodding to Hedvig.*] Good night.

GINA. Good night, Mr Werle.

HEDVIG. Good night.

HJALMAR [*who has lit a lamp*]. Just a minute. I must light you down; it's sure to be dark on the stairs.

[*Gregers and Hjalmar go out by the hall door.*]

GINA [*looking in front of her, with her sewing in her lap*]. Wasn't that a queer thing to say – that he'd like to be a dog?

HEDVIG. I tell you what, Mother. I think he meant something else by that.

GINA. What else could he mean?

HEDVIG. Well, I don't know; but it was though he meant something else all the time – and not what he said.

GINA. Was that it, do you think? It certainly was queer.

HJALMAR [*coming back*]. The lamp was still alight. [*He turns out the lamp and puts it down.*] Ah, at last one can get a bit of food. [*Beginning on the bread-and-butter.*] Now, you see, Gina. If one just keeps one's wits about one –

GINA. How do you mean 'keeps one's wits about one'?

HJALMAR. Well, anyway, wasn't it lucky that we managed to let the room in the end? And then, just think, to a person like Gregers. A good old friend.

GINA. Well, I don't quite know what to say, myself.

HEDVIG. Oh, Mother, you'll see! It'll be awfully nice.

HJALMAR. You certainly are behaving oddly. You used to be so keen on getting it let, and now you don't like it.

GINA. Oh yes, Hjalmar – if it had only been to somebody else, I would. But what do you think old Mr Werle will say?

HJALMAR. Old Werle? It's nothing to do with him.

GINA. But you may be sure they've got across each other again, as the son's leaving the house. You know well enough how things are between them.

HJALMAR. Yes, that may be, but –

GINA. And now perhaps Mr Werle will think it's you that's behind it –

HJALMAR. Let him go on thinking it, then! Mr Werle has done a great deal for me. God knows, I realize that. But I can't hold myself accountable to him for ever, just because of that.

GINA. But, Hjalmar dear, it may be Grandfather who'll suffer for it in the end. Now perhaps he'll lose the little bit he gets from Graaberg.

HJALMAR. I nearly said, 'I wish he would!' Isn't it rather humiliating for a man like me to see his grey-haired father going about like a down-and-out? But now I think the fullness of time is coming. [*Takes another piece of bread-and-butter.*] As surely as I have a task in life, I shall carry it through.

HEDVIG. Oh yes, Daddy! *Do!*

GINA. Sh! Don't wake him up.

HJALMAR [*lower*]. I shall carry it through, I say. The day

shall come, when ... And that's why it's a good thing we got the room let; it puts me in a more independent position. And a man must have that when he has a task in life. [*Going towards the arm-chair and speaking in a voice shaken by emotion.*] Poor, white-haired old father! Lean on your Hjalmar! He has broad shoulders ... strong shoulders, at any rate. One fine day you shall wake up and ... [*To Gina.*] Don't you believe it?

GINA [*getting up*]. Yes, of course I do; but let's see about getting him to bed first.

HJALMAR. Yes, let us.

[*They lift up the old man carefully.*]

ACT THREE

———— * ————

[*Hjalmar Ekdal's studio. It is morning. Daylight is coming in through the large window in the sloping roof. The curtain is pulled back.*

Hjalmar is sitting at the table retouching a photograph, with several other portraits lying in front of him. A moment later, Gina comes in from the hall door in her hat and coat; she has a covered basket on her arm.]

HJALMAR. You back again already, Gina?

GINA. Yes. One has to get a move on. [*She puts the basket down on a chair and takes off her outdoor things.*]

HJALMAR. Did you look in on Gregers?

GINA. Yes, I should think I did. Nice it looks in there! He got his room in a fine state the moment he came.

HJALMAR. Oh. How?

GINA. Oh yes! He was going to look after himself, he said! So he must needs light the fire, and shut the damper down, so that the whole room was full of smoke. Pooh! There was a stink as if –

HJALMAR. Good Lord!

GINA. But that's not the best of it. Because then he wanted to put it out, and so he emptied the jug off his washstand into the stove, so that the whole floor's a swimming mess.

HJALMAR. That *is* a nuisance!

GINA. I've just got the porter's wife to clean up after him – the pig! But the place won't be fit to go into till this afternoon.

HJALMAR. What is he doing with himself in the meantime?

GINA. He said he was going out for a little while.

HJALMAR. I went in to see him for a moment too. After you went out.

GINA. So I heard. And you've asked him to lunch.

HJALMAR. Only just for a snack at lunch-time, you know. After all, it's his first day; we can't very well help it. You must have something in the house.

GINA. I must see about finding something.

HJALMAR. Don't let it be too skimpy, though. Because I think Relling and Molvik are coming up too. I ran into Relling on the stairs, you see, so I had to –

GINA. Oh, my goodness! Have we got to have those two as well?

HJALMAR. Why, gracious! A bit more or less makes no difference either way.

OLD EKDAL [opening his door and looking in]. Look here, Hjalmar, my boy – [Notices Gina.] Oh, well ...

GINA. Is there anything you want, Grandfather?

EKDAL. Oh no; it doesn't matter. Hm. [Goes in again.]

GINA [picking up the basket]. Keep an eye on him ... see he doesn't go out.

HJALMAR. Oh yes, yes. I will. Look here, Gina; a little herring salad would be rather nice; I fancy Relling and Molvik were out on the loose last night.

GINA. So long as they don't come before I've had time –

HJALMAR. Of course they won't. You take your time.

GINA. All right, then. And you can do a bit of work in the meantime.

HJALMAR. Well, I am working, aren't I? I'm working as hard as I can.

GINA. And then you'll have that off your hands, you see. [She goes out into the kitchen with the basket.]

[Hjalmar sits a moment working on the photograph with a brush, reluctantly and making heavy weather of it.]

EKDAL [*peeping in, looking round the studio, and saying in a low voice*]. Are you busy, my boy?

HJALMAR. Yes, I'm sitting here, drudging at these portraits.

EKDAL. Oh well, all right. If you're so busy, then – Hm. [*He goes in again, leaving the door standing open. Hjalmar goes on in silence for a moment, then puts down his brush and goes across to the door.*]

HJALMAR. Are *you* busy, Father?

EKDAL [*muttering, inside the room*]. If you're busy, then I'm busy too. Hm.

HJALMAR. All right. [*Goes back to his work again.*]

EKDAL [*coming to the doorway again soon after*]. Hm. Look here, Hjalmar, I'm not so busy as all that.

HJALMAR. I thought you were writing.

EKDAL. The deuce! Can't that fellow Graaberg wait a day or two? I don't suppose it's a matter of life and death.

HJALMAR. No, and you're not a slave, either.

EKDAL. And then there was this other job in there.

HJALMAR. Yes, so there was. Would you like to go in? Shall I open it for you?

EKDAL. Wouldn't be a bad idea, really.

HJALMAR [*getting up*]. And then we'll have got *that* off our hands.

EKDAL. Exactly; yes. It's got to be ready first thing tomorrow. It *is* tomorrow, isn't it? Hm?

HJALMAR. Oh yes, it's tomorrow.

[*Hjalmar and Ekdal each pull aside one half of the door. Inside, the morning sun is shining through the skylights. A few pigeons are flying to and fro, and others sitting on the rafters cooing. From farther back in the attic comes, now and then, the clucking of hens.*]

HJALMAR. There, now you can go ahead, Father.

EKDAL [*going in*]. Aren't you coming too?

HJALMAR. Well, you know ... I rather think – [*Seeing Gina at the kitchen door.*] I? No, I haven't time; I must work. But what about our new apparatus?

[*He pulls a cord which lets down a curtain, the lower part of which consists of a strip of old sail-cloth and the rest, above that, of a piece of fishing-net stretched taut. By this means the floor of the attic can no longer be seen.*]

HJALMAR [*going across to the table*]. That's it. Now I can settle down in peace for a little while.

GINA. Don't tell me he's in there pottering about again?

HJALMAR. Would it be better, do you think, if he'd gone off to Mrs Eriksen's [*Sitting down.*] Is there anything you want? You look –

GINA. I only wanted to ask if you thought we could lay the lunch in here?

HJALMAR. Yes. No one's booked a sitting so early as that, I suppose?

GINA. No; I'm not expecting anybody except the couple that want to be taken together.

HJALMAR. Why the devil can't they be taken together some other day?

GINA. Now, Hjalmar dear, I've booked them for the afternoon, when you're having your sleep.

HJALMAR. Oh, that's all right then. Yes, then, we'll lunch here.

GINA. All right. But there's no hurry about laying the table. You can go on using it for quite a while yet.

HJALMAR. Well, I seem to be using the table as much as I can, don't I?

GINA. Because then you'll be free afterwards, you see. [*Going into the kitchen again.*]

[*Brief pause.*]

EKDAL [*at the attic-door, inside the net*]. Hjalmar!

HJALMAR. Yes?

EKDAL. Afraid we shall have to move the water-trough, after all.

HJALMAR. Yes, that's just what I've been saying all along.

EKDAL. Hm, hm, hm. [*Goes away from the door again.*]

[*Hjalmar works a little while, glances towards the attic and half gets up. Hedvig comes in from the kitchen and he sits down again quickly.*]

HJALMAR. What is it you want?

HEDVIG. I only wanted to come in to you, Daddy.

HJALMAR [*a moment later*]. You seem to be poking about. Are you on the look-out for anything?

HEDVIG. No, not a bit.

HJALMAR. What's your mother doing out there now?

HEDVIG. Oh, Mother's in the middle of making the herring salad. [*Going over to the table.*] Isn't there any little thing I could help you with, Daddy?

HJALMAR. No, no. It's best for me to manage the whole thing alone – so long as my strength holds out, I shan't want help, Hedvig. If your father can only keep his health, then –

HEDVIG. Oh, Daddy, no; you mustn't say such dreadful things!

[*She wanders about a little, stands by the opening and looks into the attic.*]

HJALMAR. What's he up to, Hedvig?

HEDVIG. He must be making a new run-way up to the water-trough.

HJALMAR. He can't possibly manage that by himself. But here am I, condemned to sit here – !

HEDVIG [*going across to him*]. Let *me* have the brush, Daddy. I can, all right.

HJALMAR. Nonsense. You'll only hurt your eyes doing it.

HEDVIG. I shan't. Not a bit. Give me the brush.

HJALMAR [*getting up*]. Well, it wouldn't be more than a minute or two.

HEDVIG. Pooh! What harm could it do, then? [*Taking the brush.*] There we are. [*Sitting down.*] And I've got one here to copy.

HJALMAR. But don't you hurt your eyes? You hear me? I'm not going to be responsible; you must take the responsibility yourself. You understand?

HEDVIG [*retouching*]. Yes, yes; of course I will.

HJALMAR. You're very clever, Hedvig. Only a minute or two, you know.

[*He slips under the corner of the curtain into the attic. Hedvig sits at her work. Hjalmar and Ekdal are heard arguing inside.*]

HJALMAR [*coming up to the net*]. Hedvig, just get me the pincers on the shelf. Oh, and the chisel, please. [*Turning back to the attic.*] Now you'll see, Father. Let me show you what I mean first. [*Hedvig has fetched the tools he wanted from the shelf and handed them in to him.*]

HJALMAR. That's it, thanks. Yes, it was just as well I came, you know.

[*He goes away from the opening. They can be heard carpentering and joking inside. Hedvig stands watching them. A moment later someone knocks at the hall door; she does not notice it. Gregers Werle, bare-headed and without an overcoat, comes in and stands for a moment by the door.*]

GREGERS. Hm.

HEDVIG [*turning and going towards him*]. Good morning. Do come in, please.

GREGERS. Thank you. [*Looking towards the loft.*] You seem to have workmen in the house.

HEDVIG. No, it's only Daddy and Grandfather. I'll go and tell them.

GREGERS. No, no. Don't do that; I'd rather wait a little while. [*Sits on the sofa.*]

HEDVIG. It's so untidy here. [*About to clear away the photographs.*]

GREGERS. Oh, let it be. Are they photographs that have to be finished?

HEDVIG. Yes. Just a little job that I'm helping Daddy with.

GREGERS. Don't let me disturb you, then.

HEDVIG. All right.

[*She moves the things over towards her and settles down to work, while Gregers watches her in silence.*]

GREGERS. Did the wild duck sleep well last night?

HEDVIG. Yes, thank you; I'm sure it did.

GREGERS [*turning towards the attic.*] It looks quite different in the daylight from last night by moonlight.

HEDVIG. Yes, it can be awfully different. It looks quite different in the morning from what it does in the afternoon, and different when it's raining from when it's fine.

GREGERS. Have you noticed that?

HEDVIG. Yes. One can't help seeing it.

GREGERS. And do you spend a good deal of time in there with the wild duck?

HEDVIG. Yes, when I can manage to.

GREGERS. But I expect you haven't so very much free time. Of course, you go to school.

HEDVIG. No, not any more. Because Daddy's afraid I shall hurt my eyes.

GREGERS. Oh, so he gives you lessons himself, then.

HEDVIG. He's promised to give me lessons, but he hasn't had time for it yet.

GREGERS. But isn't there anyone else who helps you a little?

HEDVIG. Yes, there's Mr Molvik; but he isn't always quite – altogether – er –

GREGERS. He drinks, does he?

HEDVIG. Yes, he does.

GREGERS. Ah well then, you do have time for other things. And in there it's like a world of its own, I expect?

HEDVIG. Absolutely its own! And then there are such lots of wonderful things.

GREGERS. Are there?

HEDVIG. Yes, there are big cupboards with books in them; and there are pictures in a lot of the books.

GREGERS. Ah!

HEDVIG. And then there's an old cabinet with drawers and partitions in it; and a big clock with figures that are supposed to come out. But the clock doesn't go any more.

GREGERS. Time, too, has come to a stop in there, where the wild duck lives.

HEDVIG. Yes. And then there's an old paint-box and things like that. And then all the books.

GREGERS. And do you read the books?

HEDVIG. Oh yes, when I can manage to. But most of them are in English, and I don't understand that. But then I look at the pictures. There is one very large book that is called *Harryson's History of London*; that must be quite a hundred years old. And there are a tremendous lot of pictures in that. At the beginning there's a picture of Death with an hour-glass and a girl. I think that's dreadful. But then there are all the other pictures with churches and castles and streets and great ships sailing on the sea.

GREGERS. But tell me, where did you get all these wonderful things from?

HEDVIG. Oh, an old sea captain lived here once and he brought them home. They called him 'The Flying Dutchman'. And that's queer, because he wasn't a Dutchman at all.

GREGERS. Wasn't he?

HEDVIG. No. But in the end he didn't come back, and left everything behind him.

GREGERS. Look here, tell me – when you're sitting in there looking at the pictures, don't you want to go away and really see the great world for yourself?

HEDVIG. No, not a bit! I want to stay at home here always and help Daddy and Mother.

GREGERS. Retouching photographs?

HEDVIG. No, not only that. I'd like most of all to learn to engrave pictures like those in the English books.

GREGERS. Hm. What does your father say to that?

HEDVIG. I don't think Daddy likes it. Daddy's so odd about things like that. Just think, he talks about my learning basket-weaving and straw-plaiting! But I don't see that there's anything in *that*.

GREGERS. No, I don't either.

HEDVIG. But Daddy's right in one thing. If I'd learnt to weave baskets, then I could have made the new basket for the wild duck.

GREGERS. You could, of course; and you were the proper person to do it.

HEDVIG. Yes, because it's *my* wild duck.

GREGERS. Yes, of course it is.

HEDVIG. You're quite right; it belongs to me. But Daddy and Grandpapa can borrow it as often as they want to.

GREGERS. Ah yes. And what do they do with it then?

HEDVIG. Oh, they look after it and build things for it and that sort of thing.

GREGERS. I expect they do. Because the wild duck is the most important person in there.

HEDVIG. Yes, she is. Because she is a real wild bird. And then it's so sad for her; she has no one belonging to her, poor thing.

GREGERS. No family, like the rabbits –

HEDVIG. No. The hens have got lots of others, too, that they knew as chickens, but she's so far from all her own people, poor dear! And it's all so strange about the wild duck. There's no one who knows her. And no one who knows where she's come from, either.

GREGERS. And then she has been in the ocean's depths.

HEDVIG [*giving a quick glance at him, checks a smile and asks*]. Why do you say 'the ocean's depths'?

GREGERS. What else should I say?

HEDVIG. You could say 'the bottom of the sea' or 'the sea-bed'.

GREGERS. Well, can't I just as well say 'the ocean's depths'?

HEDVIG. Only it sounds so strange to me when other people say 'the ocean's depths'.

GREGERS. Why does it? Tell me why.

HEDVIG. No, I won't. It's something so silly.

GREGERS. I'm sure it isn't. Tell me why you smiled, now.

HEDVIG. It's because, whenever I happen to remember everything in there – suddenly, as it were, in a flash – then it always seems as if that whole room, and all the things in there, ought to be called 'the ocean's depths'. But that's so silly.

GREGERS. No, you mustn't say that.

HEDVIG. It is; because it's only an attic.

GREGERS [*looking hard at her*]. Are you so sure of that?

HEDVIG [*astonished*]. That it's an attic?

GREGERS. Yes. Do you know that for certain?

[*Hedvig is silent, looking at him with open mouth. Gina comes in from the kitchen with a tablecloth.*]

GREGERS [*getting up*]. I am afraid I've come too early for you.

GINA. Well, you must be somewhere. Besides, it'll soon be ready now. Clear the table, Hedvig.

[*Hedvig tidies up. During the following dialogue she and Gina lay the table. Gregers sits in the easy-chair and turns over the leaves of an album.*]

GREGERS. I hear you can do retouching, Mrs Ekdal.

GINA [*with a side-glance*]. M – yes, I can.

GREGERS. That was very lucky, wasn't it?

GINA. How 'lucky'?

GREGERS. Seeing that Hjalmar has become a photographer, I mean.

HEDVIG. Mother can take photographs too.

GINA. Oh yes, I jolly well had to learn that job.

GREGERS. So I suppose it's you who runs the business.

GINA. Oh, when my husband hasn't time himself, I –

GREGERS. His time is very much taken up with his old father, I expect?

GINA. Yes; and besides it's not a job for a man like Hjalmar, taking photographs of every Tom, Dick and Harry.

GREGERS. I quite agree. But when once he started in that line, he –

GINA. Surely you realize, Mr Werle, that my husband isn't one of those ordinary photographers.

GREGERS. Oh yes, quite so. But –

[*A shot is fired inside the attic.*]

GREGERS [*starting up*]. What's that?

GINA. Oh! Now they're shooting again!

GREGERS. Do they shoot too?

HEDVIG. They go hunting.

GREGERS. Well, I'm damned! [*Crossing to the attic door.*] Are you out hunting, Hjalmar?

HJALMAR [*inside the net*]. Have you come in? I didn't know you had; I was so busy – [*To Hedvig.*] You didn't tell us! [*Comes into the studio.*]

GREGERS. Do you go shooting in the attic?

HJALMAR [*showing him a double-barrelled pistol*]. Oh, only with this thing here.

GINA. Yes, you and Grandfather'll end by having an accident one of these days with that gun.

HJALMAR [*irritated*]. I think I have told you that a firearm of this kind is called a pistol.

GINA. Well, I don't see that that makes it any better, myself.

GREGERS. So you've turned into a hunter too, Hjalmar?

HJALMAR. Only a little rabbit-shooting now and again. It's mostly for Father's sake, you know.

GINA. Men are so queer; they must always be having some kind of divergence.

HJALMAR [*angrily*]. Yes, quite, quite. We must always have some kind of diversion.

GINA. Yes, that's just what I say.

HJALMAR. Oh, well! [*To Gregers.*] Yes, and you see it all happens very luckily – the attic is so placed that no one can hear us shooting. [*Puts the pistol on the top shelf.*] Don't touch the pistol, Hedvig. One of the barrels is loaded, remember.

GREGERS [*looking in through the net*]. You have a sports rifle, too, I see.

HJALMAR. It's Father's old shot-gun. It doesn't shoot any more; something's gone wrong with the lock. But it's quite fun to have it, all the same, because we can take it to pieces and clean it every now and then, and grease it and put it together again. Of course, it's mostly Father who plays with that sort of thing.

HEDVIG [*going across to Gregers*]. Now you can see the wild duck properly.

GREGERS. I was just looking at it. She seems to me to drag one wing a little.

HJALMAR. Well, that's not very surprising; she's been wounded.

GREGERS. And she's a little lame in one foot, too. Or isn't she?

HJALMAR. Perhaps just the slightest bit.

HEDVIG. Well, you see, that was the foot the dog bit.

HJALMAR. But apart from that, she hasn't the slightest thing wrong with her; and that's really remarkable, considering that she's had a charge of shot in her and been held in the teeth of a dog –

GREGERS [*with a glance at Hedvig*]. – And has been in the ocean's depths – so long –

HEDVIG [*smiling*]. Yes.

GINA [*setting the table*]. That there blessed wild duck! The fuss there is over it!

HJALMAR. Hm – Will lunch be ready soon?

GINA. Yes, in just a minute. You must come and help me now, Hedvig.

[*Gina and Hedvig go out into the kitchen.*]

HJALMAR [*in an undertone*]. I don't think you'd better stay there looking at Father; he doesn't like it.

[*Gregers moves away from the loft door.*]

HJALMAR. And I'd better shut it up before the others come. [*Shooing the birds away with his hands.*] Shoo! Shoo! Get away with you! [*At the same time he draws up the curtain and pulls the doors together.*] I invented these contrivances myself. It's really very enjoyable to have a few things like this to look after and mend when they go wrong. And besides, it's absolutely necessary, you see; because Gina doesn't like having the rabbits and hens in the studio.

GREGERS. Of course not. And I suppose it's your wife who's in charge here?

HJALMAR. I generally leave the routine business to her. Then I can go away into the sitting-room in the meantime and think about more important things.

GREGERS. What things in particular, Hjalmar?

HJALMAR. I wonder you haven't asked about that before. Or perhaps you haven't heard anyone talking about the invention.

GREGERS. Invention? No.

HJALMAR. Really? You haven't? Oh well, up there in the forests and wilderness –

GREGERS. So you've invented something?

HJALMAR. Not quite *invented* it yet; but I'm on the track of it. You can quite understand that when I devoted myself to photography, it wasn't just in order to make portraits of a lot of nonentities.

GREGERS. Of course not. That's what your wife was just saying.

HJALMAR. I swore that if I dedicated my powers to that craft, I would lift it to such heights that it would become both an art and a science. So I resolved to make this notable invention.

GREGERS. And what does the invention consist in? What form is it taking?

HJALMAR. My dear fellow, you mustn't ask for details like that yet. It takes time, you know. And you mustn't think it's vanity that's driving me, either. You may be sure I'm not working for my own sake. No, it's the purpose of my life that stands before me night and day.

GREGERS. What purpose is that?

HJALMAR. Have you forgotten the white-haired old man?

GREGERS. Your poor father? Yes, but what exactly can you do for him?

HJALMAR. I can awaken his self-respect from death by raising the name of Ekdal to honour and dignity again.

GREGERS. So that is the purpose of your life.

HJALMAR. Yes. I will rescue that ship-wrecked man. For he was ship-wrecked when the storm broke loose on him. By the time this terrible inquiry took place, he was no longer himself. That pistol there, my friend – the one we use to shoot rabbits with – it has played its part in the tragedy of the House of Ekdal.

GREGERS. The pistol! Has it?

HJALMAR. When the verdict was pronounced and he was to be imprisoned, he had the pistol in his hand –

GREGERS. Was he going to – ?

HJALMAR. Yes. But he didn't dare. He was a coward. He'd become so degraded, so broken in spirit by then. Can you imagine it? He, a soldier; he, who had shot nine bears and was descended from two lieutenant-colonels – one after the other, of course. Can you imagine it, Gregers?

GREGERS. Yes, I can quite imagine it.

HJALMAR. I can't. And then the pistol played a part in our family history again. When he was dressed in prison clothes and under lock and key – ah, you will realize what a terrible time that was for me. I had the blinds down in front of both my windows. When I looked out, I saw the sun shining as usual. I could not understand it. I saw people going about the streets, laughing and talking about unimportant things. I could not understand it. I thought the whole creation should come to a stand, as in an eclipse.

GREGERS. I felt it like that, too, when my mother died.

HJALMAR. It was in such an hour that Hjalmar Ekdal held the pistol to his own heart.

GREGERS. You, too, thought of – !

HJALMAR. Yes.

GREGERS. But you didn't shoot.

HJALMAR. No. In that moment of supreme trial I won the victory over myself. I went on living. But you can well believe it takes courage to choose life in those circumstances.

GREGERS. Well, it depends how one looks at it.

HJALMAR. No, there's no question, my dear fellow; it does. But it was better so. For now I shall soon finish my invention. And Relling thinks, as I do, that then Father will

be allowed to wear his uniform again. I shall ask for that
as my sole reward.

GREGERS. So it's the question of the uniform that he – ?

HJALMAR. Yes, that's what he longs and yearns for most.
You can't realize how my heart bleeds for him. Every
time we celebrate some little family festival – our wed-
ding-day, or whatever it may be – the old man comes in,
dressed in the uniform of his happier days. But if there's
as much as a knock at the front door, he makes for his
room again as fast as his old legs will carry him. Father
daren't let strangers see him dressed like that, you see.
That's a heart-rending thing, my friend, for a son to
watch.

GREGERS. About when do you think the invention is likely
to be finished?

HJALMAR. Oh, good Lord, you mustn't ask me for details
like dates! An invention, why, that's a thing one isn't
entirely master of, oneself. It depends a great deal upon
inspiration – upon an intuition – and it's almost impossible to calculate in advance at what moment that will
come.

GREGERS. But it's making progress, isn't it?

HJALMAR. Oh yes; it's making progress. I meditate upon
my invention every day; it fills my mind. Every afternoon, after lunch, I shut myself up in the sitting-room
where I can ponder in peace. But it's simply no use their
trying to drive me; that does no good at all. That's what
Relling says, too.

GREGERS. And you don't think that all these contrivances
in the attic there take you away from it and distract your
mind?

HJALMAR. Oh no, no! Not in the least. You mustn't say
that. I can't go on everlastingly brooding over the same
exhausting train of thought. I must have something be-

sides, to fill up the intervals, Inspiration, an intuition, you see – if it is coming, it will come whatever I am doing.

GREGERS. My dear Hjalmar, I rather fancy you have a strain of the wild duck in you.

HJALMAR. Of the wild duck? How? What do you mean?

GREGERS. You've dived down and bitten fast hold of the weeds on the sea-bed.

HJALMAR. You mean, I suppose, that all but fatal blow that maimed my father, and me too?

GREGERS. Not so much that. I don't say you're wounded. But you've landed in a poisonous swamp, Hjalmar. You've got an insidious disease in you, and you've dived to the bottom to die in the dark.

HJALMAR. I? Die in the dark? Now, look here, Gregers, you really mustn't talk such nonsense.

GREGERS. Don't worry. I'll see you come up again. I have a purpose in life too now, you see; I found it yesterday.

HJALMAR. Well, that may be so; but you will please leave me out of it. I assure you that, apart from my melancholy, which is easy to understand, I find myself as well as any man can wish to be.

GREGERS. The very fact that you do is a result of the poison.

HJALMAR. Now, my dear Gregers, don't talk any more nonsense about disease and poison; I am not used to that kind of conversation; in my house people never talk to me about unpleasant things.

GREGERS. No. That I can readily believe.

HJALMAR. No, because it doesn't suit me. And there are no swamp vapours here, as you put it. In the poor photographer's home the roof is low; I know that. And my lot is humble. But I am an inventor, you know, and the bread-winner of a family. That lifts me above petty circumstance – Ah! There they are with lunch!

[*Gina and Hedvig bring in bottles of beer, a decanter of brandy, glasses and other things. At the same time Relling and Molvik come in from the hall, both without hats or overcoats; Molvik wears black.*]

GINA [*putting the things on the table*]. Well now, you two have come just at the right time.

RELLING. Molvik got an idea that he could smell herring salad and then there was no holding him. Good morning for the second time, Ekdal.

HJALMAR. Gregers, may I introduce Mr Molvik. Doctor – ah, but you know Relling?

GREGERS. Yes, slightly.

RELLING. Ah, it's young Mr Werle! Oh yes, we two have crossed swords up at the Höidal works. You've just moved in?

GREGERS. I've just moved in this morning.

RELLING. Molvik and I live downstairs. So you haven't far to go for a doctor and a priest, if you should need anything of that kind.

GREGERS. Thank you; that may happen yet. We were thirteen at table yesterday.

HJALMAR. Oh, don't start on unpleasant subjects again.

RELLING. You needn't let it worry you, Ekdal; it doesn't apply to you, heaven knows.

HJALMAR. I'll hope not, for my family's sake. But let's sit down now and eat, drink and be merry.

GREGERS. Shan't we wait for your father?

HJALMAR. No, he will have his in his own room later on. Now, then!

[*The men sit at the lunch-table and eat and drink. Gina and Hedvig go in and out and wait on them.*]

RELLING. Molvik was shockingly drunk yesterday, Mrs Ekdal.

GINA. Was he? Yesterday again?

RELLING. Didn't you hear him when I brought him home last night?

GINA. No, I can't say I did.

RELLING. That was a good thing; Molvik was simply intolerable last night.

GINA. Is that true, Mr Molvik?

MOLVIK. Let us drop a veil over the doings of last night. Such things do not emanate from my better self.

RELLING [to Gregers]. It comes over him like a possession and then I have to go out on the loose with him. Mr Molvik is a demoniac, you see.

GREGERS. Demoniac?

RELLING. Molvik's a demoniac, yes.

GREGERS. Hm!

RELLING. And demoniac temperaments are not made for steering an even course through life; they must run amuck now and again. Well, and so you're still sticking it, up there in those hideous, gloomy works?

GREGERS. I have done, until now.

RELLING. And did you get that claim honoured that you were going round with?

GREGERS. Claim? [Understanding him.] Oh, that.

HJALMAR. Have you been taking up claims, Gregers?

GREGERS. Stuff and nonsense.

RELLING. Yes indeed, he has; he went the round of the cottagers' huts and presented a thing he called 'the claim of the ideal'.

GREGERS. I was young then.

RELLING. You're right there; you were very young. And the claim of the ideal – you never got it honoured while I was up there.

GREGERS. Nor after, either.

RELLING. Well, I expect you've got enough sense now to reduce the amount a little.

GREGERS. Never, when I come upon a man that *is* a man.

HJALMAR. Well, I think that's reasonable enough. Butter, please, Gina.

RELLING. And a little piece of pork for Molvik.

MOLVIK. Ugh! Not pork!

[*There is a knock at the attic door.*]

HJALMAR. Open it, Hedvig; Father wants to come out.

[*Hedvig goes across and opens the door a little. Old Ekdal comes in with a fresh rabbit skin; he shuts the door after him.*]

EKDAL. Good morning, gentlemen! Good hunting today. Potted a big one.

HJALMAR. And you've skinned it before I came!

EKDAL. Salted it, too. It's good, tender meat, rabbit-meat. And sweet, too. Tastes like sugar. I hope you'll enjoy your lunch, gentlemen! [*Goes into his room.*]

MOLVIK [*getting up*]. Excuse me – I can't – I must get downstairs at once –

RELLING. Drink some soda-water, man!

MOLVIK [*hurrying out*]. Ugh! Ugh! [*Goes out by the hall door.*]

RELLING [*to Hjalmar*]. Let's drink a health to the old hunter.

HJALMAR [*touching glasses with him*]. Yes. To the sportsman on the brink of the grave.

RELLING. To the grey-haired – [*drinking*] ... But tell me, is it grey his hair is, or white?

HJALMAR. It's actually betwixt and between. As a matter of fact, he hasn't much hair left, in any case.

RELLING. Oh well, one can get through life in a wig. Yes, you know, Ekdal, you're a lucky man, when all's said; you've got a fine object to fight for in life –

HJALMAR. And I *am* fighting for it, believe me.

RELLING. And then you have your capable wife, padding to and fro so cosily in her felt slippers, waddling round, arranging everything comfortably for you.

HJALMAR. Yes, Gina. [*Nodding towards her.*] You are a good companion to have with one on life's way, my dear.

GINA. Oh, don't sit there making an aspersion of me.

RELLING. And then there's your Hedvig, eh, Ekdal?

HJALMAR [*touched*]. My child, yes! First and foremost, my child. Hedvig, come here to me. [*Stroking her hair.*] What day is it tomorrow, eh?

HEDVIG [*shaking him*]. Oh no, you mustn't say anything, Daddy!

HJALMAR. It cuts me to the heart when I think how poor and meagre it will be; just a little party in the attic there, to celebrate –

HEDVIG. Oh, but that will be simply lovely!

RELLING. And just wait till the great invention comes out, Hedvig!

HJALMAR. Ah yes. Then you shall see! Hedvig, I have resolved to make your future secure. You shall live in comfort all your life. I shall demand something for you, in one way or another. That shall be the poor inventor's only payment.

HEDVIG [*whispering with her arms round his neck*]. Oh, you dear, dear Daddy!

RELLING [*to Gregers*]. Well, now, doesn't it seem rather pleasant, for a change, to sit at a well-appointed table in a happy family circle?

HJALMAR. Yes, I thoroughly enjoy these meal-times.

GREGERS. I, for my part, don't thrive on swamp vapour.

RELLING. Swamp vapour?

HJALMAR. Oh, don't start that talk again!

GINA. Lord knows there's no smell of swamps here, Mr Werle; I air the place out every blessed day.

GREGERS [*getting up from the table*]. Airing it out will never get rid of the stench I mean.

HJALMAR. Stench!

GINA. Well, did you ever, Hjalmar!

RELLING. Excuse me, it couldn't be you yourself, I suppose, who's bringing the stench with you from the mines up there?

GREGERS. It's just like you to call what I bring into the house a stench.

RELLING [*going across to him*]. Look here, young Mr Werle, I have a strong suspicion that you're going about with the unabridged version of that 'claim of the ideal' still in your pocket.

GREGERS. I go about with it in my heart.

RELLING. Well, carry it where the devil you like, but I advise you not to play at producing that claim here. Not as long as I'm in the house.

GREGERS. And suppose I do, all the same?

RELLING. Then you'll go head-first down the stairs. And now you know.

HJALMAR [*getting up*]. Oh come, Relling!

GREGERS. Yes, you just throw me out –

GINA [*getting between them*]. You can't do that, Mr Relling. But I will say this, Mr Werle – you who made all that mess in your stove, you shouldn't come talking to me about smells.

[*There is a knock at the hall door.*]

HEDVIG. Mother, there's someone knocking.

HJALMAR. There we are. Now I suppose we're going to hold a reception.

GINA. Just let me go. [*She goes across and opens the door, gives a start, shivers and draws back.*] Ah! Why!

[*Werle senior, dressed in a fur coat, takes a step forward into the room.*]

WERLE. I beg your pardon. But I think my son is living here.

GINA [*with a gasp*]. Yes.

HJALMAR [*coming forward*]. Won't you be so good, Mr
    Werle, as to –

WERLE. Thank you. I merely wish to speak to my son.

GREGERS. Well, what is it? Here I am.

WERLE. I should like to speak to you in your own room.

GREGERS. In my room; very well. [*Turns to go.*]

GINA. Good Lord, no! It's not in a fit state –

WERLE. Well, outside in the passage, then. I want a word
    alone with you.

HJALMAR. You can have it here, Mr Werle. Come into the
    sitting-room, Relling.

[*Hjalmar and Relling go out to the right. Gina takes Hedvig out
into the kitchen with her.*]

GREGERS [*after a short pause*]. Well, now we are alone to-
    gether.

WERLE. You made one or two remarks yesterday evening.
    And seeing that you have taken lodgings with the Ekdals,
    I can only conclude that you have something against me
    in your mind.

GREGERS. I have it in mind to open Hjalmar Ekdal's eyes.
    He shall see his position as it is. That's all.

WERLE. Is that the purpose in life that you spoke of yester-
    day?

GREGERS. Yes. You have not left me any other.

WERLE. Did I give you your diseased mind, Gregers?

GREGERS. You have made my whole life a disease. I am
    not thinking of what happened to my mother. But it is
    you I have to thank for the restless nagging of a guilt-
    laden conscience.

WERLE. Ah, it's your conscience that's wrong with you.

GREGERS. I should have stood up to you when the trap was
    laid for Lieutenant Ekdal. I should have warned him. For
    I guessed well enough how it would end.

WERLE. Yes. You should certainly have spoken then.

GREGERS. I dared not do it. I was such a coward. I was so afraid, so unconscionably afraid of you – both then and for long after.

WERLE. That fear is gone now, it would appear.

GREGERS. Fortunately it is. The injury that has been done old Ekdal, both by me and by others, that can never be put right. But I can free Hjalmar from all the lies and deceptions he's sinking under.

WERLE. Do you think you would do him any good by that?

GREGERS. I am convinced that I should.

WERLE. You believe, then, that Ekdal, the photographer, is man enough to thank you for that friendly service?

GREGERS. Yes! He is man enough.

WERLE. Hm. We shall see.

GREGERS. And besides, if I'm to go on living I must find some cure for my sick conscience.

WERLE. It will never be cured. Your conscience has been sickly from childhood. It's an inheritance from your mother, Gregers. The only inheritance she did leave you.

GREGERS [with a half-smile of contempt]. Have you never been able to get over the shock of finding you were mistaken in expecting a fortune with her?

WERLE. Don't let us stray into irrelevances. Do you still hold to your intention, of leading this man Ekdal into what you think the right track?

GREGERS. Yes, I hold it firmly.

WERLE. Then I might as well have saved myself my journey here. For it is obviously no use to ask you whether you will come home to me again.

GREGERS. No.

WERLE. And you won't come into the firm either?

GREGERS. No.

WERLE. But as I now intend to make a second marriage, the estate will be divided between us.

GREGERS [*quickly*]. No. I don't want that.

WERLE. You don't want it?

GREGERS. No. I dare not, for my conscience' sake.

WERLE [*after a pause*]. Are you going up to the works again?

GREGERS. No. I consider myself discharged from your service.

WERLE But what are you going to do?

GREGERS. Only fulfil the purpose of my life; nothing else.

WERLE. Yes, but afterwards? What are you going to live on?

GREGERS. I have put by a little from my wages.

WERLE. But how long will that last?

GREGERS. I think it will last my time.

WERLE. What does that mean?

GREGERS. I won't answer any more.

WERLE. Good-bye, then, Gregers.

GREGERS. Good-bye.

[*Werle senior goes out.*]

HJALMAR [*peeping in*]. Has he gone?

GREGERS. Yes.

[*Hjalmar and Relling come in. Gina and Hedvig join them from the kitchen.*]

RELLING. That's settled that lunch-party.

GREGERS. Put your things on, Hjalmar. You must come for a long walk with me.

HJALMAR. Yes, certainly. What was it your father wanted? Was it anything about me?

GREGERS. Come along. There are one or two things we must talk about. I'll go in and put on my overcoat. [*Goes out by the hall door.*]

GINA. I shouldn't go out with him if I was you, Hjalmar.

RELLING. No, don't you do it, old man; you stay where you are.

HJALMAR [*putting on his hat and overcoat*]. What! When an old friend feels he must open his mind to me in private —

RELLING. But, damn it all! Don't you know the fellow's crazy, cracked, off his head?

GINA. Yes, you've only got to listen to him. His mother used to take on in the same way, every now and then.

HJALMAR. He has all the more need of a friend's watchful eye. [*To Gina.*] Just see that dinner is ready in good time. Good-bye, for the present. [*Goes out through the hall door.*]

RELLING. It's a great misfortune that fellow didn't go to hell down one of the mines at Höidal.

GINA. Gracious! Why do you say that?

RELLING [*muttering*]. Oh well, I have my own notions.

GINA. Do you think young Werle is really crazy?

RELLING. No, worse luck! He's no crazier than most people. But he's got a disease in his system, all the same.

GINA. What's wrong with him, then?

RELLING. Well, I'll tell you, Mrs Ekdal. He's suffering from acute inflammation of the conscience.

HEDVIG. Is that a kind of disease?

RELLING. Why, yes. It's a national disease; but it only breaks out sporadically. [*Bowing to Gina.*] Thank you for lunch. [*Goes out by the hall door.*]

GINA [*walking uneasily about the room*]. Ugh, that Gregers Werle! He's always been a queer fish.

HEDVIG [*standing by the table and looking hard at her*]. It all seems very odd to me.

ACT FOUR

———————— * ————————

[*Hjalmar Ekdal's studio. A photograph has just been taken; a camera covered with a cloth, a stand, a couple of chairs, a what-not and such like are standing in the middle of the room. Late afternoon light and the sun just about to set; a little later it begins to get dark.*

Gina is standing at the open door with a slide and a wet photographic plate in her hand and speaking to somebody outside.]

GINA. Yes, without fail. When I have promised something I keep my word. The first dozen shall be ready on Monday. Good afternoon; good afternoon.

[*Steps can be heard going down the stairs. Gina shuts the door, puts the plate into the slide and puts that inside the covered camera. Hedvig comes in from the kitchen.*]

HEDVIG. Have they gone now?

GINA [*tidying up*]. Yes, thank goodness. I'm finished with them at last.

HEDVIG. Can you imagine why Daddy hasn't come back yet?

GINA. Are you sure he's not down at Relling's?

HEDVIG. No, he isn't there. I ran down the back stairs to see just now.

GINA. And there's his dinner standing waiting for him and getting cold.

HEDVIG. Just think! Daddy's always so particular about getting home to dinner.

GINA. Oh, he'll soon be here, you'll see.

HEDVIG. Yes, I do wish he would. Because everything seems so queer, somehow.

GINA [*calling out*]. There he is!

[*Hjalmar Ekdal comes in from the hall door.*]

HEDVIG [*going up to him*]. Daddy! We've been waiting and waiting for you.

GINA [*glancing across*]. You *have* been out a long time, Hjalmar.

HJALMAR [*without looking at her*]. I have, rather; yes [*He takes off his overcoat. Gina and Hedvig try to help him; he waves them aside.*]

GINA. Have you had dinner with Werle?

HJALMAR [*hanging up his overcoat*]. No.

GINA [*going to the kitchen door*]. I'll bring some in for you, then.

HJALMAR. No. Don't bother with dinner. I won't have anything to eat now.

HEDVIG [*going up to him*]. Don't you feel well, Daddy?

HJALMAR. Well? Oh yes, tolerably. We had a very tiring walk together, Gregers and I.

GINA. You shouldn't have done that, Hjalmar; you're not used to it.

HJALMAR. There are a great many things a man must get used to in this world. [*Walking about for a moment.*] Has anyone been here while I was out?

GINA. No one but the engaged couple.

HJALMAR. No fresh orders?

GINA. No, not today.

HEDVIG. You'll see, Daddy! Someone'll come tomorrow all right.

HJALMAR. I should hope they would. For tomorrow I mean to turn to with all my might.

HEDVIG. Tomorrow! But surely you're not forgetting what day it is tomorrow?

HJALMAR. Oh no; that's true. Well, the day after tomorrow, then. In future I intend to do everything for myself; I wish to do all the work single-handed.

GINA. But what'll be the good of that, Hjalmar? That's only going to make your life miserable. I can manage the photographing myself; and then you'll be free to see to the invention.

HEDVIG. And the wild duck, Daddy, and all the hens and rabbits and –

HJALMAR. Don't talk to me about that rubbish. From to-morrow I shall never set foot in that attic again.

HEDVIG. Oh, but Daddy, you did promise me that to-morrow there should be a 'festivity'!

HJALMAR. Hm. That's true. Well, from the day after to-morrow, then. That accursed wild duck – I'd like to wring its neck!

HEDVIG [*with a scream*]. The wild duck!

GINA. Well, I never!

HEDVIG [*shaking him*]. Oh, but Daddy, it's *my* wild duck!

HJALMAR. That's why I'm not going to. I haven't the heart to. For your sake, Hedvig, I haven't the heart. But I feel in my inmost self that I ought to do it. I ought not to suffer under my roof a creature that has been in that man's hands.

GINA. But, my goodness! Even if Grandfather did have it from that fellow Pettersen –

HJALMAR [*walking about*]. There are certain demands – what shall I call them? – suppose we say demands of the ideal, certain claims that a man cannot put aside without hurt to his soul.

HEDVIG [*following him*]. But think, the wild duck – the poor wild duck!

HJALMAR [*pausing*]. I tell you I will spare it – for your sake. It shall not be hurt; not a hair of its – well, as I said, I will spare it. For there are, indeed, greater things than that to cope with. But you ought to go out for your usual walk, Hedvig; it's quite dusk enough for you now.

HEDVIG. No, I don't much want to go out now.

HJALMAR. Yes, you go. You seem to be blinking your eyes a good deal; all these vapours in here are bad for you. The air is heavy here, under this roof.

HEDVIG. All right, then; I'll run down the kitchen stairs and go out for a little while. My coat and hat? Oh, they're in my own room. Daddy, you simply *mustn't* do the wild duck any harm while I'm gone.

HJALMAR. Not a feather of its head shall be touched. [*Pulling her towards him.*] You and I, Hedvig – we two! Now, go along, my dear.

[*Hedvig nods to her parents and goes out by the kitchen.*]

HJALMAR [*walking about, without looking up*]. Gina.

GINA. Yes?

HJALMAR. From tomorrow onwards – or, let us say from the day after tomorrow onwards – I should like to keep the household books myself.

GINA. You want to keep the household books as well, now?

HJALMAR. Yes. Or keep account of what comes in, at any rate.

GINA. Oh, Lord love us! That's soon reckoned.

HJALMAR. I wonder. You seem to make the money go an extraordinarily long way. [*Standing still and looking at her.*] How is it done?

GINA. It's because Hedvig and I need so little.

HJALMAR. Is it true that Father is so highly paid for the copying he does for Mr Werle?

GINA. I don't know whether it's high pay. I don't know the rate for that kind of thing.

HJALMAR. Well, about how much does he get? Tell me!

GINA. It varies so much. It comes to about what he costs us and a little over for pocket-money.

HJALMAR. What he costs us! And you've never told me this before!

GINA. No, I just couldn't. You were so pleased to think everything he had came from you.

HJALMAR. Whereas, in fact, it comes from Mr Werle!

GINA. Oh, old Werle's got plenty to spare.

HJALMAR. May I have the lamp lit, please?

GINA [*lighting the lamp*]. And we can't actually tell if it's the old man; quite likely it may be Graaberg.

HJALMAR. Why are you dragging in Graaberg to evade the issue?

GINA. Well, I don't know; I just thought –

HJALMAR. Hm!

GINA. After all, it wasn't me that got Grandfather the writing. It was Berta, that time she was here.

HJALMAR. Your voice sounds a little unsteady.

GINA [*putting the shade on the lamp*]. Does it?

HJALMAR. And your hands are shaking too – aren't they?

GINA [*firmly*]. Say it straight out, Hjalmar! What sort of things has he been saying about me?

HJALMAR. Is it true – *can* it be true, that – that there was ... something between you and old Mr Werle, when you were in service there?

GINA. It's not true. Not *then*, there wasn't. Mr Werle tried to get me to; true enough. And his wife thought there was something in it, and made no end of fuss and bother. She led me a life, she did! And so I gave notice.

HJALMAR. But afterwards?

GINA. Well, then I went home. And Mother – she wasn't as straight as you thought her, Hjalmar. And she got talking at me, one thing and another. Because Werle was a widower by then.

HJALMAR. Well, and then?

GINA. Well, it's best you should know it. He never gave up till he had his way.

HJALMAR [*clasping his hands together*]. And that is my child's mother! How could you hide a thing like that from me?

GINA. Yes. It was wrong of me; I suppose I ought to have told you long ago.

HJALMAR. You ought to have told me in the beginning; then I should have known what kind of woman you were.

GINA. But would you have married me, all the same?

HJALMAR. How can you imagine such a thing!

GINA. No. ... And that's why I didn't dare tell you anything then. Because I got very fond of you, as you know. And I couldn't make myself utterly miserable –

HJALMAR [*walking about*]. And that is my Hedvig's mother! And to think that everything I see here before my eyes – [*kicking a chair*] – the whole of my home – I owe it all to a favoured predecessor! Ah, that – that seducer, Werle!

GINA. Do you regret the fourteen – fifteen years we have lived together?

HJALMAR [*standing in front of her*]. Tell me. Haven't you – every hour, every day – regretted the web of deceit you've spun round me like a spider? Answer me! Haven't you really been going about in an agony of regret and remorse?

GINA. Oh, my dear Hjalmar, I've had so much to do, looking after the house and all the everyday jobs –

HJALMAR. So you never give a thought to your past life?

GINA. No. God knows, I'd nearly forgotten all that old business.

HJALMAR. Ah, this blunt, insensitive placidity! There is something shocking about it, to my mind. Just think! Not a single regret!

GINA. But tell me, Hjalmar, what would have become of you if you hadn't had a wife like me?

HJALMAR. Like you!

GINA. Yes, because I've always been a bit more wide-awake and business-like than you. Well, that's understandable; after all, I'm a couple of years older.

HJALMAR. What would have become of me!

GINA. Because you were getting into bad ways when you first met me; you can't deny that.

HJALMAR. So that's what you call bad ways? Ah, you don't understand what it means for a man to be a prey to grief and despair, especially a man with fire and aspiration in his soul.

GINA. Well, of course, that may be so. And I don't want to make a song about it, anyway; because you made a real, good husband as soon as you had your own home. And here we'd got it all so cosy and comfortable. And Hedvig and I were just beginning to spend a little on our own food and clothes.

HJALMAR. In a swamp of deceit, yes.

GINA. Oh, why did that detestable man have to shove himself into this house!

HJALMAR. I used to think our home was a pleasant one, too. It was a delusion. Where shall I get the necessary stimulus now to make my invention a reality? It may perhaps die with me. And then it will have been your past, Gina, that will have killed it.

GINA [nearly in tears]. Oh, Hjalmar, you mustn't say things like that. I who, all my life, have only been trying to do the best I could for you.

HJALMAR. I ask you, where is the dream of the bread-winner now? When I lay in there on the sofa meditating on the invention, I realized well enough that it would drain the last of my strength. I saw clearly enough that the day I held the patent in my hands – that day would bring my ... release. And it was my dream that you should take your place as the well-to-do widow of the departed inventor.

GINA [drying her tears]. No, you *mustn't* talk like that, Hjalmar. God forbid that I should ever live to see myself a widow.

HJALMAR. Oh, it doesn't matter either way. It's all over now, anyhow. All over!

[Gregers Werle opens the hall door cautiously and looks in.]

GREGERS. May I come in?

HJALMAR. Yes; come in.

GREGERS [comes forward, his face shining with joy, and holds out his hands to them]. Now, my dear people! [He looks from one to the other and whispers to Hjalmar.] Isn't it done yet, then?

HJALMAR [aloud]. It is done.

GREGERS. It is?

HJALMAR. I have lived through the bitterest hour of my life.

GREGERS. But also the most uplifting, I imagine.

HJALMAR. Well, at any rate, we've got it off our hands, for the time being.

GINA. May God forgive you, Mr Werle.

GREGERS [in great amazement]. But I don't understand this.

HJALMAR. What don't you understand?

GREGERS. That reaching so vital an understanding – an understanding that is to be the foundation of a whole new way of life – a new way, sharing life in frankness, free from all deception –

HJALMAR. Yes, I know; I realize all that.

GREGERS. I was so sure that, when I came in at the door, I should be met by the transfiguring light of understanding in both your faces. And yet I see nothing here but this dull, gloomy, sad –

GINA. Oh, well – [*Takes the lamp-shade off.*]

GREGERS. You don't want to understand me, Mrs Ekdal. Well, well; the time will come. But you yourself, Hjalmar? Surely for you this great enlightenment has been an initiation to something higher?

HJALMAR. Why, of course it has. That is to say, to a certain extent.

GREGERS. For surely no experience in life can equal the forgiving of a sinner, lifting her up by your love to stand beside you?

HJALMAR. Do you think a man recovers so easily from the bitter draught I have just drunk?

GREGERS. Not an ordinary man, perhaps. But a man like you!

HJALMAR. Oh, I know, I know! But you mustn't *drive* me, Gregers. I must have time, you know.

GREGERS. You've a lot of the wild duck in you, Hjalmar. [*Relling has come in by the hall door.*]

RELLING. Well, well now. Talking about that wild duck again?

HJALMAR. Yes. The maimed trophy of Mr Werle's sporting prowess.

RELLING: Werle's? Is it he you're talking about?

HJALMAR. Him and – the rest of us.

RELLING [*to Gregers in an undertone*]. The devil take you!

HJALMAR. What's that you say?

RELLING. I was expressing a heartfelt wish that this quack would pack up and go home. If he stays here he's capable of ruining you both.

GREGERS. These two are not going to be ruined, Mr Relling. I won't speak of Hjalmar. We know him. But she too must surely have, in the depths of her being, something worthy of trust, something sincere –

GINA [*on the point of weeping*]. Then you might have let me alone, as I was.

RELLING [*to Gregers*]. Is it impertinent to ask what, precisely, is your business in this house?

GREGERS. To lay the foundations of a true marriage.

RELLING. So you don't think the Ekdals' marriage is good enough as it is?

GREGERS. It's probably as good a marriage as many another, unfortunately. But it has never been a true marriage, so far.

HJALMAR. You've never been sensitive to the claims of the ideal, Relling.

RELLING. Don't talk rot, my lad! If I may ask, Mr Werle, how many – at a rough estimate – how many true marriages have you seen in your life?

GREGERS. I think I've scarcely seen a single one.

RELLING. Nor I.

GREGERS. But I have seen innumerable marriages of the opposite kind. And I've had the chance of seeing at close quarters the damage that kind of marriage can do to both people.

HJALMAR. The very foundations of a man's character can give way; that is a terrible thing.

RELLING. Well, of course, I've never actually been married; so I can't very well give a judgement. But I do know this, that the child is a part of the marriage too. And you must leave the child alone.

HJALMAR. Ah, Hedvig! My poor little Hedvig.

RELLING. Yes, you will please leave Hedvig out of it. You two are grown people; you are free, God knows, to make havoc of your own affairs, if that's what you want to do. But I tell you, you must go carefully with Hedvig, else you may end by doing her serious harm.

HJALMAR. Harm?

RELLING. Yes, or she may end by doing some serious harm to herself – and perhaps to others too.

GINA. But how can you know that, Mr Relling?

HJALMAR. There's no immediate danger to her eyes, is there?

RELLING. What I'm talking about has nothing to do with her eyes. ... But Hedvig is at a difficult age. She might get hold of any idea.

GINA. Why, but that's just what she does do! She's begun to mess about in a tiresome way with the fire in the kitchen. She calls it playing at house on fire. I'm often afraid she *will* set the house on fire.

RELLING. There you are. I knew it.

GREGERS [*to Relling*]. But how do you explain that sort of thing?

RELLING [*curtly*]. Adolescence, my good man.

HJALMAR. As long as the child has *me*! as long as I'm above the ground!

[*There is a knock at the door.*]

GINA. Hush, Hjalmar! There's someone in the hall. [*Calling.*] Come in!

[*Mrs Sörby, dressed in outdoor clothes, comes in.*]

MRS SÖRBY. Good evening!

GINA [*going towards her*]. Why it's you, Berta!

MRS SÖRBY. Yes, it certainly is. But perhaps I've come at an inconvenient time?

HJALMAR. Not in the least. A messenger from *that* house –

MRS SÖRBY [*to Gina*]. To tell the truth, I hoped I shouldn't find your menfolk at home at this time of day; I slipped over to have a chat with you and say good-bye.

GINA. Really? Are you going away, then?

MRS SÖRBY. Yes, early tomorrow – up to Höidal. Mr Werle went this afternoon. [*Casually to Gregers.*] He asked to be remembered to you.

GINA. Well, fancy!

HJALMAR. So Mr Werle has gone? And now you're following him?

MRS SÖRBY. Yes. What do you say to that, Mr Ekdal?

HJALMAR. Be careful, I say.

GREGERS. I must explain. My father is marrying Mrs Sörby.

HJALMAR. Marrying!

GINA. Oh, Berta! Is he really, at last!

RELLING [with a slight tremor in his voice]. This is never true, surely?

MRS SÖRBY. Yes, my dear Mr Relling, it's perfectly true.

RELLING. Are you going to marry again?

MRS SÖRBY. Yes. That's what it's come to. Mr Werle's got a special licence, and we're going to have the wedding very quietly up at the works.

GREGERS. So I must wish you happiness, then, like a good stepson.

MRS SÖRBY. Thank you, if you mean anything by that. I certainly hope it will bring us happiness, both Mr Werle and me.

RELLING. You have every reason for hoping it. Mr Werle never gets drunk – so far as I know – and I don't suppose he's in the habit of beating his wives either, as the late lamented horse-doctor was.

MRS SÖRBY. Leave Sörby in peace in his grave, please! After all, he had his good points too.

RELLING. Mr Werle has even better points, I take it.

MRS SÖRBY. At any rate, he hasn't squandered the best that was in him. A man who does that must take the consequences.

RELLING. I shall go out with Molvik tonight.

MRS SÖRBY. You shouldn't, Mr Relling. Don't do that, for my sake!

RELLING. There's nothing else for it. [*To Hjalmar*]. You come along too, if you'd like to.

GINA. No, thanks. Hjalmar isn't going to them sorts of places with you.

HJALMAR [*in an angry undertone*]. Oh, do shut up!

RELLING. Good-bye, Mrs – Werle. [*Goes out by the hall door.*]

GREGERS [*to Mrs Sörby*]. You and Dr Relling seem to know each other pretty well.

MRS SÖRBY. Yes, we've known each other for years. At one time it looked as if something were going to come of it.

GREGERS. I suppose it was just as well for you it didn't.

MRS SÖRBY. Yes, you may well say that. But I have always been on my guard against acting impulsively. A woman can't absolutely throw herself away, either.

GREGERS. Aren't you at all afraid of my giving my father a hint about this old friendship?

MRS SÖRBY. You may be sure I've told him myself.

GREGERS. Indeed?

MRS SÖRBY. Your father knows every single thing people could find to say about me that has any truth at all in it. I've told him everything of that kind; it was the first thing I did when he showed he had intentions.

GREGERS. Then you're franker than most people, I think.

MRS SÖRBY. I've always been frank. We woman get on best that way.

HJALMAR. What do you say to that, Gina?

GINA. Oh, women are all so different. Some of us are one kind, some another.

MRS SÖRBY. Well, Gina, I think now that it's wisest to do things the way I have. And Mr Werle hasn't concealed anything in his past either Why, that's the chief thing that has brought us together. Now he can sit and talk to me as openly as a child. He's never had a chance of that before. He, a healthy, vigorous man, spent the whole of his youth and all his best years hearing nothing but sermons on his sins. And many a time, so far as I've been able to see, those sermons turned on purely imaginary transgressions.

GINA. Yes, that's true enough, that is.

GREGERS. If you ladies are going to start on that subject, I'd better go.

MRS SÖRBY. You can stay, as far as that goes. I shan't say another word. But I wanted you to realize that there's been no concealment or underhand dealings on my side. It probably seems as though I'm having a great piece of luck; and so I am, in a way. But just the same, I don't think I'm taking more than I'm giving. I shall never desert him, anyway. And it's I who can take care of him and look after him as no one else can, now that he'll soon be helpless.

HJALMAR. Be helpless?

GREGERS [to Mrs Sörby]. Oh well, don't discuss that here.

MRS SÖRBY. It's no use hiding it any longer, however much he wants to. He's going blind.

HJALMAR [amazed]. Going blind? That's very strange. He's going blind too, is he?

GINA. So many people do.

MRS SÖRBY. And one can just imagine what it will mean for a business man. Well, I shall try to use my eyes for him as far as I can. But now I mustn't stay any longer; I'm in such a rush, at the moment. Oh, and there was one thing I was to say to you, Mr Ekdal, that if there was anything Mr Werle could do for you, you had only to mention it to Graaberg.

GREGERS. An offer that Hjalmar Ekdal will certainly reject.

MRS SÖRBY. Oh? At one time, he didn't seem to –

GINA. No, Berta, Hjalmar doesn't need to take nothing from Mr Werle now.

HJALMAR [*slowly and weightily*]. Will you give my kind regards to your future husband and say that I intend in the immediate future to go to his cashier, Graaberg –

GREGERS. What! Can you really do that?

HJALMAR. – To go to his cashier, Graaberg, I repeat, and request a statement of the amount I owe his employer. I shall repay that debt of honour. Ha, ha, ha! 'Debt of honour' is the right name for it! But enough of that. I shall pay everything, with five per cent interest.

GINA. But, Hjalmar dear, we've no money for that – God knows!

HJALMAR. Will you tell your future husband that I am working indefatigably at my invention. Will you tell him that what supports me through this overwhelming toil is the desire to be freed from the burden of a painful debt. That is why I am making the invention. All that I derive from it shall be employed in discharging the debt I owe your future husband for his pecuniary outlay.

MRS SÖRBY. Something or other has certainly happened in this house.

HJALMAR. True; it has.

MRS SÖRBY. Well, then, good-bye. I still had one or two things to talk to you about, Gina; but they had better wait until another time. Good-bye.

[*Hjalmar and Gregers bow silently. Gina goes to the door with Mrs Sörby.*]

HJALMAR. Not across the threshold, Gina!

[*Mrs Sörby goes. Gina shuts the door behind her.*]

HJALMAR. There we are, Gregers. Now I've that burdensome debt off my hands.

GREGERS. You soon will have, at any rate.

HJALMAR. I think my behaviour may be called correct.

GREGERS. You are the man I always took you for.

HJALMAR. In certain circumstances it is impossible to disregard the claims of the ideal. As the bread-winner of a family, I can but writhe and groan under them. Believe me, it's no joke for a man without private means to repay a debt of many years' standing, one on which, so to speak, the dust of oblivion has settled. But, true though that is, the human being in me demands its rights too.

GREGERS [laying his hand on his shoulder]. My dear Hjalmar! Now wasn't it a good thing that I came?

HJALMAR. Ye-es.

GREGERS. So that you got a clear understanding of the whole position – wasn't that a good thing?

HJALMAR [a little impatiently]. Yes, of course it was. But there is one thing that hurts my sense of justice.

GREGERS. What's that?

HJALMAR. It's this business of – well, I don't know that I ought to speak quite so frankly about your father.

GREGERS. Don't have any scruples on my account.

HJALMAR. Well, then. ... You see, it's very disturbing to think that it isn't I, after all, but he who is to make the true marriage.

GREGERS. Why, how can you say such a thing?

HJALMAR. Yes, it's true. Your father and Mrs Sörby are entering upon a marriage founded upon complete confidence, founded on full and unqualified frankness on both sides; they are hiding nothing from each other; there is no deception at the back of it all; they have come to an agreement, if I may so express myself, for mutual forgiveness of sins.

GREGERS. Well, but what of it?

HJALMAR. Yes, but that's the whole point. You yourself said that all that was needed in this difficult business was to lay the foundations of a true marriage.

GREGERS. But that's quite a different thing, Hjalmar. Surely you are not going to compare either yourself or her with those two? Well, you know perfectly well what I mean.

HJALMAR. Yet I can't get away from the idea that there is something in this that outrages my sense of justice. It looks exactly as though there were no justice whatever in the ordering of the world.

GINA. Good gracious, Hjalmar! You musn't say things like that.

GREGERS. Hm. Don't let's enter upon that question.

HJALMAR. But, on the other hand, I do feel I can discern the guiding finger of fate, nevertheless. He is going blind.

GINA. Well, that may not be certain.

HJALMAR. There's no doubt about it. We ought not to doubt it, in any case; for in this very fact the righteous retribution is revealed. He has, in his time, blinded a trusting fellow-creature –

GREGERS. Unfortunately he has blinded several.

HJALMAR. And now comes an inexorable, mysterious fate and demands the man's own eyes.

GINA. How can you say such dreadful things? It makes me downright scared.

HJALMAR. It is salutary to immerse oneself in the dark things of life sometimes.

[*Hedvig, in her hat and coat, comes in, happy and breathless, from the hall door.*]

GINA. Are you back again?

HEDVIG. Yes, I didn't want to go any farther. And it was a good thing, because I've just met somebody at the door.

HJALMAR. I suppose it was our friend Mrs Sörby.

HEDVIG. Yes.

HJALMAR [*walking up and down*]. I hope you have seen her for the last time.

[*Silence. Hedvig looks timidly now at one, now at the other, as if trying to gauge their mood.*]

HEDVIG [*going up to Hjalmar, coaxingly*]. Daddy.

HJALMAR. Well, what is it, Hedvig?

HEDVIG. Mrs Sörby brought something for me.

HJALMAR [*stopping*]. For you?

HEDVIG. Yes. It's something for tomorrow.

GINA. Berta has always brought some little thing for your birthday.

HJALMAR. What is it?

HEDVIG. No, you're not to know anything about it yet. Because Mother is to give it me in bed first thing tomorrow.

HJALMAR. All this mystery! And I'm not to have anything to do with it!

HEDVIG [*hurriedly*]. Oh, of course you can see it. It's a big letter. [*Takes the letter out of her coat pocket.*]

HJALMAR. A letter too?

HEDVIG. Yes, there's only the letter. The rest is coming later on, I expect. But just think, a letter! I've never had a letter before. And there's 'Miss' written on the outside. [*Reading.*] 'Miss Hedvig Ekdal.' Fancy, that's me!

HJALMAR. Let me see that letter.

HEDVIG [*handing him the letter*]. There, you see.

HJALMAR. That is old Mr Werle's writing.

GINA. Are you sure of that, Hjalmar?

HJALMAR. Look for yourself.

GINA. Oh, do you think I understand that sort of thing?

HJALMAR. Hedvig, may I open the letter and read it?

HEDVIG. Yes, of course you may, if you want to.

GINA. No, not tonight, Hjalmar; it's to be for tomorrow.

HEDVIG [*softly*]. Oh, won't you let him read it! It's sure to be something nice. And then Daddy will be pleased and we can enjoy ourselves again!

HJALMAR. I may open it, then?

HEDVIG. Yes, please do, Daddy! It will be such fun to know what it is.

HJALMAR. Very well. [*Opens the letter, takes out a paper, reads it through and is obviously startled.*] Now, what does all this mean?

GINA. Why, what does it say?

HEDVIG. Yes, Daddy; tell us.

HJALMAR. Be quiet. [*Reads it through again. He has turned pale, but controls himself.*] It is a deed of gift, Hedvig.

HEDVIG. Is it really? What do I get?

HJALMAR. Read it yourself.

[*Hedvig goes across and reads for a moment by the lamp.*]

HJALMAR [*in an undertone, clenching his hands*]. The eyes! The eyes! And then that letter.

HEDVIG [*interrupts her reading*]. Yes, but it seems to me it's Grandfather who's to have it.

HJALMAR [*taking the letter from her*]. Gina, do you understand this?

GINA. I don't know anything about it. Tell me what it is.

HJALMAR. Mr Werle writes to Hedvig that her old grandfather need not trouble himself any more about his copying work, but that in future he can draw five pounds a month from the office.

GREGERS. Ah!

HEDVIG. Five pounds, Mother! I read that.

GINA. That's nice for Grandfather.

HJALMAR. – Five pounds a month as long as he needs it. That means, naturally, until his death.

GINA. Well, then, he's provided for, poor old soul.

HJALMAR. But then comes some more. You didn't read this, Hedvig. After that this gift passes to you.

HEDVIG. To me! All of it!

HJALMAR. You are assured the same amount for the whole of your life, he writes. Do you hear that, Gina?

GINA. Yes, I hear it all right.

HEDVIG. Think! I'm to get all that money! [*Giving him a shake.*] Daddy, Daddy, aren't you glad?

HJALMAR [*detaching himself*]. Glad! [*Walking about the room.*] Ah, what prospects, what vistas, it opens up before me! It is Hedvig – she is the one he provides for so liberally.

GINA. Yes, because, of course, it's Hedvig's birthday.

HEDVIG. You shall have it, just the same, Daddy! You know I'll give you and Mother all the money, of course.

HJALMAR. To your mother, yes! Of course.

GREGERS. Hjalmar, this is a trap that is laid for you.

HJALMAR. Do you think it could be another trap?

GREGERS. When he was here this morning he said, 'Hjalmar Ekdal is not the man you imagine.'

HJALMAR. Not the man!

GREGERS. 'You'll come to see that,' he said.

HJALMAR. What you were to see was that I would let myself be bought off with a bribe!

HEDVIG. But, Mother, what is it all about?

GINA. Go and take your things off.

[*Hedvig, nearly in tears, goes out by the kitchen door.*]

GREGERS. Yes, Hjalmar. Now we shall see which of us is right, he or I.

HJALMAR [*slowly tears the paper in two and lays both pieces on the table*]. There is my answer.

GREGERS. What I expected.

HJALMAR [*goes across to Gina who is standing by the stove and says quietly.*] And now no more deception. If the connexion between you and him was at an end when you – became 'fond of me', as you call it – why did he put us in a position to marry?

GINA. I suppose he thought he would have the entrance to our house.

HJALMAR. Only that? Wasn't he afraid of a certain possibility?

GINA. I don't know what you mean.

HJALMAR. I want to know whether – your child has the right to live under my roof.

GINA [drawing herself up, with her eyes flashing]. And you ask that?

HJALMAR. You're to answer this question. Does Hedvig belong to me – or ... Well?

GINA [looking at him with cold defiance]. I don't know.

HJALMAR [trembling]. You don't know that?

GINA. How can I know that? The sort of woman I am –

HJALMAR [quietly, turning away from her]. Then I have nothing more to do in this house.

GINA. Think what you are doing, Hjalmar.

HJALMAR [putting on his overcoat]. There is nothing here to think about, for a man like me.

GREGERS. On the contrary, there is a very great deal to think about. You three must be together if you are to win the great sacrament of forgiveness.

HJALMAR. That I will not. Never! Never! My hat! [Picks it up.] My home has collapsed in ruins about me. [Bursting into tears.] Gregers! I have no child!

HEDVIG [who has opened the kitchen door]. What are you saying? [Going across to him.] Daddy, Daddy!

GINA. There, now!

HJALMAR. Don't come near me, Hedvig! Go away! Right away! I can't bear to look at you. Ah, the eyes! Goodbye. [Making towards the door.]

HEDVIG [clinging tightly to him and screaming]. No, no! Don't go away from me!

GINA [*crying out*]. Look at the child, Hjalmar! Look at the child!

HJALMAR. I won't. I can't. I must get out, away from all this!

[*He tears himself free from Hedvig and goes out by the hall door.*]

HEDVIG [*with despair in her eyes*]. He's going away from us, Mother! He's going away from us! He'll never come back again.

GINA. Don't cry, now, Hedvig. Father will come back again.

HEDVIG [*throwing herself down on the sofa, sobbing*]. No, no, he'll never come back to us again.

GREGERS. You do believe, Mrs Ekdal, that I meant it all for the best?

GINA. Yes, I half believe you did; but God forgive you, all the same.

HEDVIG [*lying on the sofa*]. I think I'm going to die of all this. What have I done to him? Mother, you must make him come home again.

GINA. Yes, yes. Just be quiet, and I'll go out and look for him. [*Putting on her outdoor coat.*] Perhaps he's gone down to Relling. But you mustn't lie there and cry, now. Will you promise me that?

HEDVIG [*sobbing convulsively*]. Yes, I'll stop crying, if only Daddy comes back.

GREGERS [*to Gina, who is just going*]. Wouldn't it be better, all the same, to let him fight his bitter fight to the end first?

GINA. Oh, he can do that afterwards. First and foremost we must get the child quieted down. [*She goes out by the hall door.*]

HEDVIG [*sitting up and drying her tears*]. Now you must tell me what is the matter. Why doesn't Daddy want to see me any more?

GREGERS. You mustn't ask about that till you are big and grown-up.

HEDVIG [*with a sob*]. But I can't go on being absolutely miserable till I'm big and grown-up. I think I know what it is. Perhaps I'm not Daddy's real child.

GREGERS [*uneasily*]. How could that happen?

HEDVIG. Mother may have found me. And now perhaps Daddy has found it out. I've read about that sort of thing.

GREGERS. Well, but even so –

HEDVIG. Yes, I think he might be just as fond of me, for all that. Almost more. The wild duck was sent us as a present, too; and I'm tremendously fond of that, just the same.

GREGERS [*distracting her attention*]. Yes, the wild duck; that reminds me. Let's talk about the wild duck a little, Hedvig.

HEDVIG. The poor wild duck! He can't bear to look at that any more, either. Just think, he wanted to wring its neck.

GREGERS. Oh, he certainly won't.

HEDVIG. No, but he said it. And I think it was dreadful of Daddy to say that. Because I say a prayer for the wild duck every night and ask that it shall be protected from death and everything bad.

GREGERS [*looking at her*]. Do you say your prayers at night?

HEDVIG. Of course.

GREGERS. Who taught you?

HEDVIG. I taught myself; because there was a time when Daddy was very ill and had leeches on his neck and said he was lying at death's door.

GREGERS. What, really?

HEDVIG. So I said a prayer for him, when I'd gone to bed. And I've gone on with it ever since.

GREGERS. And now you pray for the wild duck, too?

HEDVIG. I thought I'd better put in the wild duck, because she was so delicate at first.

GREGERS. Do you say prayers in the morning, too?

HEDVIG. Oh no, of course not.

GREGERS. But why not in the morning, just as much?

HEDVIG. Why, in the morning it's light, and there is nothing to be afraid of any more.

GREGERS. And the wild duck that you are so fond of – your father would like to wring its neck.

HEDVIG. No, he said it would be best for him to, but he would spare it for my sake. And that was good of Daddy.

GREGERS [coming a little nearer]. But suppose, now, that you, of your own free will, sacrificed the wild duck for *his* sake?

HEDVIG [getting up]. The wild duck!

GREGERS. Supposing that you were to give up, as a sacrifice to him, the most precious thing you have in the world?

HEDVIG. Do you think that would help?

GREGERS. Try it, Hedvig.

HEDVIG [quietly, with shining eyes]. Yes, I will try it.

GREGERS. Have you strength of mind enough, do you think?

HEDVIG. I will ask Grandfather to shoot the wild duck for me.

GREGERS. But not a word to your mother about this kind of thing.

HEDVIG. Why not?

GREGERS. She doesn't understand us.

HEDVIG. The wild duck? I will try it first thing tomorrow.

[Gina comes in from the hall door.]

HEDVIG [going to her]. Did you meet him, Mother?

GINA. No, but I heard he'd been down there and had taken Relling with him.

GREGERS. Are you sure of that?

GINA. Yes, the porter's wife said so. Molvik had gone with them too, she said.

GREGERS. And that at this moment, when his spirit so sorely needs to fight in solitude!

GINA [*taking off her coat*]. Yes, you never know where you are with men. Lord knows where Relling has carted him off to. I ran over to Mrs Eriksen's, but they weren't there.

HEDVIG [*fighting with her tears*]. Oh, suppose he never comes home any more!

GREGERS. He'll come home again. I'm going to take a message to him tomorrow, and then you'll see how he'll come. You can go to sleep and trust to that, Hedvig. Good night.

[*He goes out through the hall door.*]

HEDVIG [*throwing herself sobbing on her mother's neck*]. Mother! Mother!

GINA [*patting her on the back and sighing*]. Ah yes; Relling was right, he was. This is what happens when these fools of people come around presenting these here 'Idol's claims'.

ACT FIVE

———————— * ————————

[*Hjalmar Ekdal's studio in a cold, grey morning light. Wet snow is lying on the large panes of the skylight. Gina, dressed in an overall, comes in from the kitchen with a brush and a duster and goes across towards the sitting-room door. At the same moment Hedvig rushes in from the hall.*]

GINA [*stopping*]. Well?

HEDVIG. Mother, I wonder if he isn't down at Relling's –

GINA. There you are, you see!

HEDVIG. – Because the porter's wife said she heard two people come home with Relling last night.

GINA. That's just what I thought.

HEDVIG. But that doesn't help at all if he won't come up to us.

GINA. At least I can go down and have a word with him.

[*Old Ekdal, in a dressing-gown and slippers and smoking a pipe, comes to the door of his room.*]

EKDAL. Hjalmar, my boy! Isn't Hjalmar at home?

GINA. No, he's gone out.

EKDAL. So early? And in a blinding snow-storm like this! Oh well, all right. I can take my morning walk alone, thank you.

[*He pushes the attic door aside; Hedvig helps him; he goes in and she shuts it after him.*]

HEDVIG [*in an undertone*]. Oh, Mother, think, when poor Grandfather hears that Daddy is going away from us!

GINA. Oh fiddlesticks! Grandfather mustn't hear anything

about it. It was a mercy he wasn't at home yesterday in all that to-do.

HEDVIG. Yes, but –

[*Gregers comes in at the hall door.*]

GREGERS. Well? Have you got any news of him?

GINA. He seems to be down at Relling's, so they say.

GREGERS. At Relling's! Has he really been out with those fellows?

GINA. He obviously has.

GREGERS. Yes, but he had such profound need of solitude and serious reflection –

GINA. Yes, you may well say that.

[*Relling comes in from the hall.*]

HEDVIG [*going to him*]. Is Daddy in your rooms?

GINA [*simultaneously*]. Is he there?

RELLING. Yes, he's there all right.

HEDVIG. And you never told us!

RELLING. Yes, I am a brute. But to begin with I had that other brute to look after – our demoniac, of course. And then I slept so heavily that –

GINA. What does Hjalmar say today?

RELLING. He doesn't say a thing.

HEDVIG. Hasn't he talked at all?

RELLING. Not a blessed word.

GREGERS. Ah no. I can quite understand that.

GINA. But what is he doing, then?

RELLING. He's lying on the sofa, snoring.

GINA. Is he? Oh well, Hjalmar's a great one for snoring.

HEDVIG. Is he asleep? Can he sleep?

RELLING. It certainly seems so.

GREGERS. It's understandable. After the conflict of spirit that has torn him –

GINA. And then he's never been used to wandering about out of doors at night.

HEDVIG. Perhaps it's a good thing, you know, Mother, that he's getting some sleep.

GINA. I think so, too. But it's no good us waking him up too soon, in that case. Thanks, Mr Relling. Now I must see about getting the house cleaned up and tidied a bit, and then – Come and help me, Hedvig.

[*Gina and Hedvig go out into the sitting-room.*]

GREGERS [*turning to Relling*]. Can you explain the spiritual upheaval which is taking place in Hjalmar Ekdal?

RELLING. Damned if I've noticed any spiritual upheaval taking place in him.

GREGERS. What! At such a turning-point, when the whole of his life has taken on a new meaning! How can you imagine that a personality like Hjalmar's – ?

RELLING. Bah! Personality! *He!* If he did at one time have the rudiments of anything so abnormal as a personality, as you call it, it was grubbed up, root and branch, in his childhood. I can assure you of that.

GREGERS. That would be extraordinary – with the tender and affectionate upbringing he received.

RELLING. From those two warped, hysterical maiden-aunts, do you mean?

GREGERS. Let me tell you, they were women who never lost sight of the claim of the ideal. Now, of course, you are going to jeer at me again.

RELLING. No, I don't feel much like that. Besides, I know what I am talking about, because he has thrown up a good deal of rhetoric about his 'twin soul-mothers'. But I don't think he has much to thank them for. Ekdal's misfortune is that in his circle he has always been taken for a shining light –

GREGERS. And don't you think he is? In his innermost being, I mean?

RELLING. I have never noticed anything of the kind. That

his father thought so – that's nothing. The old Lieutenant has been an ass all his days.

GREGERS. He has, all his days, been a man with the spirit of a child; that's a thing you don't understand.

RELLING. Probably not. But when our dear, precious Hjalmar became a student of sorts, he was at once accepted by the others as the great light of the future. Of course he was handsome, the scamp – pink and white – what silly young girls like men to be; and as he had that susceptible mind and that winning voice, and as he had a charming way of declaiming other people's verse and other people's ideas –

GREGERS [angrily]. Is it Hjalmar Ekdal you are speaking of like this?

RELLING. Yes, with your permission. For that's what he is, seen from inside, this idol that you're grovelling in front of.

GREGERS. I didn't think I was totally blind, either. ...

RELLING. Well, not far short of it. For you're a sick man too, you know.

GREGERS. There you are right.

RELLING. Quite so. You're suffering from a complication of maladies. First there's this troublesome inflamed conscience of yours, and then, what's worse, you are always in a raging fever of hero-worship; you must always have something to admire that's no business of yours.

GREGERS. Yes, I certainly have to look for it somewhere outside my own business.

RELLING. But you're so shockingly deceived over these marvellous beings you think you see all round you. Here you are again, coming to a cottage door with that claim of the ideal; there are no solvent people in this house.

GREGERS. If you have no better idea of Hjalmar Ekdal than

that, how can you take pleasure in being everlastingly with him?

RELLING. Lord bless you, I'm supposed – to my shame – to be some kind of a doctor; I must pay some attention to the wretched sick folk I live in the house with.

GREGERS. Oh, really! Is Hjalmar Ekdal a sick man, too?

RELLING. Almost everybody is sick, unfortunately.

GREGERS. And what cure are you prescribing for Hjalmar?

RELLING. My usual one. I am trying to keep up the saving lie in him.

GREGERS. The saving lie? Did I hear you properly?

RELLING. Oh yes. I said 'the saving lie'. Because that lie is the stimulating principle of life, you see.

GREGERS. May I ask what sort of saving lie Hjalmar is infected with?

RELLING. Thank you; I don't betray secrets like that to quacks. You'd be in a position to make an even worse wreck of him for me. My method has been tested. I've applied it to Molvik, too. I've made him a 'demoniac'. That's the cure I've had to use for him.

GREGERS. Isn't he demoniac, then?

RELLING. What the devil does it mean, to be demoniac? It's just a piece of nonsense I hit upon to keep the life going in him. If I hadn't done it, the poor simple creature would have collapsed years ago under his self-contempt and despair. And there's the old Lieutenant, too. But he hit upon the cure all right for himself.

GREGERS. Lieutenant Ekdal? What about him?

RELLING. Well, what do you make of it – a bear-hunter going rabbit-shooting in that dark attic? There isn't a happier sportsman in the world than that old man, pottering about in there among all that rubbish. The four or five dried-up Christmas trees that he's kept are the same to him as all the great, growing forests of Höidal;

the cock and the hens are wild birds in the pine tops; and
the rabbits loping about the floor of the loft, those are
the bears he grappled with when he was a vigorous man
under the open sky.

GREGERS. Poor, unhappy old Lieutenant Ekdal; yes. He's
certainly had to let go the ideals of his youth.

RELLING. While I remember it, young Mr Werle – don't
use that exotic word 'ideals'. We have a good enough
native word: 'lies'.

GREGERS. Do you mean that the two things are related?

RELLING. Yes. Like typhus and typhoid fever.

GREGERS. Dr Relling, I shan't give up until I have rescued
Hjalmar from your clutches.

RELLING. All the worse for him. Take the saving lie from
the average man and you take his happiness away, too.
[*To Hedvig, who comes in from the living-room.*] Well, little
wild-duck mother, I'm going down now to see whether
your father is still lying and meditating on the wonderful
invention. [*Goes out by the hall door.*]

GREGERS [*coming up to Hedvig*]. I can see by your look that
it is not done yet.

HEDVIG. What? Oh, about the wild duck. No.

GREGERS. Your courage failed you, when it came to doing
it, I expect.

HEDVIG. No, it's not really that. But when I woke up early
this morning and remembered what we'd talked about,
it seemed so queer to me.

GREGERS. Queer?

HEDVIG. Yes, I don't know. ... Last night, at the time, it
seemed such a beautiful idea. But when I had been asleep
and remembered it again, it didn't seem to mean very
much.

GREGERS. Ah no. You haven't grown up here without
something being damaged in you.

HEDVIG. Well, I don't mind about that; if only Daddy would come up, then –

GREGERS. Ah, if your eyes had really been opened to what makes life worth while, if you had the real, joyous, courageous spirit of sacrifice, you would see that he would come up to you, all right. But I still believe in you, Hedvig. [*He goes out by the hall door.*]

[*Hedvig walks about the room. She is about to go out into the kitchen. At that moment there is a knock on the inside of the attic door. She goes across and opens it a little way. Old Ekdal comes out and she pushes the door to again.*]

EKDAL. Hm. It's poor fun, going for one's morning walk alone.

HEDVIG. Didn't you feel like shooting, Grandpapa?

EKDAL. It's not shooting weather today. So dark in there you can hardly see in front of you.

HEDVIG. Don't you ever feel like shooting anything besides the rabbits?

EKDAL. Surely the rabbits are good enough, aren't they?

HEDVIG. Yes, but what about the wild duck?

EKDAL. Ha, ha! Are you afraid I shall shoot your wild duck for you? Not for the world, bless you! Never!

HEDVIG. No, I expect you couldn't. Because it must be difficult to shoot wild ducks.

EKDAL. Couldn't? I should jolly well think I could!

HEDVIG. How would you manage it, Grandpapa? I don't mean with *my* wild duck, but with others.

EKDAL. I should make sure of shooting it in the breast, you know; that's the surest place. And then, you must shoot *against* the lie of the feathers, you see, not *with* the feathers.

HEDVIG. Do they die, then, Grandpapa?

EKDAL. Oh yes, they die all right, so long as you shoot

properly. Well, I must go in and tidy myself. Hm – you see – hm. [*Goes into his room.*]

[*Hedvig waits a moment, glances towards the door, goes across to the bookcase, stretches up on tip-toes, takes the double-barrelled pistol down from the shelf and looks at it. Gina, with her brush and duster, comes in from the living-room. Hedvig puts down the pistol quickly and unnoticed.*]

GINA. Don't go meddling with your father's things, Hedvig.

HEDVIG [*moving away from the shelves*]. I only wanted to tidy up a little.

GINA. You'd better go into the kitchen and see if the coffee's keeping hot; I'll take the tray with me when I go down to him.

[*Hedvig goes out; Gina begins to sweep and dust the studio. A moment later the hall door is opened, hesitantly, and Hjalmar Ekdal looks in. He has his overcoat on but no hat. He is unwashed, with tumbled, uncombed hair. His eyes are sleepy and dull.*]

GINA [*standing with the broom in her hand and looking at him*]. Well, now, Hjalmar! Have you come back, after all?

HJALMAR [*coming in and answering in a gloomy voice*]. I've come – to go away again immediately.

GINA. Oh yes. I can quite understand that. But, good Lord! What *do* you look like!

HJALMAR. Look like?

GINA. And your good winter overcoat, too! Why, it's absolutely done for!

HEDVIG [*at the kitchen door*]. Mother, shall I – ? [*Sees Hjalmar, screams with joy and runs to him.*] Oh, Daddy! Daddy!

HJALMAR [*turning aside and waving her away*]. Go away! Go away! [*To Gina.*] Make her go away from me, I tell you.

GINA [*in an undertone*]. Go into the living-room, Hedvig. [*Hedvig goes in silently.*]

HJALMAR [*looking busy, and pulling out the table drawer*]. I must have my books with me. Where are my books?

GINA. Which books?

HJALMAR. My scientific works, naturally; the technical periodicals I use for my invention.

GINA [*looking in the bookcase*]. Are they these unbound books here?

HJALMAR. Yes, of course.

GINA [*putting a pile of paper-covered books on the table*]. Shan't I tell Hedvig to cut the pages for you?

HJALMAR. No one need cut pages for me.

GINA. Then it's settled that you're going away from us, Hjalmar?

HJALMAR [*looking among the books*]. I should think that was obvious.

GINA. Oh, well.

HJALMAR [*angrily*]. I can't stay here, having my heart wrung every hour of the day.

GINA. God forgive you for thinking so badly of me.

HJALMAR. Prove that –

GINA. I think it is for you to prove.

HJALMAR. After a past like yours? There are certain claims ... I'm almost tempted to call them claims of the ideal –

GINA. But what about Grandfather? What's to become of him, poor old thing?

HJALMAR. I know my duty; the helpless old man goes with me. I will go out into the town, and make the arrangements. Hm. [*Hesitating.*] Didn't anybody find my hat on the stairs?

GINA. No. Have you lost your hat?

HJALMAR. I had it on, of course, when I came in last night; there's no doubt about that. But today I couldn't find it.

GINA. Oh, Lord! Wherever did you go with those two good-for-nothings?

HJALMAR. Oh, don't ask me about trivialities. Do you think I am in the state of mind to remember details?

GINA. If only you haven't caught cold, Hjalmar. [*Goes out to the kitchen.*]

HJALMAR [*talking to himself in an angry undertone, while he empties the table-drawer*]. You're a wretch, Relling! A scoundrel, that's what you are! Shameless and treacherous! I wish to heaven I could get someone to murder you. [*He puts aside some old letters, finds the torn document from the day before, takes it up and looks at the pieces. He puts it hastily aside as Gina comes in.*]

GINA [*putting a tray with coffee things down on the table*]. Here's a drop of something hot, if you'd like it. And there's bread-and-butter and a little salt meat with it.

HJALMAR [*glancing at the tray*]. Salt meat! Never, under this roof! It's true I've had practically no solid food for almost four-and-twenty hours; but that does not matter. My notes! The beginning of my autobiography. Where shall I find my diary and all my important papers? [*Opens the living-room door, but shrinks back.*] There she is again!

GINA. Well, good gracious, the child must be somewhere!

HJALMAR. Come out. [*He stands aside. Terrified, Hedvig comes into the studio.*]

HJALMAR [*with his hand on the door-handle, to Gina*]. In the last moments I spend in my former home I wish to be spared contact with things which are not my concern. [*He goes into the room.*]

HEDVIG [*darting towards her mother and speaking in a low and trembling voice*]. Is that me?

GINA. Stay in the kitchen, Hedvig. Or, no – go into your own room. [*Speaking to Hjalmar, as she goes in to him.*]

Wait a minute, Hjalmar. Don't rummage about in the chest-of-drawers; I know where everything is. [*Hedvig stands motionless for a moment, in terror and confusion, biting her lips to stop herself crying. Then she clenches her hands convulsively and says in a low voice*]: The wild duck! [*She steals across and takes the pistol from the shelf, opens the attic door a little way, slips in and pulls the door to after her. Hjalmar and Gina begin to argue in the living-room.*]

HJALMAR [*bringing in some note-books and old loose papers which he lays on the table*]. Oh! What's the use of the hold-all! There are a hundred and one things I've got to drag about with me.

GINA [*following him with the hold-all*]. Well, leave all the rest for the present and just take a shirt and a pair of pants with you.

HJALMAR. Phew! These exhausting preparations! [*Takes off his overcoat and throws it on the sofa.*]

GINA. And there's the coffee getting cold, too.

HJALMAR. Hm. [*Drinks a gulp without thinking what he is doing, and then another.*]

GINA [*dusting the backs of the chairs*]. The worst job will be finding an attic as big as this one for the rabbits.

HJALMAR. Good God! Have I got to drag all those rabbits with me, too?

GINA. Why, yes. Grandfather can't do without his rabbits, I'm sure.

HJALMAR. He'll just have to get used to it. There are things that matter more in life than rabbits; and I am having to give them up.

GINA [*dusting the bookcase*]. Shall I put your flute in the hold-all for you?

HJALMAR. No. No flute for me. But give me the pistol.

GINA. Do you want to take that gun with you?

HJALMAR. Yes. My loaded pistol.

GINA [*looking for it*]. It's gone. He must have taken it in there with him.

HJALMAR. Is he in the attic?

GINA. Yes. Sure to be.

HJALMAR. Hm. Poor, lonely old man. [*He takes a piece of bread-and-butter, eats it and finishes the cup of coffee.*]

GINA. Now if we hadn't let the room, you could have moved in there.

HJALMAR. I should be living under the same roof as – ! Never! Never!

GINA. But couldn't you make do in the living-room for a day or two? You'd have all your own things to yourself there.

HJALMAR. Never inside these walls!

GINA. Well, down with Relling and Molvik, then?

HJALMAR. Don't mention the names of those scoundrels. It almost takes my appetite away, just to think of them. Oh no; I'll go out in the storm and the snow – go from house to house seeking shelter for my father and myself.

GINA. But you haven't got a hat, Hjalmar! You've lost it, you know.

HJALMAR. Oh, those two wretches! Sunk in depravity! I must get a hat on the way. [*Taking another piece of bread-and-butter.*] The necessary arrangements must be made. I have no intention of risking my life. [*Looking for something on the tray.*]

GINA. What is it you are looking for?

HJALMAR. Butter.

GINA. You shall have some directly. [*Goes out to the kitchen.*]

HJALMAR [*calling after her*]. Oh, it doesn't matter; I can just as well eat dry bread.

GINA [*bringing in a butter-dish*]. Here you are; it's freshly churned.

[*She pours him out a fresh cup of coffee; he sits down on the sofa, puts more butter on the bread, and eats and drinks for a while in silence.*]

HJALMAR. Would I, without being interfered with by any-body ... by anybody at all ... be able to put up in the living-room for a day or two?

GINA. Yes you could, perfectly well. If only you would.

HJALMAR. Because I don't see that it is possible to get all Father's things out in one move.

GINA. And then there's this, too – you've got to tell him first that you won't live with the rest of us no longer.

HJALMAR [*pushing his coffee-cup away from him*]. That too, yes. Having to open up all these complicated matters again. I must think things out; I must have a breathing-space. I can't bear all these burdens in one single day.

GINA. No, and in such awful weather as it is, too.

HJALMAR [*turning over Werle's letter*]. I see this paper's still lying about here.

GINA. Yes, *I* haven't touched it.

HJALMAR. That bit of paper's nothing to do with me –

GINA. Well, I've no intention of doing anything with it.

HJALMAR. – But there's no point in letting it get lost, all the same. In all the disturbance of my moving it could so easily –

GINA. I'll take care of it all right, Hjalmar.

HJALMAR. After all, the deed of gift belongs first and fore-most to Father; and it's his affair whether he'll use it or not.

GINA [*sighing*]. Yes, poor old Father.

HJALMAR. Just to be on the safe side – where shall I find some paste?

GINA [*going to the bookcase*]. Here's the paste-pot.

HJALMAR. And a brush?

GINA. Here's the brush, too. [*Brings him the things.*]

HJALMAR [*taking a pair of scissors*]. Just a strip of paper at the back. [*Cutting and pasting.*] Far be it from me to want to lay hands on someone else's property, and least of all on a poverty-stricken old man's. And not on the ... other person's, either. There it is. Let it lie there a little while. And when it's dry, then put it away. I don't want that paper to meet my eyes again. Never!

[*Gregers Werle comes in from the hall.*]

GREGERS [*a little surprised*]. What! Are you sitting here, Hjalmar?

HJALMAR [*getting up quickly*]. I had sunk down from exhaustion.

GREGERS. You've had breakfast, though, I see.

HJALMAR. Even the body's claims must be met occasionally.

GREGERS. What have you decided on, then?

HJALMAR. For a man such as I am there is only one way to take. I am in process of putting together my most important possessions. But it takes time, you realize.

GINA [*a little impatiently*]. Well, shall I get the room ready for you or shall I pack the bag?

HJALMAR [*after an irritated side-glance at Gregers*]. Pack – and get the room ready.

GINA [*taking the hold-all*]. All right. I'll put the shirt and the other things in, then. [*Goes into the living-room and pulls the door to after her.*]

GREGERS [*after a short silence*]. I should never have thought that this would be the end of it. Is it really necessary for you to leave house and home?

HJALMAR [*wandering uneasily about*]. Well, what would you have me do? I am not built for unhappiness, Gregers. I must have things comfortable and safe and peaceful about me.

GREGERS. But can't you, though? Just have a try. It seems to me there's a good foundation now for building on.

So begin from now. And remember, you have your invention to live for, too.

HJALMAR. Oh, don't talk about the invention. That may be a long way off yet.

GREGERS. May it?

HJALMAR. Oh, good Lord! What exactly do you expect me to invent? Other people have invented nearly everything already. It gets more difficult every day –

GREGERS. But you, who have done so much work on it –

HJALMAR. It was that beast Relling who inveigled me into it.

GREGERS. Relling?

HJALMAR. Yes, it was he who first persuaded me that I was capable of some notable invention in photography.

GREGERS. Aha! It was Relling!

HJALMAR. I was so thoroughly happy with that invention. Not so much because of the invention itself as because Hedvig believed in it – believed in it with all the power and strength a child's mind is capable of. Well, that's to say that I, fool that I was, went about fancying that she believed in it.

GREGERS. Can you really believe Hedvig was deceiving you?

HJALMAR. I can believe anything in the world now. It's Hedvig who stands in my way. She'll end by taking all the sunshine out of my life.

GREGERS. Hedvig! Is it Hedvig you mean? How could she do that?

HJALMAR [without answering]. Such inexpressible love as I had for that child! So inexpressibly happy as I felt, every time I came home to my poor room and she flew to meet me with her precious, delicate eyes. Trusting fool, I was! I was so inexpressibly devoted to her. And so, romanticizing and dreaming, I built up the delusion that she was just as deeply attached to me.

GREGERS. Are you saying that that was only a delusion?

HJALMAR. How can I know? I can't get anything out of
Gina at all. And besides, she's completely insensitive to
the ideal side of these complications. But to you I feel
driven to open my mind, Gregers. There is this terrible
doubt; perhaps Hedvig has never really loved me at all.

GREGERS. Well, you may possibly have some proof as to
that. [Listening.] What is that? I think it's the wild duck's
cry.

HJALMAR. It's the wild duck quacking. Father is in the loft.

GREGERS. Is he? [Joy lights up his face.] I tell you, you may
yet have proof of the love of your poor, misunderstood
Hedvig!

HJALMAR. Ah, what proof can she offer me? I daren't trust
any assurance of hers.

GREGERS. Hedvig does not know the meaning of deception.

HJALMAR. Ah, Gregers, that's just it; that's by no means
certain. Who knows what Gina and this Mrs Sörby have
sat here buzzing and whispering about? And Hedvig has
her ears about her, all right. Perhaps the deed of gift was
not so unexpected, after all. I rather thought I noticed
something.

GREGERS. What devil is this that has got into you?

HJALMAR. I have had my eyes opened. You wait; you'll
see the deed of gift is only a beginning. Mrs Sörby has
always had a great fondness for Hedvig, and now she has
it in her power to do whatever she wants for the child.
They can take her away from me whenever they like.

GREGERS. Hedvig will never leave you, never in the world.

HJALMAR. Don't be so sure about that. Suppose they stand
and beckon to her with full hands – ? Oh, I have loved
her so inexpressibly! I would have found my highest
happiness in taking her tenderly by the hand and leading

her, as one leads a child that is afraid of the dark, through a great, empty room. Now I feel the bitter certainty that the poor photographer up in his garret has never meant anything to her at all. She has only been shrewd and taken care to keep on a good footing with him until the hour came.

GREGERS. You don't believe this yourself, Hjalmar.

HJALMAR. That's just the ghastly part of it; I don't know what to believe – I shall never find out. But can you really doubt that it must be as I say? Ha, ha! You're relying too much on the claims of the ideal, my dear Gregers. Suppose the others were to come with full hands and call to the child: Come away from him! Life lies before you with us –

GREGERS [quickly]. Well what then, do you think?

HJALMAR. If I asked her then, 'Hedvig, are you willing to give up life for my sake?' [Laughing sarcastically.] Oh yes, I dare say! You'd soon hear what answer I got!

[A pistol shot is heard in the attic.]

GREGERS [loud and joyfully]. Hjalmar!

HJALMAR. There we are. Now he must needs go shooting!

GINA [coming in]. Oh, Hjalmar, I think Grandfather's banging about in the attic there by himself.

HJALMAR. I'll look inside.

GREGERS [quickly and with exaltation]. Wait a moment! Do you know what that was?

HJALMAR. Yes, of course I know.

GREGERS. No, you don't. But I know. It was the proof.

HJALMAR. What proof?

GREGERS. It was a child's sacrifice. She has got your father to shoot the wild duck –

HJALMAR. Shoot the wild duck!

GINA. Well, just think – !

HJALMAR. What's the point of that?

GREGERS. She wanted to sacrifice for you the best thing she had in the world; because she thought it would make you love her again.

HJALMAR [*softly, touched*]. Bless the child!

GINA. The things she thinks of!

GREGERS. She only wanted you to love her again, Hjalmar; she didn't feel as if she could live without it.

GINA [*struggling with her tears*]. Now you see, Hjalmar.

HJALMAR. Gina, where has she gone?

GINA [*sniffing*]. Poor child, she's sitting out in the kitchen, I expect.

HJALMAR [*going across and throwing the kitchen door open*]. Hedvig, come along! Come in here to me! [*Looking round.*] No, she's not here.

GINA. Then she's in her own little room.

HJALMAR [*from outside*]. No, she isn't here either. [*Coming in.*] She must have gone out.

GINA. Well, you didn't want her anywhere about the house.

HJALMAR. Ah, if only she'd come home soon – so that I can really tell her. ... Now all will be well, Gregers; for now I really believe we can begin life over again.

GREGERS [*quietly*]. I knew it; it will all come right through the child.

[*Old Ekdal comes to the door of his room; he is in full uniform and is busy fastening on his sabre.*]

HJALMAR [*amazed*]. Father! Are you there?

GINA. Were you shooting in your room, Father?

EKDAL [*indignantly, coming forward*]. So you go shooting alone, do you, Hjalmar?

HJALMAR [*anxious, bewildered*]. So it wasn't you who fired the shot in the attic?

EKDAL. I? Fire a shot? Hm.

GREGERS [*calling to Hjalmar*]. She has shot the wild duck herself, don't you see?

HJALMAR. What is all this? [*Rushes across to the door of the attic, pulls it aside, looks in and gives a scream.*] Hedvig!

GINA [*running to the door*]. Heavens! What is it?

HJALMAR [*going in*]. She is lying on the floor!

GREGERS. Hedvig! On the floor! [*He goes in to Hjalmar.*]

GINA [*at the same time*]. Hedvig! [*Inside the attic.*] No, no, no!

EKDAL. Oh, indeed! Is she taking to shooting, too?

[*Hjalmar, Gina and Gregers carry Hedvig into the studio; her right hand is hanging down and the pistol is clasped tight in her fingers.*]

HJALMAR [*in desperation*]. The pistol has gone off! She has shot herself. Call for help! Help!

GINA [*running out into the hall and calling down*]. Mr Relling! Dr Relling! Come up as quick as you can!

[*Hjalmar and Gregers lay Hedvig down on the sofa.*]

EKDAL [*quietly*]. The forests avenge themselves.

HJALMAR [*on his knees beside her*]. She's just coming to now. She's coming to. Yes. Yes.

GINA [*who has come back again*]. Where has she shot herself? I can't see anything.

[*Relling comes quickly in with Molvik at his heels, the latter without waistcoat or collar and with his jacket unfastened.*]

RELLING. What's the matter?

GINA. They say Hedvig has shot herself.

HJALMAR. Come here and help!

RELLING. Shot herself! [*He pushes the table aside and begins to examine her.*]

HJALMAR [*still kneeling, looking anxiously up at him*]. But it can't be dangerous? Eh, Relling? She's hardly bleeding at all. So it can't be dangerous?

RELLING. How did it happen?

HJALMAR. I can't think.

GINA. She wanted to shoot the wild duck.

RELLING. The wild duck?

HJALMAR. The pistol must have gone off.

RELLING. Yes. Quite.

EKDAL. The forests avenge themselves. But I'm not afraid, all the same. [*Goes into the attic and shuts the door behind him.*]

HJALMAR. Why, Relling – why don't you say anything?

RELLING. The bullet has entered the breast.

HJALMAR. Yes, but she's coming to.

RELLING. Can't you see Hedvig isn't alive?

GINA [*bursting into tears*]. My child, my child!

GREGERS [*huskily*]. In the ocean's depths.

HJALMAR [*springing up*]. No, no, she must live! Oh, for heaven's sake, Relling – only a moment – just long enough to let me tell her how inexpressibly I loved her all the time!

RELLING. It has reached the heart. Internal haemorrhage. She died on the spot.

HJALMAR. And I drove her from me like a hunted animal! And she crept into the loft in terror and died, for love of me. [*Sobbing.*] Never able to put it right now! Never able to tell her! [*Clenching his hands and shrieking to heaven.*] Ah, Thou above! If Thou *art* there! Why hast Thou done this thing to me!

GINA. Hush, hush; you mustn't say dreadful things like that. We didn't deserve to keep her, I expect.

MOLVIK. The child is not dead, but sleepeth.

RELLING. Nonsense.

HJALMAR [*becoming quieter, goes over to the sofa, folds his arms and looks at Hedvig*]. There she lies, so stiff and still.

RELLING [*trying to loosen the pistol*]. She's got so fast hold of it ... so fast.

GINA. No, no, Mr Relling, don't force her fingers. Let the gun be.

HJALMAR. She shall take it with her.

GINA. Yes, let her. But the child can't lie here for everybody to see. She shall go into her own little room, she shall. Help me with her, Hjalmar.

[*Hjalmar and Gina lift Hedvig between them.*]

HJALMAR [*as they carry her away*]. Oh, Gina, Gina, can you bear it?

GINA. We must help one another. Now we have equal shares in her, haven't we?

MOLVIK [*stretching out his arms and muttering*]. Praised be the Lord. Earth to earth. Earth to earth.

RELLING [*in a whisper*]. Shut up, you fool; you're drunk.

[*Hjalmar and Gina carry the body out through the kitchen door. Relling shuts it after them. Molvik slips out into the hall.*]

RELLING [*going over to Gregers*]. No one is ever going to persuade me this was an accident.

GREGERS [*who has stood horror-stricken, his face twitching*]. No one can say how this terrible thing happened.

RELLING. The charge has burnt her dress. She must have held the pistol right against her breast and fired.

GREGERS. Hedvig has not died in vain. Did you see how sorrow called out what was noblest in him?

RELLING. Most people are noble in the presence of death. But how long do you suppose this nobility will last in him?

GREGERS. Surely it will last and increase all his life!

RELLING. Before the year is out little Hedvig will be nothing more to him than a fine subject to declaim on.

GREGERS. And you dare to say that of Hjalmar Ekdal!

RELLING. We will talk about it again when the first grass is showing on her grave. Then you'll hear him delivering himself of fine phrases about 'the child torn untimely from her father's heart', and see him wallowing in emotion and self-pity.

GREGERS. If you are right and I am wrong, then life is not worth living.

RELLING. Oh, life would be tolerable enough, even so, if we could only be rid of these infernal duns who come to us poor people's doors with their claim of the ideal.

GREGERS [*looking in front of him*]. In that case, I am glad my destiny is what it is.

RELLING. May I ask – what *is* your destiny?

GREGERS [*on the point of going*]. To be thirteenth at table.

RELLING. I wonder. ...

CHARACTERS

———— * ————

JÖRGEN TESMAN, a scholar engaged in research in the
    history of civilization
HEDDA TESMAN, his wife
JULIANE TESMAN, his aunt
MRS ELVSTED
BRACK, a puisne judge
EJLERT LÖVBORG
BERTE, the Tesmans' servant

The action takes place in the Tesmans' villa on the
west side of the town

ACT ONE

————————— * —————————

[*A large drawing-room, well furnished, in good taste, and decorated in dark colours. In the back wall there is a wide doorway with its curtains pulled back. This opening leads into a smaller room decorated in the same style as the drawing-room. In the right wall of this outer room is a folding door that leads into the hall. In the opposite wall, left, is a glass door also with curtains pulled back. Through its panes can be seen part of a veranda outside and autumn foliage. In the middle of the stage is an oval table with a cloth on it and chairs round it. Downstage, against the right wall are a large, dark porcelain stove, a high-backed arm-chair, a padded foot-rest and two stools. Up in the right corner are a corner sofa and a little round table. Downstage, left, a little way from the wall, is a sofa. Above the glass door, a piano. On each side of the doorway at the back stands a what-not with terra-cotta and majolica ornaments. Against the back wall of the inner room can be seen a sofa, a table and a chair or two. Over this sofa hangs the portrait of a handsome, elderly man in a general's uniform. Over the table a hanging lamp with a soft, opal glass shade. All round the drawing-room are bouquets of flowers in vases and glasses; others are lying on the tables. The floors in both rooms are covered with thick carpets. Morning light: the sun shines in through the glass doors.*

Miss Juliane Tesman, wearing her hat and carrying a parasol, comes in from the hall followed by Berte carrying a bouquet wrapped in paper. Miss Tesman is a comely, sweet-tempered-looking woman of about sixty-five, well but simply dressed in grey outdoor clothes. Berte is a servant getting on in years, with a homely, rather countrified look.]

MISS TESMAN [*stops just inside the door, listens and says softly*]. Why, I don't believe they're up yet!

BERTE [*softly, too*]. That's what I said, Miss. Think how late the boat came in last night. And on top of that, my goodness! All the things the young mistress *would* unpack before she'd settle down.

MISS TESMAN. Well, well. Let them have their sleep out, of course. But they must have fresh morning air to breathe when they do come out. [*She goes over to the glass door and throws it wide open.*]

BERTE [*standing by the table, not knowing what to do with the bouquet in her hand*]. Well, upon my word, there just isn't anywhere left for it. I think I'd better put it here, Miss. [*She stands it up on the piano.*]

MISS TESMAN. Well now, Berte my dear, you've got a new mistress. Heaven knows it was dreadfully hard for me to part with you!

BERTE [*nearly crying*]. What do you think it was for *me*, Miss? I just can't tell you. After all these many years I've been with you two ladies.

MISS TESMAN. We must try to be contented, Berte. There's really nothing else to be done. You know, Jörgen must have you in the house with him. He simply *must*. You have been used to looking after him ever since he was a little boy.

BERTE. Yes, Miss. But I keep thinking of her lying there at home. Poor thing! So helpless and all. And that new girl, too! *She'll* never learn to look after a sick person properly. Never!

MISS TESMAN. Oh, I shall manage to train her. And, you know, I shall take over most of it myself. Berte dear, there's no need for you to worry so much about my poor sister.

BERTE. Yes, but there's another thing, Miss. I'm really afraid I'll never manage to suit the young mistress.

MISS TESMAN. Oh, come now! Just at first, perhaps, there may be one or two things ...

BERTE. Because, of course, she's a fine lady – and that particular!

MISS TESMAN. You can understand that, can't you, with General Gabler's daughter? Think what she was accustomed to in the General's day. Do you remember her riding along the road with her father? In that long black habit? And feathers in her hat?

BERTE. My, yes! I should think I do. But, upon my word, I never thought it would be a match between her and Mr Jörgen. Not in those days.

MISS TESMAN. Nor did I. But that reminds me, Berte, while I think of it – you mustn't call Jörgen 'Mr' any more. You must say 'Doctor'.

BERTE. Yes, the young mistress said something about that, too, as soon as they got in last night. Is it true, then, Miss?

MISS TESMAN. Yes, perfectly true. Just think of it, Berte, they made him a doctor abroad! While he was away this time, you know. I didn't know a single word about it, not till he told me down at the pier.

BERTE. Oh, of course, he can be anything – he can. Clever, like he is. But I never thought he'd take up doctoring, too.

MISS TESMAN. Oh, it's not *that* kind of doctor he is. [*With a nod full of meaning.*] Come to that, you may soon be able to call him something else – something even grander.

BERTE. You don't say, Miss! What would that be, Miss?

MISS TESMAN [*smiling*]. Ah! If you only knew! [*Touched.*] God bless us! If poor dear Jochum could look up from his grave and see what his little boy has grown up to be! [*Looking about her.*] Oh, but – I say, Berte! Why *have* you done that? Taken all the covers off the furniture?

BERTE. The mistress said I was to. Says she can't do with covers on the chairs.

MISS TESMAN. Are they going to use this room for every day, then?

BERTE. So it seemed, from what the mistress said. The master – the Doctor – he didn't say anything.

[*Jörgen Tesman, humming to himself, comes into the inner room from the right. He is carrying an empty, unfastened suit-case. He is a youngish-looking man of thirty-three, middle-sized, stoutish, with a round, frank, happy face. His hair and beard are fair; he wears glasses. He is comfortably – almost carelessly – dressed, in an indoor suit.*]

MISS TESMAN. Good morning, good morning, Jörgen!

TESMAN [*in the doorway between the rooms*]. Aunt Julle! My dear Aunt Julle! [*Goes up and shakes her hand affectionately.*] All the way out here so early! Eh?

MISS TESMAN. Well, you can just imagine! I *had* to have a look at you both.

TESMAN. Although you haven't had anything like a proper night's rest!

MISS TESMAN. Oh, that doesn't make a bit of difference to me.

TESMAN. But you did get home from the pier all right? Eh?

MISS TESMAN. Oh yes, quite all right, I'm glad to say. Mr Brack was so very kind and saw me right to my door.

TESMAN. We *were* so sorry we couldn't give you a lift. But you saw how it was yourself. Hedda had so much luggage that she had to have with her.

MISS TESMAN. Yes, she certainly did have a tremendous lot of luggage.

BERTE [*to Tesman*]. Shall I go in and ask the mistress if there's anything I could help her with?

TESMAN. No, thanks, Berte, you needn't do that. If she wants you for anything, she says she'll ring.

BERTE [*to the right*]. Very well.

TESMAN. Oh, but, here – take this suit-case, will you?

BERTE [*taking it*]. I'll put it up in the attic. [*Goes out by the hall door.*]

TESMAN. Just think, Aunt Julle, I had that whole suit-case crammed full, just with the stuff I'd copied. You wouldn't believe what I've managed to collect, going through the archives. Curious old things that no one really knows about.

MISS TESMAN. Well, well, Jörgen, you certainly haven't wasted your time on your honeymoon.

TESMAN. No, I jolly well haven't! But take your hat off, Aunt Julle. Here, let me unfasten the bow. Eh?

MISS TESMAN [*while he is doing it*]. Bless me! It's just as though you were still at home with us.

TESMAN [*turning and twisting the hat in his hand*]. Why! What a fine, smart hat you've bought yourself!

MISS TESMAN. I got it because of Hedda.

TESMAN. Because of Hedda? Eh?

MISS TESMAN. Yes. So that Hedda shan't be ashamed of me if we go out together.

TESMAN [*patting her cheek*]. *Dear* Aunt Julle! You think of absolutely everything. [*Puts the hat on a chair by the table.*] Now, look here; let's sit on the sofa and have a little chat till Hedda comes.

[*They sit down. She puts her parasol in the sofa-corner.*]

MISS TESMAN [*taking both his hands and looking at him*]. What a blessing it is to have you again, Jörgen, as large as life! My dear! Poor Jochum's own boy!

TESMAN. So it is for me, Aunt Julle, to see *you* again! You who've been my father and my mother.

MISS TESMAN. Yes, I know you'll always have a corner in your heart for your old aunts.

TESMAN. But I suppose there's no improvement in Aunt Rina, eh?

MISS TESMAN. Well, you know, we can't really expect any improvement in her, poor dear. She just lies there, the same as she has all these years. But I hope the good Lord will let me keep her a little longer. For I shan't know what to do with my life otherwise, Jörgen. Especially now, you know, that I haven't got you to look after any more.

TESMAN [*patting her on the back*]. Come, come, come!

MISS TESMAN [*with a sudden change*]. But just think, Jörgen, you're a married man! And to think it was you who carried off Hedda Gabler! The lovely Hedda Gabler! To think of it! She, who always had so *many* admirers.

TESMAN [*humming a little, with a satisfied smile*]. Yes, I expect a certain number of my good friends are going about this town feeling pretty envious. Eh?

MISS TESMAN. And to think that you were able to have such a long honeymoon! Over five months. Nearly six.

TESMAN. Well, for me it's been a kind of research tour as well – with all those old records I had to hunt through. And then, you know, the enormous number of books I had to read.

MISS TESMAN. Yes, that's quite true. [*Dropping her voice a little and speaking confidentially.*] But look here, Jörgen, haven't you anything ... anything, well, *special* to tell me?

TESMAN. About the trip?

MISS TESMAN. Yes.

TESMAN. No, I don't think there's anything else, except what I told you in my letters. About my taking my doctorate down there – well, I told you that yesterday.

MISS TESMAN. Oh yes, that kind of thing. Yes. But, I mean, haven't you any ... well, any hopes ... er ... ?

TESMAN. Hopes?

MISS TESMAN. Oh, come, Jörgen! After all, I *am* your old aunt!

TESMAN. Well, yes, of course I have hopes ...

MISS TESMAN. Ah!

TESMAN. ... I've the very best hopes of getting a professorship one of these days.

MISS TESMAN. Oh yes, a professorship. Yes.

TESMAN. Or I might say, rather, there's a certainty of my getting it. But, my dear Aunt Julle, you know that yourself perfectly well!

MISS TESMAN [*with a little laugh*]. Yes, of course I do. You're quite right. [*Changing her tone.*] But we were talking about your travels. It must have cost a lot of money, Jörgen?

TESMAN. Ye-es. But, you know, that big fellowship took us a good bit of the way.

MISS TESMAN. But I don't see how you can possibly have made that do for two.

TESMAN. Well, no; one could hardly expect that. Eh?

MISS TESMAN. Especially when it's a lady one's travelling with. For that usually comes more expensive – very much more, I've heard.

TESMAN. Well, yes, of course. It does come rather more expensive. But Hedda had to have that trip, Aunt Julle. She really had to. Nothing else would have done.

MISS TESMAN. No, no. Of course it wouldn't. A honeymoon abroad seems quite a matter of course, nowadays. But tell me, now. Have you had a chance yet to have a good look at the house?

TESMAN. You bet I have! I have been wandering round ever since it was light.

MISS TESMAN. And what do you think of it, on the whole?

TESMAN. Splendid! Absolutely splendid! There's only one thing I can't see – what we're going to do with the two empty rooms there between the back sitting-room and Hedda's bedroom.

MISS TESMAN [*with a little laugh*]. Oh, my dear Jörgen, there may be a use for them – all in good time.

TESMAN. Yes, you're perfectly right, Aunt Julle! Because, by degrees, as I get a bigger library, well – Eh?

MISS TESMAN. Of course, my dear boy. It was the library I was thinking of.

TESMAN. I'm specially glad for Hedda's sake. She often said, before we were engaged, that she'd never care to live anywhere except in Mrs Falk's house.

MISS TESMAN. Yes, just fancy! And then its happening like that – the house being for sale! Just as you had started.

TESMAN. Yes, Aunt Julle, the luck certainly was with us. Eh?

MISS TESMAN. But expensive, my dear Jörgen! It will be expensive for you, all this.

TESMAN [*looking at her, a little disheartened*]. Yes, I suppose it will, perhaps.

MISS TESMAN. Goodness, yes!

TESMAN. How much do you think? Roughly. Eh?

MISS TESMAN. Oh, I can't possibly tell till all the bills come in.

TESMAN. But fortunately Mr Brack has arranged the easiest possible terms for me. He wrote and told Hedda so himself.

MISS TESMAN. Well, don't you worry about it, my child. And as for the furniture and carpets, I have given security for them.

TESMAN. Security? You? My dear Aunt Julle, what kind of security could you give?

MISS TESMAN. I have given a mortgage on the annuity.

TESMAN [*jumping up*]. What! On yours and Aunt Rina's annuity?

MISS TESMAN. Yes. I didn't know what else to do, you see.

TESMAN [*standing in front of her*]. But, Aunt Julle, have you gone crazy? The annuity! The only thing you and Aunt Rina have to live on!

MISS TESMAN. Now, now – don't get so upset about it. The whole thing is just a formality, you know. That's what Mr Brack said, too. For it was he who so kindly arranged it for me. Just a formality, he said.

TESMAN. Yes, that may be so. But all the same ...

MISS TESMAN. Because you've got your own salary to rely on now. And – goodness me! – suppose we did have to spend a little too – help a little just at first? Why, it would only be a pleasure for us.

TESMAN. Oh, Aunt Julle, you will never be tired of sacrificing yourself for me.

MISS TESMAN [*getting up and laying her hands on his shoulders*]. Have I any other joy in this world but in smoothing the way for you, my dear boy? You who've had neither father nor mother to turn to. And now we've reached our goal, my dear! Things may have looked black now and again. But, thank goodness, you're through that now, Jörgen.

TESMAN. Yes, it's wonderful, really, how everything has worked out.

MISS TESMAN. Yes, and the people who stood in your way, who would have stopped your getting on, you have them at your feet. They have gone down before you, Jörgen – most of all, the person who was most dangerous to you. And there he lies now, on the bed he made for himself, the poor misguided creature.

TESMAN. Have you heard anything of Ejlert? Since I went away, I mean?

MISS TESMAN. No, only that he's supposed to have brought out a new book.

TESMAN. *What?* Ejlert Lövborg? Just recently? Eh?

MISS TESMAN. Yes, so they say. I shouldn't think there can be much in it, would you? Now when *your* new book comes out, that will be quite another story, Jörgen. What is it going to be about?

TESMAN. It's going to be about domestic crafts in Brabant in the Middle Ages.

MISS TESMAN. Well, well! To think you can write about a thing like that!

TESMAN. As a matter of fact, the book may take some time yet. I've got to arrange those enormous collections of material first, you know.

MISS TESMAN. Ah yes. Arranging and collecting – that's what you're so good at. You're not dear Jochum's son for nothing.

TESMAN. I'm looking forward immensely to getting down to it. Especially now that I've got a charming house of my own, my own home to work in.

MISS TESMAN. And first and foremost, my dear, now that you've got the wife your heart was set on.

TESMAN [*giving her a hug*]. Why, of course, Aunt Julle! Hedda! Why, that's the loveliest thing of all! [*Looking towards the centre doorway.*] I think she's coming. Eh?

[*Hedda comes in from the left, through the inner room. She is a woman of twenty-nine. Her face and figure show breeding and distinction, her complexion has an even pallor. Her eyes are steel-grey; cold, clear and calm. Her hair is a beautiful light brown, though not noticeably abundant. The loose-fitting morning costume she is wearing is in good style.*]

MISS TESMAN [*going up to Hedda*]. Good morning, Hedda dear! A very good morning to you!

HEDDA [*holding out her hand*]. Good morning, my dear Miss Tesman. What an early visit! It was kind of you.

MISS TESMAN [*seeming a little taken aback*]. Well, has the bride slept well in her new home?

HEDDA. Oh yes, thank you. Tolerably.

TESMAN. Tolerably! I like that, Hedda! You were sleeping like a log when I got up.

HEDDA. Fortunately. In any case, one has to get used to anything new, Miss Tesman. By degrees. [*Looking to the left.*] Oh! The maid has gone and opened the veranda door! There's a perfect flood of sunlight coming in.

MISS TESMAN [*going towards the door*]. Well, we'll shut it, then.

HEDDA. Oh no, don't do that, please. [*To Tesman.*] Just draw the blinds, my dear, will you? That gives a softer light.

TESMAN [*at the door*]. Yes, yes. All right. There you are, Hedda. Now you've got shade *and* fresh air.

HEDDA. Yes, we certainly need fresh air in here. All these precious flowers! But – won't you sit down, Miss Tesman?

MISS TESMAN. No, thank you very much. Now I know everything is going on all right here – thank goodness! – I must see about getting home again. Poor dear, she finds the time very long, lying there.

TESMAN. Give her my love and my best wishes, won't you? And tell her I'll come over and see her later on today.

MISS TESMAN. Yes, yes, I certainly will. But that reminds me, Jörgen. [*Feeling in her bag.*] I nearly forgot it. I've brought something of yours.

TESMAN. What is it, Aunt Julle? Eh?

MISS TESMAN [*bringing out a flat newspaper package and handing it to him*]. Look there, my dear boy.

TESMAN [*opening it*]. Well, I'm blessed! You've kept them for me, Aunt Julle! That really is sweet of her, Hedda, isn't it? Eh?

HEDDA [*by the what-not on the right*]. Yes, my dear. What is it?

TESMAN. My old morning shoes. My slippers – look!

HEDDA. Oh yes. I remember, you often spoke about them while we were away.

TESMAN. Yes, I missed them dreadfully. [*Going up to her.*] Now you shall see them, Hedda.

HEDDA [*going over to the stove*]. No, thanks. It really doesn't interest me.

TESMAN [*following her*]. Just think, Aunt Rina embroidered them for me in bed, lying ill like that. Oh, you can't imagine how many memories are worked into them!

HEDDA. Not for me, particularly.

MISS TESMAN. Hedda's right about that, Jörgen.

TESMAN. Yes, but I think, now she belongs to the family –

HEDDA [*interrupting*]. My dear, we shall never be able to manage with this maid.

MISS TESMAN. Not manage with Berte?

TESMAN. What makes you say that, my dear? Eh?

HEDDA [*pointing*]. Look there. She's left her old hat behind her on the chair.

TESMAN [*dropping his slippers on the floor in his dismay*]. But, *Hedda* –

HEDDA. Suppose anyone were to come in and see it?

TESMAN. But – but, Hedda, that is Aunt Julle's hat!

HEDDA. Oh! Is it?

MISS TESMAN [*picking up the hat*]. Yes, it's certainly mine. And it isn't old, either, my dear little Hedda.

HEDDA. I really didn't look at it closely, Miss Tesman.

MISS TESMAN [*putting on the hat*]. As a matter of fact, it's the first time I've worn it. The very first, it is.

TESMAN. And a beautiful hat it is, too. Really grand!

MISS TESMAN. Oh, it's not all that, my dear Jörgen. [*Looking round her.*] Parasol? Ah, here it is. [*Picking it up.*] For that's mine, too. [*Under her breath.*] Not Berte's.

TESMAN. A new hat and a new parasol! Think of that, Hedda.

HEDDA. Yes, it's very nice. Charming.

TESMAN. Yes, isn't it? Eh? But, Aunt Julle, take a good look at Hedda before you go. See how nice and charming *she* is.

MISS TESMAN. Ah, my dear, there's nothing new in *that*. Hedda has been lovely all her life. [*She nods and goes towards the right.*]

TESMAN [*following her*]. Yes, but have you noticed how plump she's grown, and how well she is? How much she's filled out on our travels?

HEDDA [*crossing the room*]. Oh, be quiet – !

MISS TESMAN [*who has stopped and turned round*]. Filled out?

TESMAN. Of course, you can't see it so well, Aunt Julle, now she has that dress on. But I, who have the opportunity of –

HEDDA [*at the glass door, impatiently*]. Oh, you haven't any opportunity !

TESMAN. It must be the mountain air, down there in the Tyrol –

HEDDA [*interrupting curtly*]. I am exactly the same as I was when I went away.

TESMAN. Yes, so you keep on saying. But you certainly aren't. Don't you think so too, Aunt Julle?

MISS TESMAN [*gazing at her with clasped hands*]. Hedda is lovely – lovely – lovely ! [*She goes up to Hedda, takes her head in both hands, and, bending it down, kisses her hair.*] May God bless and take care of our Hedda. For Jörgen's sake.

HEDDA [*freeing herself gently*]. Oh – let me go.

MISS TESMAN [*quietly, but with emotion*]. I shall come over and see you two every single day.

TESMAN. Yes, do, *please*, Aunt Julle ! Eh?

MISS TESMAN. Good-bye. Good-bye.

[*She goes out by the hall door. Tesman goes with her, leaving the door half open. He can be heard repeating his messages to Aunt Rina and thanking her for the shoes. In the meanwhile Hedda crosses the room, raising her arms and clenching her hands, as if in fury. Then she pulls back the curtains from the glass door and stands there looking out.*

After a moment Tesman comes in again, shutting the door behind him.]

TESMAN [*picking up the slippers from the floor*]. What are you looking at, Hedda?

HEDDA [*calm and controlled again*]. I'm just looking at the leaves. They're so yellow, and so withered.

TESMAN [*wrapping up the shoes and putting them on the table*]. Well, after all, we're well on in September now.

HEDDA [*disturbed again*]. Yes, just think. We're already in – in September.

TESMAN. Don't you think Aunt Julle was rather unlike herself, my dear? A little bit – almost formal? Whatever do you think was the matter? Eh?

HEDDA. I hardly know her, you see. Isn't she like that as a rule?

TESMAN. No, not like she was today.

HEDDA [*moving away from the glass door.*] Do you think she was really upset about that business with the hat?

TESMAN. Oh, not much. Perhaps a little, just at the moment.

HEDDA. But what extraordinary manners! To throw her hat down here in the drawing-room. One doesn't do that kind of thing.

TESMAN. Well, you can be sure Aunt Julle won't do it again.

HEDDA. Anyway, I'll make it all right with her.

TESMAN. That's sweet of you, Hedda dear! If you would!

HEDDA. When you go in to see them presently, you might ask her over here for the evening.

TESMAN. Yes, I certainly will. And there's another thing you could do that would please her enormously.

HEDDA. Oh? What?

TESMAN. If you could bring yourself to speak a little more affectionately to her – as if you were one of the family. For my sake, Hedda? Eh?

HEDDA. No, no. You mustn't ask me to do that. I've told you that once already. I'll try to call her 'Aunt', and that must be enough.

TESMAN. Oh well, all right. Only it seems to me now that you belong to the family –

HEDDA. Well, I really don't know. ... [*She goes up towards the centre doorway.*]

TESMAN [*after a pause*]. Is there anything the matter, Hedda? Eh?

HEDDA. I'm just looking at my old piano. It doesn't go very well with all these other things.

TESMAN. When I get my first salary cheque, we'll see about an exchange.

HEDDA. Oh no, not an exchange. I don't want to get rid of it. We can put it in there, in the back room. And we can have another in its place here. Some time or other, I mean.

TESMAN [*a little subdued*]. Yes. We can do that, of course.

HEDDA [*picking up the bouquet from the piano*]. These flowers weren't here when we came in last night.

TESMAN. Aunt Julle must have brought them for you.

HEDDA [*looking into the bouquet*]. A visiting-card. [*Taking it out and reading it.*] 'Will call again later on today.' Can you guess who it's from?

TESMAN. No. Who is it? Eh?

HEDDA. It says, 'Mrs Elvsted'.

TESMAN. Really? The wife of the District Magistrate. Miss Rysing that was.

HEDDA. Yes. Exactly. That girl with the tiresome hair, that she was always showing off. An old flame of yours, I've heard.

TESMAN [*laughing*]. Oh, it didn't last long! And it was before I knew you, Hedda. But fancy her being in town.

HEDDA. Odd, that she should call on us. I hardly know her, except that we were at school together.

TESMAN. Yes, I haven't seen her either for – heaven knows how long. I wonder she can bear it up there, in that hole of a place. Eh?

HEDDA [*thinks a moment and says suddenly*]. Tell me, isn't it somewhere up there that he lives – er – Ejlert Lövborg?

TESMAN. Yes it is. Up in those parts.

[*Berte comes in at the hall door.*]

BERTE. She's here again, ma'am. The lady who came and left the flowers an hour ago. [*Pointing.*] The ones you've got in your hand, ma'am.

HEDDA. Oh, is she? Show her in, will you?

[*Berte opens the door for Mrs Elvsted and goes out herself. Mrs Elvsted is a slender little thing with pretty, soft features. Her eyes are light blue, large, round and slightly prominent, with a startled, questioning expression. Her hair is remarkably fair, almost silver-gilt, and exceptionally thick and wavy. She is a couple of years younger than Hedda. She is wearing a dark calling costume, of a good style but not quite of the latest fashion.*]

HEDDA [*going to meet her in a friendly way*]. How are you, my dear Mrs Elvsted? It's nice to see you once more.

MRS ELVSTED [*nervous, and trying to control herself*]. Yes, it's a very long time since we met.

TESMAN [*giving her his hand*]. Or we two either. Eh?

HEDDA. Thank you for your lovely flowers.

MRS ELVSTED. Oh, please! I would have come here at once, yesterday afternoon. But I heard that you were away.

TESMAN. Have you only just come to town? Eh?

MRS ELVSTED. I got here about midday yesterday. I was absolutely in despair when I heard that you weren't at home.

HEDDA. In despair? But why?

TESMAN. But my dear, dear Mrs Rysing – Mrs Elvsted, I mean –

HEDDA. There isn't anything the matter, is there?

MRS ELVSTED. Yes, there is. And I don't know a living soul to turn to here in town, except you.

HEDDA [putting the bouquet down on the table]. Come now, let's sit here on the sofa.

MRS ELVSTED. No, I feel too worried and restless to sit down.

HEDDA. Oh no, you don't. Come along here. [She pulls Mrs Elvsted down on to the sofa and sits beside her.]

TESMAN. Well now, what is it, Mrs Elvsted?

HEDDA. Has anything gone wrong up there, at home?

MRS ELVSTED. Well, it has and it hasn't. Oh, I do so want you not to misunderstand me.

HEDDA. Then the best thing you can do, Mrs Elvsted, is to tell us all about it.

TESMAN. Because that's what you've come for, isn't it? Eh?

MRS ELVSTED. Yes, yes, it is, of course. Well, then, I must explain – if you don't know already – that Ejlert Lövborg is in town too.

HEDDA. Lövborg is!

TESMAN. Really? So Ejlert Lövborg's come back again! Fancy that, Hedda!

HEDDA. Quite. I heard all right.

MRS ELVSTED. He's been here a week now, already. Think of it! A whole week in this dangerous town. And alone! And all the bad company he could get into here!

HEDDA. But, my dear Mrs Elvsted, why does *he* specially matter to you?

MRS ELVSTED [*gives her a frightened glance and says quickly*]. He used to be the children's tutor.

HEDDA. Your children's?

MRS ELVSTED. My husband's. I haven't got any.

HEDDA. Your step-children's, then.

MRS ELVSTED. Yes.

TESMAN [*hesitantly*]. Was he ... er ... tolerably ... then ... I don't quite know how to put it ... fairly steady in his habits – enough to be given *that* job? Eh?

MRS ELVSTED. For the last two years there hasn't been a word against him.

TESMAN. Really! Think of that, Hedda!

HEDDA. I heard.

MRS ELVSTED. Not the least thing, I assure you. Nothing of any kind. But still now, when I know he's here – in this great city – and with plenty of money in his pockets ... I'm desperately anxious about him now.

TESMAN. But why didn't he stay up there where he was, then? With you and your husband? Eh?

MRS ELVSTED. Once the book was out he was too restless and excited to stay up there with us.

TESMAN. Oh yes, that reminds me. Aunt Julle said he'd brought out a new book.

MRS ELVSTED. Yes, a big new book on the history of civilization; a sort of general survey. It's been out a fortnight now. And now that it's gone so well and made such a tremendous stir –

TESMAN. It has, has it? It must be something he had by him from his better days, then.

MRS ELVSTED. From some time ago, you mean?

TESMAN. Exactly.

MRS ELVSTED. No, he wrote the whole thing up at our place. Just lately – within the last year.

TESMAN. That's good news, isn't it, Hedda? Just fancy!

MRS ELVSTED. Yes, indeed. If only it would last.

HEDDA. Have you met him here in town?

MRS ELVSTED. No, not yet. I had a lot of trouble finding his address. But I got it at last, this morning.

HEDDA [*looking searchingly at her*]. You know, it seems a little odd of your husband to ... er ...

MRS ELVSTED [*starting nervously*]. Of my husband? What does?

HEDDA. To send you to town on an errand like this. Not to come in and look after his friend himself.

MRS ELVSTED. Oh, not at all! My husband hasn't time for that. And then there – there was some shopping I had to do.

HEDDA [*with a slight smile*]. Ah well, that's a different matter.

MRS ELVSTED [*getting up quickly, in some distress*]. So I do implore you, Mr Tesman, be good to Ejlert Lövborg if he comes to you! And he's sure to, because you were such good friends in the old days. And besides, you're both working in the same field. On the same subjects, as far as I can make out.

TESMAN. Well anyway, we were at one time.

MRS ELVSTED. Yes. And that's why I do beseech you – you really will keep a watchful eye on him too, won't you, Mr Tesman? You do promise me?

TESMAN. Yes, I'll be only too glad to, Mrs Rysing –

HEDDA. Elvsted.

TESMAN. I really will do what I can for Ejlert. Everything I possibly can. You can be sure of that.

MRS ELVSTED. Oh, you *are* being kind! [*Clasping his hands.*] Thank you, again and again. [*Frightened.*] Because my husband is so attached to him.

HEDDA [*getting up*]. You ought to write to him, my dear. He may not come to see you of his own accord.

TESMAN. Yes, Hedda, that probably would be best.
Eh?

HEDDA. And the sooner the better. Now – at once – I
think.

MRS ELVSTED [*beseechingly*]. Oh yes! If you *would!*

TESMAN. I'll write this very minute. Have you his address,
Mrs – Elvsted?

MRS ELVSTED [*taking a small slip of paper out of her pocket
and handing it to him*]. Here it is.

TESMAN. Good. Good. I'll go in, then. [*Looking round him.*]
That reminds me – my slippers? Ah, here they are. [*Picks
up the parcel and is just going.*]

HEDDA. Now write really kindly and affectionately. And
a good long letter, too.

TESMAN. Yes, I certainly will.

MRS ELVSTED. But, please, don't say a word about my
having asked you to!

TESMAN. Of course not. That goes without saying. Eh?
[*He goes through the inner room to the right.*]

HEDDA [*goes up to Mrs Elvsted and says softly*]. That's
right. Now we've killed two birds with one stone.

MRS ELVSTED. How do you mean?

HEDDA. Didn't you realize I wanted to get rid of him?

MRS ELVSTED. Yes, to write his letter.

HEDDA. And also so that I could talk to you alone.

MRS ELVSTED [*confused*]. About this business?

HEDDA. Exactly. About that.

MRS ELVSTED [*alarmed*]. But there isn't anything more,
Mrs Tesman! Nothing at all!

HEDDA. Oh yes there is, now. There's a lot more. That
much I do realize. Come over here, and we'll sit and be
cosy and friendly together.

[*She pushes Mrs Elvsted into the easy-chair by the stove and sits
on one of the stools herself.*]

MRS ELVSTED [*looking anxiously at her watch*]. But my dear Mrs Tesman, I really meant to go now.

HEDDA. Oh, surely there's no hurry. Now then, suppose you tell me a little about what your home's like.

MRS ELVSTED. But that's the last thing in the world I wanted to talk about!

HEDDA. Not to me, my dear? After all, we were at school together.

MRS ELVSTED. Yes, but you were a class above me. How dreadfully frightened of you I was in those days!

HEDDA. Were you frightened of me?

MRS ELVSTED. Yes. Dreadfully frightened. Because when we met on the stairs you always used to pull my hair.

HEDDA. No, *did* I?

MRS ELVSTED. Yes, and once you said you would burn it off.

HEDDA. Oh, that was only silly talk, you know.

MRS ELVSTED. Yes, but I was so stupid in those days. And since then, anyhow, we have drifted such a long, long way apart. Our circles were so entirely different.

HEDDA. Well, then, we'll see if we can come together again. Now, look here. When we were at school we used to talk like real close friends and call each other by our Christian names.

MRS ELVSTED. Oh no, you're making quite a mistake.

HEDDA. I certainly am *not*. I remember it perfectly well. So we are going to tell each other everything, as we did in the old days. [*Moving nearer with her stool.*] There we are! [*Kissing her cheek.*] Now you're to talk to me like a real friend and call me 'Hedda'.

MRS ELVSTED [*clasping and patting her hands*]. All this goodness and kindness – it's not a bit what I'm used to.

HEDDA. There, there, there! And I'm going to treat *you* like a friend, as I did before, and call you my dear Thora.

MRS ELVSTED. My name's Thea.

HEDDA. Yes, of course. Of course. I meant Thea. [*Looking sympathetically at her.*] So you're not used to much goodness or kindness, aren't you, Thea? Not in your own home?

MRS ELVSTED. Ah, if I *had* a home! But I haven't one. Never have had. ...

HEDDA [*looking at her a moment*]. I rather thought it must be something of that sort.

MRS ELVSTED [*gazing helplessly in front of her*]. Yes. Yes. Yes.

HEDDA. I can't quite remember now, but wasn't it as housekeeper that you went up there in the beginning – to the District Magistrate's?

MRS ELVSTED. Actually it was to have been as governess. But his wife – his late wife – was an invalid and was ill in bed most of the time. So I had to take charge of the house too.

HEDDA. But then, in the end, you became the mistress of the house.

MRS ELVSTED [*drearily*]. Yes, I did.

HEDDA. Let me see. ... About how long ago is it now?

MRS ELVSTED. Since I was married?

HEDDA. Yes.

MRS ELVSTED. It's five years ago now.

HEDDA. Yes, of course. It must be that.

MRS ELVSTED. Ah! Those five years – or rather the last two or three. Oh, if you could only imagine, Mrs Tesman –

HEDDA [*giving her a little slap on the hand*]. Mrs Tesman! Come, Thea!

MRS ELVSTED. Oh yes; I will try! Yes, Hedda, if you had any idea – if you understood –

HEDDA [*casually*]. Ejlert Lövborg was up there too for three years or so, I believe?

MRS ELVSTED [*looking at her doubtfully*]. Ejlert Lövborg? Why yes. He was.

HEDDA. Did you know him already? From the old days in town?

MRS ELVSTED. Hardly at all. Well I mean – by name, of course.

HEDDA. But when you were up there – then, he used to visit you and your husband?

MRS ELVSTED. Yes, he came over to us every day. You see, he was giving the children lessons. Because, in the long run, I couldn't manage it all myself.

HEDDA. No, I should think not. And your husband? I suppose he is often away from home?

MRS ELVSTED. Yes. You see, Mrs – er – you see, Hedda, being District Magistrate he's always having to go out on circuit.

HEDDA [*leaning against the arm of the chair*]. Thea, my poor little Thea. Now you're going to tell me all about it. Just how things are.

MRS ELVSTED. Very well. You ask me about it, then.

HEDDA. What is your husband really like, Thea? You know what I mean – in everyday life? Is he nice to you?

MRS ELVSTED [*evasively*]. He's quite sure himself that he does everything for the best.

HEDDA. Only, it seems to me, he must be much too old for you. More than twenty years older, surely?

MRS ELVSTED [*irritably*]. Yes, there's that too. What with one thing and another, I'm miserable with him. We haven't an idea in common, he and I. Not a thing in the world.

HEDDA. But isn't he fond of you, all the same? I mean, in his own way?

MRS ELVSTED. Oh, I don't know *what* he feels. I think I'm

just useful to him. After all, it doesn't cost much to keep me. I'm cheap.

HEDDA. That's silly of you.

MRS ELVSTED [shaking her head]. It can't be any different. Not with him. He isn't really fond of anyone but himself. And perhaps the children – a little.

HEDDA. And of Ejlert Lövborg, Thea.

MRS ELVSTED [looking at her]. Of Ejlert Lövborg? What makes you think that?

HEDDA. But, my dear – it seems to me, when he sends you all the way into town after him. ... [Smiling almost imperceptibly.] And besides, you said so yourself to my husband.

MRS ELVSTED [with a nervous start]. What? Oh yes, so I did. [Breaking out, but in a lowered voice.] No. I might as well tell you now as later. It'll all come out, anyway.

HEDDA. But, my dear Thea –

MRS ELVSTED. Well, to be quite frank, my husband had no idea I was coming.

HEDDA. What! Didn't your husband know about it?

MRS ELVSTED. No, of course not. And, anyway, he wasn't at home. He was away too. Oh, I couldn't stand it any longer, Hedda! It was simply impossible. I should have been absolutely alone up there in future.

HEDDA. Well? So then?

MRS ELVSTED. So I packed up some of my things, you see – the ones I needed most. Very quietly, of course. And so I left the place.

HEDDA. Just like that? Nothing more?

MRS ELVSTED. No ... And then I took the train straight in to town.

HEDDA. But, my dear, precious child! How did you dare risk it?

MRS ELVSTED [*getting up and moving across the room*]. Well, what on earth could I do?

HEDDA. But what do you think your husband will say when you go back again?

MRS ELVSTED [*by the table, looking at her*]. Back there, to him?

HEDDA. Yes, of course. What then?

MRS ELVSTED. I'm never going back there to him.

HEDDA [*getting up and going nearer to her*]. Then you've left in real earnest, for good and all?

MRS ELVSTED. Yes. There didn't seem to be anything else for me to do.

HEDDA. And then – your doing it quite openly!

MRS ELVSTED. Oh, you can't keep that kind of thing secret, in any case.

HEDDA. But, Thea, what do you think people will say about you?

MRS ELVSTED. Heaven knows, they must say what they like. [*Sitting down on the sofa wearily and sadly*.] I have only done what I *had* to do.

HEDDA [*after a short silence*]. What do you mean to do now? What kind of job are you going to get?

MRS ELVSTED. I don't know yet. I only know that I must live here, where Ejlert Lövborg lives. That is, if I *must* live. ...

HEDDA [*moves a chair from the table, sits beside her and strokes her hands*]. Thea, my dear, how did it happen? This – this friendship between you and Ejlert Lövborg?

MRS ELVSTED. Oh, it happened by degrees, somehow. I came to have some kind of power over him.

HEDDA. Indeed? And then?

MRS ELVSTED. He gave up his old habits. Not because I asked him to. I never dared do that. But of course he noticed I didn't like that kind of thing. And so he left off.

HEDDA [*masking an involuntary sneer*]. In fact, you've what they call 'reclaimed him', you have, little Thea.

MRS ELVSTED. Yes. At least, he says so himself. And he, for his part, has made me into a real human being! Taught me to think ... and to understand ... one thing after another.

HEDDA. Perhaps he gave *you* lessons, too, did he?

MRS ELVSTED. No, not exactly lessons. ... But he used to talk to me about such endless numbers of things. And then came the glorious, happy moment when I began to share his work! When he let me help him.

HEDDA. And you did, did you?

MRS ELVSTED. Yes. When he was writing anything, we always had to work at it together.

HEDDA. I see. Like two good comrades.

MRS ELVSTED [*eagerly*]. Comrades! Why, Hedda, that's just what he called it! Oh, I ought to feel so perfectly happy. But I can't, though. Because I really don't know whether it will last.

HEDDA. Aren't you surer of him than that?

MRS ELVSTED [*drearily*]. There's the shadow of a woman standing between Ejlert Lövborg and me.

HEDDA [*looking intently at her*]. Who can that be?

MRS ELVSTED. I don't know. Someone or other from – from his past. Someone he's never really forgotten.

HEDDA. What has he said ... about it?

MRS ELVSTED. He only touched on it once – and quite vaguely.

HEDDA. Oh. And what did he say, then?

MRS ELVSTED. He said that when they parted she wanted to shoot him with a pistol.

HEDDA [*cold and controlled*]. How absurd! People don't do that kind of thing here.

MRS ELVSTED. No. And that's why I thought it must be that red-haired singer that he once –

HEDDA. Yes, that may be.

MRS ELVSTED. Because I remember people used to talk about her carrying loaded firearms.

HEDDA. Oh well, then, it's obviously she.

MRS ELVSTED [*wringing her hands*]. Yes, but just think, Hedda, now I hear that that singer – she's in town again! Oh, I'm simply desperate!

HEDDA [*glancing towards the inner room*]. Sh! Here comes my husband. [*Getting up and whispering.*] Thea, all this must be between our two selves.

MRS ELVSTED [*springing up*]. Why, yes! For heaven's sake!

[*Jörgen Tesman, with a letter in his hand, comes in from the right through the inner room.*]

TESMAN. There we are! The letter's finished and ready.

HEDDA. That's good. But I think Mrs Elvsted wants to go now. Wait a minute. I'm going to the garden gate with her.

TESMAN. I say, Hedda, I wonder if Berte could see to this?

HEDDA [*taking the letter*]. I'll tell her to.

[*Berte comes in from the hall.*]

BERTE. Mr Brack's here and would like to see the master and mistress, please.

HEDDA. Ask Mr Brack if he will please come in. And – look here – put this letter in the post, will you?

BERTE [*taking the letter*]. Certainly, ma'am.

[*She opens the door for Brack and goes out herself. He is a man of forty-five, square but well built and light in his movements. His face is roundish, with a fine profile. His hair, still almost black, is short and carefully waved. His eyes are lively and bright. His eyebrows are thick and so is his moustache with its clipped ends. He is dressed in a well-cut outdoor suit – a little too young for his age. He wears an eye-glass, which he now and then lets fall.*]

BRACK [*bowing, with his hat in his hand*]. May one call so early as this?

HEDDA. One certainly may!

TESMAN [*clasping his hand*]. You will always be welcome [*Introducing him.*] Mr Brack, Miss Rysing.

HEDDA. Oh!

BRACK [*bowing*]. A great pleasure.

HEDDA [*looking at him and laughing*]. It's very nice to have a look at you by daylight, Mr Brack.

BRACK. Any difference, do you think?

HEDDA. Yes; I think a little younger.

BRACK. Thank you – very much.

TESMAN. But what do you say to Hedda? Eh? Doesn't she look well? She's positively –

HEDDA. Oh, do leave me out of it, please. What about thanking Mr Brack for all the trouble he has taken?

BRACK. Oh, no, no. It was only a pleasure.

HEDDA. Yes. You're a good friend. But here's Mrs Elvsted longing to be off. Excuse me a moment; I shall be back again directly.

[*Mutual good-byes. Mrs Elvsted and Hedda go out by the hall door.*]

BRACK. Well now; is your wife fairly satisfied?

TESMAN. Rather! We can't thank you enough. Of course, I gather there will have to be a little rearranging. And there's a certain amount needed still. We shall have to get a few little things.

BRACK. Is that so? Really?

TESMAN. But you're not to have any trouble over that. Hedda said she would see to what was needed herself. But why don't we sit down? Eh?

BRACK. Thanks. Just for a minute. [*He sits by the table.*] There's something I rather wanted to talk to you about, Tesman.

TESMAN. Is there? Ah, I understand! [*Sits down.*] I expect it's the serious part of the fun that's coming now. Eh?

BRACK. Oh, there's no great hurry about the financial side. However, I could wish we'd managed things a little more economically.

TESMAN. But that wouldn't have done at all! Think of Hedda, my dear man. You, who know her so well. I couldn't possibly ask her to live in some little suburban house.

BRACK. No. That's just the difficulty.

TESMAN. Besides, luckily it can't be long now before I get my appointment.

BRACK. Well you know, a thing like that can often be a slow business.

TESMAN. Have you heard anything further? Eh?

BRACK. Well, nothing definite – [*Breaking off.*] But that reminds me, there's one piece of news I can tell you.

TESMAN. Oh?

BRACK. Your old friend, Ejlert Lövborg, has come back to town.

TESMAN. I know that already.

BRACK. Do you? How did you come to know?

TESMAN. She told us. The lady who went out with Hedda.

BRACK. Oh, I see. What was her name? I didn't quite catch it.

TESMAN. Mrs Elvsted.

BRACK. Oh yes; the District Magistrate's wife. Of course, it's up there he's been living.

TESMAN. And just think! I hear, to my great delight, that he's become perfectly steady again.

BRACK. Yes, so I'm assured.

TESMAN. And that he's brought out a new book. Eh?

BRACK. Oh yes.

TESMAN. And it's made quite an impression, too.

BRACK. It's made quite an extraordinary impression.

TESMAN. Well, now! Isn't that good news? He, with his

remarkable gifts – I was terribly afraid he'd gone under for good.

BRACK. Yes. That was the general opinion about him.

TESMAN. But I can't imagine what he'll do now? What on earth can he be going to live on? Eh?

[*During the last words, Hedda has come in by the hall door.*]

HEDDA [*to Brack, laughing, with a touch of contempt*]. My husband's always worrying about what one's going to live on.

TESMAN. Oh but, my dear, we were talking about poor Ejlert Lövborg.

HEDDA [*looking quickly at him*]. Oh, were you? [*Sits in the easy-chair by the stove and asks, with a casual manner.*] What's wrong with him?

TESMAN. Well, he must have run through that money he inherited long ago. And he can't very well write a new book every year. Eh? So, you see, I really wonder what will become of him.

BRACK. Perhaps I could tell you something about that.

TESMAN. Really?

BRACK. You must remember that he has relatives with a good deal of influence.

TESMAN. Ah, but unfortunately, his relatives have completely washed their hands of him.

BRACK. Once upon a time they called him the hope of the family.

TESMAN. Once upon a time, yes! But he's wrecked all that himself.

HEDDA. Who knows? [*With a slight smile.*] After all, they've 'reclaimed' him up at the Elvsteds' place.

BRACK. And then this book that's come out –

TESMAN. Ah well, let's hope to goodness they'll get something or other for him. I've just written to him. Hedda, my dear, I asked him to come out to us this evening.

BRACK. But, my dear fellow, you're coming to my bachelor party this evening. You promised last night at the pier.

HEDDA. Had you forgotten it, my dear?

TESMAN. Yes, by Jove, I had!

BRACK. In any case, you needn't worry. He isn't likely to come.

TESMAN. Why do you think he won't? Eh?

BRACK [*hesitating a little. Gets up and rests his hands on the back of the chair*]. Mr dear Tesman – and you too, Mrs Tesman – I can't, in fairness, leave you in ignorance of something that ... er ... that –

TESMAN. Something that has to do with Ejlert?

BRACK. That has to do both with you and with him.

TESMAN. But, my dear Brack, tell me what it is!

BRACK. You must be prepared for your appointment not to come so quickly, perhaps, as you wish or expect it to.

TESMAN [*jumping up, uneasily*]. Has anything gone wrong? Eh?

BRACK. There may be some competition – perhaps – before the post is filled.

TESMAN. Competition! Fancy that, Hedda!

HEDDA [*leaning farther back in the easy-chair*]. Well, well, now!

TESMAN. But with whom? Surely, never with – ?

BRACK. Yes. Just so. With Ejlert Lövborg.

TESMAN [*clasping his hands*]. No, no! That's absolutely unthinkable! It's simply impossible! Eh?

BRACK. Well ... That's what we may see, all the same.

TESMAN. But look here, Brack, it would be incredibly inconsiderate to me! [*Gesticulating with his arms.*] Because – why, just think! – I'm a married man. We married on our prospects, Hedda and I. Went and got thoroughly in debt, and borrowed money from Aunt Julle too. Why good Lord, the appointment was as good as promised to me! Eh?

BRACK. Steady, old man! No doubt you'll get the job, all right. But it will be contested first.

HEDDA [*motionless in the easy-chair*]. Think of that, my dear. It will be almost like a kind of sport.

TESMAN. But, Hedda dearest, how can you take it all so casually?

HEDDA [*as before*]. I'm not doing that at all. I'm quite excited about the result.

BRACK. At any rate, Mrs Tesman, it's as well you should know now how things stand. I mean, before you start making those little purchases I hear you have in mind.

HEDDA. This can't make any difference.

BRACK. Oh, indeed? Then there's no more to be said. Good-bye. [*To Tesman.*] When I go for my afternoon stroll, I'll come in and fetch you.

TESMAN. Oh yes. Yes. I really don't know *what* I'm going to do. ...

HEDDA [*lying back and reaching out her hand*]. Good-bye, Mr Brack. And do come again.

BRACK. Many thanks! Good-bye, good-bye.

TESMAN [*going to the door with him*]. Good-bye, my dear Brack. You must excuse me. ...

[*Brack goes out by the hall door.*]

TESMAN [*crossing the room*]. Well, Hedda, one should never venture into the land of romance. Eh?

HEDDA [*looking at him and smiling*]. Do *you* do that?

TESMAN. Why, my dear, it can't be denied. It *was* romantic to go and get married and set up house, simply and solely on our prospects.

HEDDA. You may be right, there.

TESMAN. Well, we have our charming home, anyhow.

Think, Hedda, it's the home we both used to dream of –
that we fell in love with, I might almost say. Eh?

HEDDA [*getting up slowly and wearily*]. It was understood of
course, that we should entertain – keep up some sort of
establishment.

TESMAN. Goodness, yes! How I used to look forward to it,
seeing you as hostess to a chosen circle of friends! Well,
well, well. For the present we two must get along by
ourselves, Hedda. Just have Aunt Julle out here every
now and then. ... Oh, my dear, it was to have been so
very, very different for you.

HEDDA. Naturally, now I shan't get a man-servant just at
first.

TESMAN. No, I'm afraid you can't. There can be no question of keeping a man-servant, you know.

HEDDA. And the saddle-horse that I was going to –

TESMAN [*horrified*]. Saddle-horse!

HEDDA. I suppose it's no use even thinking of that now.

TESMAN. Good heavens, no! That goes without saying.

HEDDA [*crossing the room towards the back*]. Well, anyhow,
I still have one thing to kill time with.

TESMAN [*beaming with pleasure*]. Thank heavens for that!
But what is it, Hedda? Eh?

HEDDA [*at the centre doorway, looking at him with lurking
contempt*]. My pistols, Jörgen.

TESMAN [*anxiously*]. Your pistols!

HEDDA [*with cold eyes*]. General Gabler's pistols. [*She goes
through the inner room and out to the left.*]

TESMAN [*running to the centre doorway and calling after her*].
For goodness' sake! Hedda, darling! Don't touch those
dangerous things! For my sake, Hedda! Eh?

ACT TWO

———————— * ————————

[*The room at the Tesmans', as in the First Act, except that the piano has been taken away and a graceful little writing-table with a book case put in its place. A smaller table has been put by the sofa on the left; most of the bouquets are gone, but Mrs Elvsted's stands on the large table in the front of the stage. It is afternoon.*

Hedda, in an afternoon dress, is alone in the room. She is standing by the open glass door, loading a pistol. The fellow to it lies in an open pistol-case on the writing-table.]

HEDDA [*looking down the garden and calling*]. How do you do again, Mr Brack?

BRACK [*is heard from below, at a little distance*]. And you, Mrs Tesman?

HEDDA [*lifting the pistol and aiming*]. I'm going to shoot you, sir!

BRACK [*calling from below*]. No, no, no! Don't stand there aiming straight at me.

HEDDA. That comes of using the back way in. [*She shoots*].

BRACK [*nearer*]. Are you quite crazy?

HEDDA. Dear me! I didn't hit you, did I?

BRACK [*still outside*]. Now stop this nonsense!

HEDDA. Well, come in then.

[*Brack, dressed as for an informal party, comes in by the glass door. He is carrying a light overcoat on his arm.*]

BRACK. The deuce! Do you still play that game? What are you shooting at?

HEDDA. Oh, I just stand and shoot up into the blue.

BRACK [*taking the pistol gently out of her hand*]. If you don't mind, my dear lady. [*Looking at it.*] Ah, this one. I know it well. [*Looking round him.*] Now, where have we got the case? Ah yes, here. [*Puts the pistol away and shuts the case.*] Because we're not going to play that game any more today.

HEDDA. Well, what in heaven's name do you expect me to do with myself?

BRACK. Haven't you had any visitors?

HEDDA [*shutting the glass door*]. Not a soul. I suppose everybody we know is still in the country.

BRACK. And isn't Tesman at home either?

HEDDA [*at the writing-table, shutting up the pistol-case in the drawer*]. No, the minute he had finished lunch he tore off to his aunts. He didn't expect you so soon.

BRACK. Hm – and I didn't think of that. That was stupid of me.

HEDDA [*turning her head and looking at him*]. Why stupid?

BRACK. Because if I had, I should have come here a little – earlier.

HEDDA [*crossing the room*]. Well, then you wouldn't have found anyone at all. I was in my room changing after lunch.

BRACK. And there isn't so much as a tiny chink in the door that one could have communicated through?

HEDDA. You've forgotten to arrange anything like that.

BRACK. That was stupid of me, too.

HEDDA. Well, we shall just have to sit down here and wait. My husband won't be home yet awhile.

BRACK. Well, never mind. I'll be patient.

[*Hedda sits down in the corner of the sofa. Brack lays his coat over the back of the nearest chair and sits down, keeping his hat in his hand. There is a short pause. They look at each other.*]

HEDDA. Well?

BRACK [*in the same tone*]. Well?

HEDDA. It was I who asked first.

BRACK [*leaning forward a little*]. Come now, let's have a cosy little gossip all to ourselves – Madam Hedda.

HEDDA [*leaning farther back on the sofa*]. Doesn't it feel like a whole eternity since we last talked to each other? Oh, of course, a word or two last night and this morning – but I don't count that.

BRACK. Not like this, between ourselves? Alone together, you mean?

HEDDA. Yes. More or less that.

BRACK. Here was I, every blessed day, wishing to goodness you were home again.

HEDDA. And there was I, the whole time, wishing exactly the same.

BRACK. You? Really, Madam Hedda! And I, thinking you had thoroughly enjoyed yourself on your travels!

HEDDA. You may be sure I did!

BRACK. But Tesman was always saying so in his letters.

HEDDA. Oh, *he* did all right. Rummaging in libraries is the most entrancing occupation he knows. Sitting and copying out old parchments, or whatever they are.

BRACK [*with a touch of malice*]. After all, that is his vocation in life. Partly, at least.

HEDDA. Oh yes, quite; it is. And of course then one can – But as for me! No, my dear sir. I was excruciatingly bored.

BRACK. Do you really mean it? In sober earnest?

HEDDA. Well, you can just imagine it for yourself. To go a whole six months and never meet a soul even remotely connected with our circle. Not a soul to talk to about the things we're interested in.

BRACK. Well, yes. I should feel the lack of that too.

HEDDA. And then, what's the most intolerable thing of all ...

BRACK. Well?

HEDDA. Everlastingly having to be with ... with one and the same person. ...

BRACK [*nodding agreement*]. Early and late; I know. At every conceivable moment.

HEDDA. What I said was 'everlastingly'.

BRACK. Quite. But with our good friend Tesman, I should have thought one would be able ...

HEDDA. Jörgen Tesman is – a learned man, you must remember.

BRACK. Admittedly.

HEDDA. And learned men are *not* entertaining as travelling companions. Not in the long run, anyhow.

BRACK. Not even a learned man one is in love with?

HEDDA. Oh! Don't use that sentimental word.

BRACK [*slightly taken aback*]. Why, what's the matter, Madam Hedda?

HEDDA [*half laughing, half annoyed*]. Well, you just try it yourself! Listening to someone talking about the history of civilization, early and late –

BRACK. – Everlastingly –

HEDDA. Yes, exactly! And all this business about domestic crafts in the Middle Ages! That's the most awful part of all.

BRACK [*looking searchingly at her*]. But, tell me ... I don't quite see why, in that case ... er ...

HEDDA. Why Jörgen and I ever made a match of it, you mean?

BRACK. Well, let's put it that way; yes.

HEDDA. After all, do you think that's extraordinary?

BRACK. Yes – and no, Madam Hedda.

HEDDA. I had simply danced myself out, my dear sir. My time was up. [*With a little start.*] Ah, no! I'm not going to say that. Nor think it, either.

BRACK. And by Jove, you have no reason to!

HEDDA. Oh, reason! [*Watching him rather carefully.*] And Jörgen Tesman ... one must admit that he's a thoroughly good creature.

BRACK. Good and reliable. No question.

HEDDA. And I can't see that there's anything actually ridiculous about him. Do you think there is?

BRACK. Ridiculous? No-o. I wouldn't exactly say that.

HEDDA. Quite so. But, anyway, he's an indefatigable researcher. And it's always possible that he may get somewhere in time, after all.

BRACK [*looking at her a little uncertainly*]. I thought you believed, like everyone else, that he was going to become a really eminent man.

HEDDA [*with a weary expression*]. Yes, so I did. And since he insisted with might and main on being allowed to support me, I don't know why I shouldn't have accepted the offer.

BRACK. No, no. Looking at it from that point of view. ....

HEDDA. Anyhow, it was more than my other friends and admirers were prepared to do, my dear sir.

BRACK [*laughing*]. Well, I can't answer for all the others. But as far as I myself am concerned, you know quite well that I have always preserved a – a certain respect for the marriage-tie. In a general way; in the abstract, at least, Madam Hedda.

HEDDA [*jesting*]. Ah, but I never had any hopes with regard to you.

BRACK. All I want is to have a pleasant, intimate circle of friends where I can be useful, in one way and another, and can come and go freely like – like a trusted friend.

HEDDA. Of the husband, you mean?

BRACK [*leaning forward*]. To be quite frank, preferably of the wife. But of the husband, too, in the second place, of course. I assure you that sort of – shall I call it triangular relationship? – is actually a very pleasant thing for everybody concerned.

HEDDA. Yes. Many a time I longed for a third person on that trip. Driving side by side with just one other person ...!

BRACK. Fortunately the wedding-journey is over now.

HEDDA [shaking her head]. The journey will go on for a long time yet. I have only come to a stopping-place on the way.

BRACK. Why, then one jumps out and walks about a little, Madam Hedda.

HEDDA. I never jump out.

BRACK. Don't you really?

HEDDA. No. Because there is always someone at hand who –

BRACK [laughing]. – Who looks when you leap, you mean?

HEDDA. Precisely.

BRACK. Oh come, you know!

HEDDA [with a gesture of disagreement]. I don't care for that. I prefer to remain sitting where I am, alone with the other person.

BRACK. But suppose, now, a third person were to get in and join the other two?

HEDDA. Ah well, that's quite a different matter.

BRACK. A trusted and sympathetic friend –

HEDDA. – Someone who could talk entertainingly about all sorts of interesting things –

BRACK. – And nothing learned about him!

HEDDA [with an audible sigh]. Well, that certainly is a relief.

BRACK [hearing the hall door open and glancing towards it]. The triangle is complete.

HEDDA [half aloud]. And so the train goes on.

[Jörgen Tesman, in a grey outdoor suit and a soft felt hat, comes

*in from the hall. He has a number of unbound books under his
arm and in his pockets.*]

TESMAN [*going up to the table by the corner sofa*]. It was pretty
hot carrying that load. [*Putting the books down.*] I'm absolutely streaming, Hedda. Why, there you are, come
already, Brack. Eh? Berte didn't say anything about it.

BRACK [*getting up*]. I came up through the garden.

HEDDA. What are those books you've brought?

TESMAN [*standing and dipping into them*]. They are some
new learned publications that I simply had to have.

HEDDA. Learned publications?

BRACK. Ah yes. Learned publications, Mrs Tesman.

[*Brack and Hedda exchange an understanding smile.*]

HEDDA. Do you need any more learned publications?

TESMAN. Why, my dear Hedda, one can never have too
many of them. One has to keep up with everything that's
written and printed.

HEDDA. Yes, of course one does.

TESMAN [*turning over the books*]. And look here – I've got
hold of Ejlert Lövborg's new book too. [*Holding it out.*]
Perhaps you'd like to have a look at it, Hedda. Eh?

HEDDA. No, thank you very much. Or ... well perhaps
later on.

TESMAN. I dipped into it on the way.

BRACK. Well, what do you think of it – as a learned man?

TESMAN. I think it's remarkable – the balance and judgement it has. He never used to write like this before.
[*Gathering the books together.*] Now, I'll take all this in
with me. It'll be a treat to cut the pages! And then I must
tidy myself up a little, too. [*To Brack.*] I say, we don't
need to start at once? Eh?

BRACK. Goodness no! There's no hurry for some time yet.

TESMAN. Ah well, I'll take my time, then. [*Is going out
with the books, but stops in the centre doorway and turns.*]

Oh, while I think of it, Hedda, Aunt Julle won't be coming out to you this evening.

HEDDA. Won't she? Perhaps it's that business with the hat that's the trouble?

TESMAN. Oh Lord, no! How can you think that of Aunt Julle? No, the thing is Aunt Rina's very ill.

HEDDA. So she always is.

TESMAN. Yes, but today she was particularly bad, poor dear.

HEDDA. Oh, then it's only natural for the other one to stay with her. I must make the best of it.

TESMAN. And you can't imagine, my dear, how glad Aunt Julle was, in spite of that, that you'd got so plump on your holiday.

HEDDA [half audibly, getting up]. Oh! These everlasting aunts!

TESMAN. Eh?

HEDDA [going to the glass door]. Nothing.

TESMAN. Oh, all right.

[He goes through the inner room and out to the right.]

BRACK. What hat was it you were talking about?

HEDDA. Oh, that was something that happened with Miss Tesman this morning. She had put her hat down there on the chair. [Looking at him and smiling.] And I pretended I thought it was the servant's.

BRACK [shaking his head]. But my dear Madam Hedda, how could you do that? And to that nice old lady?

HEDDA [nervously, walking across the room]. Well, you know, that kind of thing comes over me – just like that. And then I can't stop myself. [Throwing herself down in the easy-chair by the stove.] I don't know, myself, how to explain it.

BRACK [behind the easy-chair]. You're not really happy. That's the trouble.

HEDDA [looking straight in front of her]. And I don't know

why I should be – happy. Perhaps you can tell me, can you?

BRACK. Well, among other things, because you've got the very home you wished for.

HEDDA [*looking up at him and laughing*]. Do you believe that fantasy too?

BRACK. Isn't there something in it, though?

HEDDA. Oh yes ... *Something*.

BRACK. Very well?

HEDDA. There's this much in it. Last summer I used Jörgen Tesman to see me home from evening parties.

BRACK. Unfortunately I was going quite another way.

HEDDA. True enough. You certainly were going another way last summer.

BRACK [*laughing*]. You ought to be ashamed of yourself, Madam Hedda! Well, but you and Tesman, then?

HEDDA. Why, we came past here one evening. And he, poor creature, was tying himself in knots because he didn't know how to find anything to talk about. And so I felt sorry for the poor, learned man.

BRACK [*smiling doubtfully*]. You did, did you? H'm.

HEDDA. Yes. I really did. And so, to help him out of his misery, I just said – quite casually – that I should like to live here, in this villa.

BRACK. No more than that?

HEDDA. Not that evening.

BRACK. But ... afterwards?

HEDDA. Yes; my thoughtlessness had its consequences, my dear sir.

BRACK. Unfortunately, our thoughtlessness all too often has, Madam Hedda.

HEDDA. Thank you. But, you see, it was through this passion for the villa of the late Mrs Falk that Jörgen Tesman and I found our way to an understanding. *That* led to our

engagement and marriage and wedding trip and everything. Well, well. As one makes one's bed one must lie
on it, I was just going to say.

BRACK. This is delightful! And all the time, it seems, you
weren't interested in the least?

HEDDA. No. Heaven knows, I wasn't.

BRACK. Well, but now? Now that we have made it more
or less comfortable for you?

HEDDA. Oh! I seem to smell lavender and dried roses in all
the rooms. But perhaps Aunt Julle brought the smell
with her.

BRACK [laughing]. No, I should think it's more likely the
late Mrs Falk bequeathed it to you!

HEDDA. It reminds one of the departed, all right. Like one's
bouquet, the day after a ball. [Clasping her hands at the
back of her neck, leaning back in her chair and looking at him.]
My friend, you can't imagine how horribly bored I'm
going to be out here.

BRACK. But won't there be some object or other in life for
you to work for, like other people, Madam Hedda?

HEDDA. An object ... that would have something fascinating about it?

BRACK. Preferably, of course.

HEDDA. Lord knows what kind of an object it could be.
I very often wonder – [Breaking off.] But that's no use
either.

BRACK. It might be. Tell me about it.

HEDDA. Whether I could get my husband to go into
politics, I was going to say.

BRACK [laughing]. Tesman! Oh, come now! Things like
politics aren't a bit – they're not at all his line of country.

HEDDA. No, I quite believe you. But suppose I could get
him to, all the same?

BRACK. Well, but what satisfaction would you get out of

it? When he isn't made that way? Why do you want to make him do it?

HEDDA. Because I'm bored, I tell you. [*After a pause.*] Then you think, do you, it would be absolutely impossible for him to get into the Government?

BRACK. Well you see, my dear Madam Hedda, to do that he'd need to be a fairly rich man in the first place.

HEDDA [*getting up impatiently*]. Yes. There we have it. It's this middle-class world that I've got into. [*Crossing the stage.*] It's that that makes life so wretched! So absolutely ludicrous! Because that's what it *is*.

BRACK. I rather fancy the trouble lies somewhere else.

HEDDA. Where?

BRACK. You have never gone through anything that really roused you.

HEDDA. Nothing serious, you mean?

BRACK. Yes, that's one way of putting it, certainly. But now perhaps that may come.

HEDDA [*with a jerk of her head*]. Oh, you're thinking of all the bother over that wretched professorship. But that's my husband's affair entirely. I'm not wasting so much as a thought on it.

BRACK. No, no. That wasn't what I was thinking of either. But suppose now there comes what, in rather solemn language, is called a serious claim on you, one full of responsibility? [*Smiling.*] A new claim, little Madam Hedda.

HEDDA [*angrily*]. Be quiet! You'll never see anything of the kind.

BRACK [*gently*]. We'll talk about it in a year's time – at most.

HEDDA [*shortly*]. I have no gift for that kind of thing, Mr Brack. Not for things that make claims on me!

BRACK. Why shouldn't you have a gift, like most other women, for the calling that – ?

HEDDA [*over by the glass door*]. Oh, be quiet, I tell you! It often seems to me that I've only got a gift for one thing in the world.

BRACK [*going nearer*]. And what is that, if I may ask?

HEDDA [*stands looking out*]. For boring myself to death. Now you know. [*Turning and looking towards the inner room with a laugh*.] Ah, just so! Here is our professor.

BRACK [*quietly, and with a warning*]. Now then, Madam Hedda!

[*Jörgen Tesman, dressed for the party, carrying his gloves and hat, comes through the inner room from the right.*]

TESMAN. Hedda, Ejlert Lövborg hasn't sent to say he isn't coming? Eh?

HEDDA. No.

TESMAN. Ah, you'll see, then. We shall have him along in a little while.

BRACK. Do you really think he'll come?

TESMAN. Yes, I'm almost sure he will. Because that's only a vague rumour, you know – what you told us this morning.

BRACK. Is it?

TESMAN. Yes. At least, Aunt Julle said she didn't for one moment believe he'd stand in my way again. Just think of it!

BRACK. Oh well, then, everything's quite all right.

TESMAN [*putting his hat, with his gloves in it, on a chair to the right*]. Yes, but I really must wait as long as possible for him, if you don't mind.

BRACK. We've plenty of time for that. No one will turn up at my place before seven, or half past.

TESMAN. Oh well, we can keep Hedda company till then. And see what happens.

HEDDA [*putting Brack's overcoat and hat over on the corner sofa*]. And if the worst comes to the worst, Mr Lövborg can stay here with me.

BRACK [*trying to take his things himself*]. Please let me, Mrs Tesman! What do you mean by 'the worst'?

HEDDA. If he won't go with you and my husband.

TESMAN [*looking at her dubiously*]. But, Hedda dear, do you think that would quite do, for him to stay here with you? Eh? Remember, Aunt Julle can't come.

HEDDA. No, but Mrs Elvsted's coming. So the three of us will have tea together.

TESMAN. Oh, that'll be all right, then.

BRACK [*smiling*]. And perhaps that might be the wisest plan for him too.

HEDDA. Why?

BRACK. Good gracious, my dear lady, you've often enough said hard things about my little bachelor parties. They weren't suitable for any but men of the strongest principles.

HEDDA. But surely Mr Lövborg is a man of strong enough principles now? A converted sinner –

[*Berte appears at the hall door.*]

BERTE. There's a gentleman, ma'am, who'd like to see you.

HEDDA. Yes, show him in.

TESMAN [*quietly*]. I'm sure it's he. Just fancy!

[*Ejlert Lövborg comes in from the hall. He is slight and thin, the same age as Tesman but looking older and played out. His hair and beard are dark brown, his face is long and pale but with two patches of colour on the cheek-bones. He is dressed in a well-cut black suit, quite new, and is carrying dark gloves and a top-hat. He remains standing near the door and bows abruptly. He seems a little embarrassed.*]

TESMAN [*crossing to him and shaking his hand*]. Well, my dear Ejlert, so at last we meet once more!

EJLERT LÖVBORG [*speaking with lowered voice*]. Thank you for your letter, Jörgen. [*Approaching Hedda.*] May I shake hands with you too, Mrs Tesman?

HEDDA [*taking his hand*]. I am glad to see you, Mr Lövborg. [*With a gesture.*] I don't know whether you two –

LÖVBORG [*with a slight bow*]. Mr Brack, I think.

BRACK [*returning it*]. Of course we do. Some years ago –

TESMAN [*to Lövborg, with his hands on his shoulders*]. And now you're to make yourself absolutely at home, Ejlert. Musn't he, Hedda? For you're going to settle down in town again, I hear. Eh?

LÖVBORG. I am.

TESMAN. Well, that's only natural. Oh, look here, I've got hold of your new book. But I really haven't had the time to read it yet.

LÖVBORG. You may as well save yourself the trouble.

TESMAN. Why may I?

LÖVBORG. Because there isn't much in it.

TESMAN. Well! Fancy your saying that!

BRACK. But it's very highly spoken of, I hear.

LÖVBORG. That's exactly what I wanted. So I wrote a book that everybody could agree with.

BRACK. Very wise.

TESMAN. Yes, but my dear Ejlert –

LÖVBORG. Because now I'm going to try and build myself up a position again. To begin over again.

TESMAN [*a little embarrassed*]. I see; that's what it is? Eh?

LÖVBORG [*smiling puts down his hat and takes a packet wrapped in paper out of his pocket*]. But when this one comes out, Jörgen Tesman, you must read it. For this is my first real book – the first I have put myself into.

TESMAN. Really? And what kind of book is that?

LÖVBORG. It's the continuation.

TESMAN. Continuation? Of what?

LÖVBORG. Of the book.

TESMAN. Of the new one?

LÖVBORG. Of course.

TESMAN. But my dear Ejlert, that one comes down to our own times!

LÖVBORG. It does. And this one deals with the future.

TESMAN. With the future? But, good gracious, we don't know anything about that.

LÖVBORG. No. But there are one or two things to be said about it, all the same. [*Opening the package.*] Here, you see –

TESMAN. But that's not your handwriting?

LÖVBORG. I dictated it. [*Turning over the pages.*] It's divided into two sections. The first is about the factors that will control civilization in the future. And the second part, here [*turning over the later pages*], this is about the probable direction civilization will take.

TESMAN. Amazing! It would never occur to me to write about a thing like that.

HEDDA [*drumming on the panes of the glass door*]. Hm. No ... it wouldn't.

LÖVBORG [*puts the MS. into the envelope and lays the packet on the table*]. I brought it with me because I thought of reading you a little of it this evening.

TESMAN. My dear fellow, that was very good of you. But, this evening ... ? [*He looks across at Brack.*] I don't quite know how it's to be managed.

LÖVBORG. Well, another time then. There's no hurry.

BRACK. I'll explain, Mr Lövborg. There's a little affair at my place tonight. Chiefly for Tesman, you know –

LÖVBORG [*looking for his hat*]. Ah, then I won't keep you –

BRACK. No, look here; won't you give me the pleasure of joining us?

LÖVBORG [*shortly and decidedly*]. No, I can't do that. Thank you very much.

BRACK. Oh, nonsense! Please do. We shall be a small,

select circle. And, believe me, we shall have quite a 'gay'
time, as Mad – Mrs Tesman puts it.

LÖVBORG. I don't doubt it. But all the same –

BRACK. So you could take your manuscript along and read
it to Tesman there, at my place. I've got plenty of rooms.

TESMAN. Yes, what about it, Ejlert? You could do that!
Eh?

HEDDA [*intervening*]. But, my dear, if Mr Lövborg really
doesn't want to! I'm sure he would much rather stay
here and have supper with me.

LÖVBORG [*looking at her*]. With you, Mrs Tesman?

HEDDA. And with Mrs Elvsted.

LÖVBORG. Oh. [*Casually.*] I met her for a moment this
morning.

HEDDA. Did you? Yes, she's coming out. So it's almost
imperative for you to stay, Mr Lövborg. Otherwise
she'll have no one to see her home.

LÖVBORG. That's true. Well, thank you very much, Mrs
Tesman; then I'll stay here.

HEDDA. I'll just have a word with the maid.

[*She goes to the hall door and rings. Berte comes in. Hedda talks
to her in an undertone and points to the inner room. Berte nods
and goes out again.*]

TESMAN [*at the same time, to Ejlert Lövborg*]. Look here,
Ejlert, is it this new material – about the future – that
you're going to lecture on?

LÖVBORG. Yes.

TESMAN. Because I heard at the book-shop that you are
going to give a course of lectures here in the autumn.

LÖVBORG. I am. You mustn't think hardly of me for it,
Tesman.

TESMAN. Good gracious, no! But –

LÖVBORG. I can quite understand that it must be rather
annoying for you.

TESMAN [*dispiritedly*]. Oh, I can't expect you to ... for my sake ...

LÖVBORG. But I'm waiting till you've got your appointment.

TESMAN. Waiting? Yes, but – but aren't you going to try for it, then? Eh?

LÖVBORG. No. I only want a *succès d'estime*.

TESMAN. But, good Lord! Aunt Julle was right after all, then! Of course that was it, I knew! Hedda! Think of it, my dear! Ejlert Lövborg isn't going to stand in our way at all!

HEDDA [*shortly*]. Our way? Please leave me out of it.

[*She goes up towards the inner room where Berte is putting a tray with decanters and glasses on the table. Hedda nods approvingly and comes down again. Berte goes out.*]

TESMAN [*at the same time.*] But what about you, Judge? What do you say to this? Eh?

BRACK. Why, I should say that honour and a *succès d'estime* ... they can be very pleasant things –

TESMAN. They certainly can. But all the same –

HEDDA [*looking at Tesman with a cold smile*]. You look to me as though you'd been thunderstruck.

TESMAN. Well, something like that. ... I almost feel ...

BRACK. As a matter of fact, a thunderstorm has just passed over us, Mrs Tesman.

HEDDA [*with a gesture towards the inner room*]. Wouldn't you men like to go in and have a glass of cold punch?

BRACK [*looking at his watch*]. By way of a stirrup-cup? That wouldn't be a bad idea.

TESMAN. Good, Hedda! Excellent! I feel so light-hearted now, that –

HEDDA. Won't you too, Mr Lövborg?

LÖVBORG [*with a gesture of refusal*]. No, thank you very much. Not for me.

BRACK. But, good Lord! Cold punch isn't poison, so far as I know.

LÖVBORG. Not for everybody, perhaps.

HEDDA. I'll entertain Mr Lövborg in the meantime.

TESMAN. That's right, Hedda dear. You do that.

[*He and Brack go into the inner room and sit down. During what follows they drink punch, smoke cigarettes and carry on a lively conversation. Ejlert Lövborg remains standing by the stove. Hedda goes to the writing-table.*]

HEDDA [*raising her voice a little*]. I'll show you some photographs, if you like. My husband and I made a trip through the Tyrol on our way home.

[*She brings an album and puts it on the table by the sofa, sitting down herself in the farthest corner. Ejlert Lövborg goes nearer, stands and looks at her. Then he takes a chair and sits down on her left with his back to the inner-room.*]

HEDDA [*opening the album*]. Do you see this mountain range, Mr Lövborg? It's the Ortler Group. My husband has written it underneath. Here it is: 'The Ortler Group at Meran.'

LÖVBORG [*who has been looking intently at her, speaking softly and slowly*]. Hedda – Gabler.

HEDDA [*glancing quickly at him*]. Hush, now!

LÖVBORG [*repeating softly*]. Hedda Gabler.

HEDDA [*looking at the album*]. Yes, that was my name once upon a time. In the days – when we two knew one another.

LÖVBORG. And in future – for the whole of my life – then, I must break myself of the habit of saying Hedda Gabler?

HEDDA [*going on turning over the pages*]. Yes, you must. And I think you'd better practise it in good time. The sooner the better, I should say.

LÖVBORG [*with resentment in his voice*]. Hedda Gabler married? And married to – Jörgen Tesman.

HEDDA. Yes. That's what happened.

LÖVBORG. Oh, Hedda, Hedda, how could you throw your-self away like that?

HEDDA [*looking sharply at him*]. Now! None of that, please.

LÖVBORG. None of what?

[*Tesman comes in and goes towards the sofa.*]

HEDDA [*hearing him coming, and speaking indifferently*]. And this one, Mr Lövborg, is from the Vale of Ampezzo. Just look at the mountain peaks there. [*Looking affection-ately up at Tesman.*] What is it these queer peaks are called, my dear?

TESMAN. Let me see. Oh, those are the Dolomites.

HEDDA. Oh, of course! Those are the Dolomites, Mr Lövborg.

TESMAN. Hedda, dear, I just wanted to ask if we shouldn't bring you a little punch? For you, at any rate. Eh?

HEDDA. Well, yes; thank you. And a few cakes, perhaps.

TESMAN. No cigarettes?

HEDDA. No, thanks.

TESMAN. Right.

[*He goes into the inner room and out to the right. Brack stays sitting in the inner room, with an eye on Hedda and Lövborg from time to time.*]

LÖVBORG [*in a low voice, as before*]. Answer me, now, Hedda my dear. How could you go and do this?

HEDDA [*apparently intent on the album*]. If you go on saying 'dear' to me, I won't talk to you.

LÖVBORG. Mayn't I even do it when we are alone?

HEDDA. No. You can think it if you like. But you mustn't say it.

LÖVBORG. Ah, I understand. It offends ... your love for Jörgen Tesman.

HEDDA [*glancing at him and smiling*]. Love? That's good!

LÖVBORG. Isn't it love, then?

HEDDA. There isn't going to be any kind of disloyalty, anyhow. I won't have that sort of thing.

LÖVBORG. Hedda, answer me just one thing –

HEDDA. Hush!

[*Tesman, with a tray, comes from the inner room.*]

TESMAN. Look at the good things we've got here. [*He puts the tray on the table.*]

HEDDA. Why are you bringing it yourself?

TESMAN [*filling the glasses*]. Why, because I think it's so jolly waiting on you, Hedda.

HEDDA. Oh, but you've filled both glasses now. And Mr Lövborg won't have any.

TESMAN. No, but Mrs Elvsted will be here soon.

HEDDA. Oh, of course; Mrs Elvsted –

TESMAN. Had you forgotten her? Eh?

HEDDA. We've got so absorbed in this. [*Showing him a picture.*] Do you remember that little village?

TESMAN. Ah, that's the one below the Brenner Pass! It was there we stayed the night –

HEDDA. – And met all those jolly tourists.

TESMAN. That's it. It was there. Just think, if we could have had *you* with us, Ejlert! Well, well!

[*He goes in again and sits down with Brack.*]

LÖVBORG. Answer me just this one thing, Hedda.

HEDDA. Well?

LÖVBORG. Was there no love in your feeling for me either? Not a touch – not a flicker of love in that either?

HEDDA. I wonder if there actually was? To me it seems as if we were two good comrades. Two real, close friends. [*Smiling.*] You, especially, were absolutely frank.

LÖVBORG. It was you who wanted that.

HEDDA. When I look back at it, there really was something fine, something enthralling. There was a kind of courage

about it, about this hidden intimacy, this comradeship
that not a living soul so much as guessed at.

LÖVBORG. Yes, there was, Hedda! Wasn't there? When I
came up to see your father in the afternoons. ... And the
General used to sit right over by the window reading the
papers, with his back to us ...

HEDDA. And we used to sit on the corner sofa.

LÖVBORG. Always with the same illustrated paper in front
of us.

HEDDA. Yes, for lack of an album.

LÖVBORG. Yes, Hedda; and when I used to confess to you!
Told you things about myself that no one else knew in
those days. Sat there and owned up to going about
whole days and nights blind drunk. Days and nights
on end. Oh, Hedda, what sort of power in you was it –
that forced me to confess things like that?

HEDDA. Do you think it was some power in me?

LÖVBORG. Yes, how else can I account for it? And all these
– these questions you used to put to me ... indirectly.

HEDDA. And that you understood so perfectly well.

LÖVBORG. To think you could sit and ask questions like
that! Quite frankly.

HEDDA. Indirectly, mind you.

LÖVBORG. Yes, but frankly, all the same. Cross-question
me about ... about all that kind of thing.

HEDDA. And to think that you could answer, Mr Lövborg.

LÖVBORG. Yes, that's just what I can't understand, looking
back. But tell me now, Hedda, wasn't it love that was
at the bottom of that relationship? Wasn't it, on your
side, as though you wanted to purify and absolve me,
when I made you my confessor? Wasn't it that?

HEDDA. No, not quite.

LÖVBORG. What made you do it, then?

HEDDA. Do you find it so impossible to understand,

that a young girl, when there's an opportunity ... in secret ...

LÖVBORG. Well?

HEDDA. That one should want to have a glimpse of a world that ...

LÖVBORG. That ... ?

HEDDA. That one isn't allowed to know about?

LÖVBORG. So that was it, then?

HEDDA. That ... that as well, I rather think.

LÖVBORG. The bond of our common hunger for life. But why couldn't that have gone on, in any case?

HEDDA. That was your own fault.

LÖVBORG. It was you who broke it off.

HEDDA. Yes, when there was imminent danger of our relationship becoming serious. You ought to be ashamed of yourself, Ejlert Lövborg. How could you take advantage of – your unsuspecting comrade!

LÖVBORG [*clenching his hands*]. Oh, why didn't you make a job of it! Why didn't you shoot me down when you threatened to!

HEDDA. Yes ... I'm as terrified of scandal as all that.

LÖVBORG. Yes, Hedda; you are a coward at bottom.

HEDDA. An awful coward. [*Changing her tone.*] But it was lucky enough for you. And now you have consoled youself so delightfully up at the Elvsteds'.

LÖVBORG. I know what Thea has told you.

HEDDA. And you have told her something about us two?

LÖVBORG. Not a word. She's too stupid to understand a thing like that.

HEDDA. Stupid?

LÖVBORG. She is stupid about that sort of thing.

HEDDA. And I'm a coward. [*She leans nearer to him, without meeting his eyes, and says more softly*]. But now *I* will confess something to *you*.

LÖVBORG [*eagerly*]. Well?

HEDDA. That, my not daring to shoot you down –

LÖVBORG. Yes?

HEDDA. That wasn't my worst piece of cowardice ... that night.

LÖVBORG [*looks at her a moment, understands and whispers passionately*]. Ah, Hedda! Hedda Gabler! Now I see a glimpse of the hidden foundation of our comradeship. You and I! Then it *was* your passion for life –

HEDDA [*quietly, with a sharp, angry glance*]. Take care! Don't assume anything like that.

[*It has begun to get dark. The hall door is opened from outside by Berte.*]

HEDDA [*shutting the album with a snap and calling out with a smile*]. There you are at last, Thea darling! Come along in!

[*Mrs Elvsted comes in from the hall, dressed for the evening. The door is closed behind her.*]

HEDDA [*on the sofa, stretching her arms towards her*]. My precious Thea – you can't think how I've been longing for you to come!

[*Mrs Elvsted, in the meanwhile, exchanges slight greetings with the men in the inner room and then comes across to the table holding her hand out to Hedda. Ejlert Lövborg has got up. He and Mrs Elvsted greet each other with a silent nod.*]

MRS ELVSTED. Oughtn't I to go in and say a word or two to your husband?

HEDDA. Not a bit of it! Let them be. They're going out directly.

MRS ELVSTED. Are they going out?

HEDDA. Yes, they're going to make a night of it.

MRS ELVSTED [*quickly, to Lövborg*]. You're not, are you?

LÖVBORG. No.

HEDDA. Mr Lövborg – is staying here with us.

MRS ELVSTED [*takes a chair and is going to sit beside him*]. Oh, it *is* nice to be here!

HEDDA. No, no, Thea my child! Not there. You're coming over here, right beside me. I want to be in the middle.

MRS ELVSTED. All right; just as you like. [*She goes round the table and sits on the sofa on Hedda's right. Lövborg sits down on his chair again.*]

LÖVBORG [*to Hedda, after a little pause*]. Isn't she lovely, just to look at?

HEDDA [*stroking her hair lightly*]. Only to look at?

LÖVBORG. Yes. Because *we* two – she and I – we really *are* comrades. We trust each other absolutely. That's how it is we can sit and talk to each other quite frankly.

HEDDA. Nothing indirect about it, Mr Lövborg?

LÖVBORG. Oh well ...

MRS ELVSTED [*softly, leaning close to Hedda*]. Oh, Hedda, I am so happy! Just think, he says I have inspired him, too!

HEDDA [*looking at her with a smile*]. He says that, does he?

LÖVBORG. And then she has the courage that leads to action, Mrs Tesman.

MRS ELVSTED. Good gracious! *Me?* Courage?

LÖVBORG. Immense – when her comrade is concerned.

HEDDA. Ah, courage. Yes. If one only had that.

LÖVBORG. What do you mean?

HEDDA. Then perhaps one could even *live* at last. [*Changing her tone suddenly.*] But now, Thea, my dear, you must have a nice glass of cold punch.

MRS ELVSTED. No, thank you. I never drink anything like that.

HEDDA. Well you, then, Mr Lövborg.

LÖVBORG. Thank you, I don't either.

MRS ELVSTED. No, he doesn't either.

HEDDA [*looking at him steadily*]. But suppose I want you to?

LÖVBORG. That wouldn't alter it.

HEDDA [*laughing*]. So I, poor thing, have no power over you at all?

LÖVBORG. Not where that's concerned.

HEDDA. But, joking apart, I think you ought to, all the same. For your own sake.

MRS ELVSTED. Oh, but, Hedda!

LÖVBORG. How do you mean?

HEDDA. Or, rather, on account of other people.

LÖVBORG. Really?

HEDDA. Otherwise people might easily get the idea that you didn't feel absolutely secure. Not really sure of yourself.

MRS ELVSTED [*softly*]. Oh *no*, Hedda!

LÖVBORG. People may think what they like, for the present.

MRS ELVSTED [*happily*]. Exactly!

HEDDA. I saw it so plainly with Judge Brack just this minute.

LÖVBORG. What did you see?

HEDDA. That contemptuous smile of his when you were afraid to go in there with them.

LÖVBORG. Afraid! Naturally I preferred to stay here and talk to you.

MRS ELVSTED. That was quite understandable, Hedda!

HEDDA. But Judge Brack couldn't be expected to guess that. And I noticed too that he smiled and glanced at my husband when you were afraid to go to this harmless little party with them either.

LÖVBORG. Afraid! Did you say I was afraid?

HEDDA. I don't. But that's how Judge Brack understood it.

LÖVBORG. Let him, then.

HEDDA. So you're not going with them?

LÖVBORG. I am staying here with you and Thea.

MRS ELVSTED. Why, yes, Hedda; of course.

HEDDA [*smiling and nodding approvingly at Lövborg*]. There! Quite immovable. A man of unshaken principles, always. You know, that's what a man should be. [*Turning to Mrs Elvsted and patting her.*] Now, wasn't that what I said, when you came in here this morning in such a state of distraction –

LÖVBORG [*with surprise*]. Distraction?

MRS ELVSTED [*in terror*]. Hedda! Oh, Hedda!

HEDDA. Now you see for yourself! There's not the slightest need for you to go about in this deadly anxiety – [*Breaking off.*] There! Now we can all three be cheerful.

LÖVBORG [*who has made a startled gesture*]. What on earth is all this, Mrs Tesman?

MRS ELVSTED. Oh heavens, heavens, Hedda! What are you saying? What are you doing?

HEDDA. Keep quiet. That detestable Judge Brack has got his eye on you.

LÖVBORG. So it was deadly anxiety ... on my behalf.

MRS ELVSTED [*softly and in misery*]. Oh, Hedda! How *could* you!

LÖVBORG [*looking intently at her for a moment, his face haggard*]. So *that* was my comrade's absolute faith in me.

MRS ELVSTED [*beseeching*]. Oh, my dear, my dear – you must listen to me before –

LÖVBORG [*takes one of the filled glasses, lifts it and says softly in a strained voice*]: Your health, Thea! [*He empties his glass, puts it down and takes the other.*]

MRS ELVSTED [*softly*]. Oh, Hedda, Hedda! Did you *want* this to happen?

HEDDA. Want it? I? Are you crazy?

LÖVBORG. And a health to you too, Mrs Tesman. Thank you for the truth. Here's to it. [*He drains his glass and is about to fill it again.*]

HEDDA [*laying a hand on his arm*]. Now, then. No more for the moment. Remember you're going to a party.

MRS ELVSTED. No, no, no!

HEDDA. Hush! They're looking at you.

LÖVBORG [*putting down his glass*]. Now, Thea, my dear, tell the truth!

MRS ELVSTED. Yes!

LÖVBORG. Did your husband know that you had followed me?

MRS ELVSTED [*wringing her hands*]. Oh, Hedda! You hear what he's asking me?

LÖVBORG. Was it an understanding between you and him, that you should come to town and spy on me? Perhaps it was he himself who made you do it? Ah yes, no doubt he wanted me in the office again! Or did he miss me at the card-table?

MRS ELVSTED [*softly, with a moan*]. Oh, Ejlert, Ejlert!

LÖVBORG [*seizing a glass and about to fill it*]. A health to the old District Magistrate, too!

HEDDA [*checking him*]. No more now. Remember, you're going out to read your book to my husband.

LÖVBORG [*calmly, putting down the glass*]. It was stupid of me, Thea, all this. To take it like that, I mean. And don't be angry with me, dear old friend. You shall see, you and the others, that even if I came to grief once, yet ... Now I'm on my feet again. Thanks to your help, Thea!

MRS ELVSTED [*radiant with joy*]. Thank heaven!

[*Brack, in the meantime, has looked at his watch. He and Tesman get up and come into the drawing-room.*]

BRACK [*getting his hat and overcoat*]. Well, Mrs Tesman, our time's up now.

HEDDA. I expect it is.

LÖVBORG [*getting up*]. Mine too, Mr Brack.

MRS ELVSTED [*softly, and imploring*]. Oh, Ejlert, don't!

HEDDA [*pinching her arm*]. They can hear what you're saying.

MRS ELVSTED [*with a faint cry*]. Oh!

LÖVBORG [*to Brack*]. You were so kind as to ask me to join you.

BRACK. Oh, are you coming, after all?

LÖVBORG. Yes, thank you very much.

BRACK. I'm delighted.

LÖVBORG [*putting his parcel in his pocket and speaking to Tesman*]. Because I should like to show you one or two things before I hand it in.

TESMAN. Fancy! That will be jolly. But, Hedda dear, how are you going to get Mrs Elvsted home, eh?

HEDDA. We'll manage that somehow.

LÖVBORG [*looking towards the women*]. Mrs Elvsted? I'll come back again and fetch her, of course. [*Coming nearer.*] Round about ten o'clock, Mrs Tesman? Will that do?

HEDDA. Certainly. That will do beautifully.

TESMAN. Oh well, everything's all right, then. But you mustn't expect *me* as early as that, Hedda.

HEDDA. My dear, stay – as long as ever you like.

MRS ELVSTED [*in suppressed anxiety*]. I shall wait here, then, Mr Lövborg, till you come.

LÖVBORG [*with his hat in his hand*]. All right, Mrs Elvsted.

BRACK. And so the procession starts, gentlemen. I hope we shall have a gay time, as a certain charming lady puts it.

HEDDA. Ah, if only that charming lady could be there, invisible –

BRACK. Why invisible?

HEDDA. So as to hear a little of your gaiety – uncensored, Mr Brack.

BRACK [*laughing*]. I shouldn't advise the charming lady to try!

TESMAN [*laughing, too*]. Oh, Hedda, you're simply price-less! Just think!

BRACK. Well, good-bye, good-bye, ladies.

LÖVBORG [*taking leave with a bow*]. About ten o'clock, then.

[*Brack, Lövborg and Tesman go out by the hall door. At the same time Berte comes in from the inner room with a lighted lamp, which she puts on the drawing-room table. She goes out again the same way.*]

MRS ELVSTED [*who has got up and is wandering restlessly about the room*]. Hedda, Hedda, where is all this going to end?

HEDDA. Ten o'clock – then he will come. I can see him. With vineleaves in his hair. Flushed and confident.

MRS ELVSTED. Yes, if only it would be like that.

HEDDA. And then, you see, then he'll have got control of himself again. Then he will be a free man for the rest of his days.

MRS ELVSTED. Heavens, yes. If only he would come like that. As you see him.

HEDDA. He'll come like that – 'so and no otherwise'. [*Getting up and going nearer.*] Go on doubting him as long as you like. I believe in him. And now we'll try ...

MRS ELVSTED. There's something behind all this, Hedda.

HEDDA. True; there is. I want, for once in my life, to have power over a human being's fate.

MRS ELVSTED. But haven't you got that?

HEDDA. I have not. And never have had.

MRS ELVSTED. Not over your husband's?

HEDDA. That *would* be worth having, wouldn't it? Ah, if you could only realize how poor I am. And here are you, offered such riches! [*Throwing her arms passionately round her.*] I think I shall burn your hair off, after all.

MRS ELVSTED. Let go! Let go! I'm frightened of you, Hedda!

BERTE [*in the doorway between the rooms*]. Tea's laid in the dining-room, ma'am.

HEDDA. Good. We're coming.

MRS ELVSTED. No, no, no! I'd rather go home alone. At once!

HEDDA. Nonsense! You must have tea first, you little goose. And then, at ten o'clock, Ejlert Lövborg will come – with vineleaves in his hair.

[*She pulls Mrs Elvsted, almost by force, towards the doorway.*]

ACT THREE

——————— * ———————

[*The room at the Tesmans'. The curtains across the middle door-way are closed and so are those in front of the glass door. The lamp, with its shade on, is burning, turned half-down, on the table. The door of the stove is open and there has been a fire in it, which is now nearly out.*

Mrs Elvsted, wrapped up in a large shawl with her feet on a footstool, is close to the stove, lying sunk in the easy-chair. Hedda is lying asleep on the sofa with her clothes on and a rug over her.

After a pause, Mrs Elvsted sits up quickly in her chair and listens intently. Then she sinks back wearily again, crying softly.]

MRS ELVSTED. Not yet! Oh, heavens, heavens! Not yet!
[*Berte comes stealing in cautiously by the hall door. She has a letter in her hand.*]
MRS ELVSTED [*turning and whispering eagerly*]. Well? Has anyone come?
BERTE. Yes. A girl's just been with this letter.
MRS ELVSTED [*quickly, holding out her hand*]. A letter! Give it to me!
BERTE. No, ma'am, it's for the Doctor.
MRS ELVSTED. Oh.
BERTE. It was Miss Tesman's maid who came with it. I'll put it here on the table.
MRS ELVSTED. Yes, do.
BERTE [*putting down the letter*]. I think I'd better put the lamp out. It's smoking.

MRS ELVSTED. Yes, put it out. It'll very soon be light now.

BERTE [*putting it out*]. It's quite light, ma'am.

MRS ELVSTED. Why, it's broad daylight! And still not back!

BERTE. Lord bless you, ma'am, I thought this was how it would be.

MRS ELVSTED. You thought so?

BERTE. Yes. When I saw that a certain person had come back to town again, well ... And when he went off with them ... One's heard enough about that gentleman before today.

MRS ELVSTED. Don't speak so loud. You'll wake Mrs Tesman.

BERTE [*looking towards the sofa and sighing*]. Gracious, yes; let her sleep, poor thing. Shall I put a bit more on the fire?

MRS ELVSTED. No, thank you; not for me.

BERTE. Very good. [*She goes out quietly by the hall door.*]

HEDDA [*waking as the door shuts and looking up*]. What's that?

MRS ELVSTED. It was only the maid.

HEDDA [*looking round her*]. In here? Oh yes, I remember now. [*She sits up on the sofa, stretches and rubs her eyes.*] What's the time, Thea?

MRS ELVSTED [*looking at her watch*]. It's past seven.

HEDDA. What time did my husband come back?

MRS ELVSTED. He isn't back.

HEDDA. He hasn't come home yet?

MRS ELVSTED [*getting up*]. No one's come back at all.

HEDDA. And we sat here and kept ourselves awake, waiting up for them till nearly four o'clock!

MRS ELVSTED [*wringing her hands*]. And *how* I waited for him!

HEDDA [*yawning and speaking with her hand in front of her*

mouth]. Ah, well, we might have saved ourselves that trouble.

MRS ELVSTED. Did you get a little sleep afterwards?

HEDDA. Oh yes. I slept quite well, I think. Didn't you?

MRS ELVSTED. Not a wink! I couldn't, Hedda! It was absolutely impossible.

HEDDA [*getting up and going across to her*]. There, there, there! There's nothing to worry about. I can see perfectly well what's happened.

MRS ELVSTED. Why, what do you think then? Tell me! Please!

HEDDA. Well, of course they kept things up frightfully late at the Judge's.

MRS ELVSTED. Heavens, yes. They must have done. But, all the same –

HEDDA. And then, you see, my husband didn't like to come home and disturb us by ringing in the middle of the night. [*Laughing.*] Perhaps he didn't much care to show himself either – not straight after making a gay night of it.

MRS ELVSTED. But, Hedda dear, where would he have gone?

HEDDA. He's gone up to his aunts', of course, and slept there. They keep his old room ready.

MRS ELVSTED. No, he can't be with them. Because a letter came for him a little while ago from Miss Tesman. There it is.

HEDDA. Really? [*Looking at the address.*] Yes. That's certainly from Aunt Julle; it's her handwriting. Well, then, he's stayed on at the Judge's place. And Ejlert Lövborg, he's sitting reading to him – with vineleaves in his hair.

MRS ELVSTED. Oh, Hedda, you're just saying things you don't believe yourself.

HEDDA. You really are a little goose, Thea.

MRS ELVSTED. Well, I suppose I am – worse luck.

HEDDA. And you look simply tired to death.

MRS ELVSTED. Yes, I am tired to death.

HEDDA. Well then, you're going to do as I tell you. You're going into my room and you're going to lie down on the bed for a little while.

MRS ELVSTED. Oh no. I shan't sleep, anyway.

HEDDA. Yes, you *are* to.

MRS ELVSTED. Yes, but surely your husband must be home soon. And then I must find out at once ...

HEDDA. I'll let you know all right when he comes.

MRS ELVSTED. Well; you promise me, Hedda?

HEDDA. Yes, you can be sure I will. You just go in and go to sleep in the meantime.

MRS ELVSTED. Thank you. I'll try to, then. [*She goes out through the inner room.*]

[*Hedda goes over to the glass door and pulls back the curtains. Broad daylight pours into the room. She takes a small hand-mirror from the writing-table, looks at herself in it and tidies her hair. Then she crosses to the hall door and presses the bell. After a moment Berte comes to the door.*]

BERTE. Is there anything you want, ma'am?

HEDDA. Yes, will you make up the fire? I'm simply freezing here.

BERTE. Bless us! I'll have it warm in no time.

[*She rakes the remains of the fire together and puts some wood on.*]

BERTE [*stopping to listen*]. There was a ring at the front door, ma'am.

HEDDA. You go and answer it, then. I'll see to the fire myself.

BERTE. It'll soon burn up. [*She goes out by the hall door.*]

[*Hedda kneels on the footstool and puts some more wood into the*

stove. After a short pause, Jörgen Tesman comes in from the hall.
He looks tired and rather grave. He steals towards the middle
doorway on tiptoe and is about to slip through the curtains.]

HEDDA [*at the stove, without looking up*]. Good morning.

TESMAN [*turning*]. Hedda! [*Coming towards her.*] But what
    on earth! You up as early as this! Eh?

HEDDA. Yes, I got up very early today.

TESMAN. And I was so certain you were lying asleep still!
    Just fancy, Hedda!

HEDDA. Don't speak so loudly. Mrs Elvsted is lying down
    in my room.

TESMAN. Did Mrs Elvsted stay the night here?

HEDDA. Of course. Nobody came to fetch her.

TESMAN. That's true; nobody did.

HEDDA [*shutting the door of the stove and getting up*]. Well,
    did you have a good time at the Judge's?

TESMAN. Have you been worrying about me, eh?

HEDDA. No, that would never occur to me. I was just
    asking whether you had a good time.

TESMAN. Not bad. It was rather jolly for once. Mostly at
    the beginning, as far as I was concerned. Because then
    Ejlert read me some of his book. We got there more
    than an hour too soon. Just fancy! And Brack had so
    much to see to. But then Ejlert read to me.

HEDDA [*sitting down on the right-hand side of the table*]. Well
    now, tell me about it.

TESMAN [*sitting down on a footstool by the stove*]. My good-
    ness, Hedda! You can't think what a book that's going to
    be! I should think it's one of the most remarkable things
    that's ever been written. Just think!

HEDDA. No doubt. That doesn't interest me.

TESMAN. I must admit one thing, Hedda. When he had
    read it, a perfectly detestable feeling came over me.

HEDDA. Detestable?

TESMAN. There I was *envying* Ejlert for having been able to write a thing like that! Just think, Hedda!

HEDDA. Yes, yes. I am.

TESMAN. And then to know that he, with the gifts he has ... Yet he's quite irreclaimable. What a tragedy!

HEDDA. You mean, I suppose, that he has more spirit than other people.

TESMAN. Oh no. The point is – there's no moderation in him.

HEDDA. And what happened, then, in the end?

TESMAN. Well, I really think the best way to describe it is an orgy, Hedda.

HEDDA. Did he have vineleaves in his hair?

TESMAN. Vineleaves? No, I didn't notice any. But he made a long, wandering speech in honour of the woman who had inspired him in his work. Well, that was how he put it.

HEDDA. Did he say who she was?

TESMAN. No, he didn't do that. But I can't imagine it could be anybody but Mrs Elvsted. You watch!

HEDDA. Oh, well. ... Where did you part from him, then?

TESMAN. On the way back. We broke up – the last of us – at the same time. And Brack came along with us to get a breath of fresh air. And so, you see, we agreed to see Ejlert home. Because, to tell the truth, he'd had far more than he could carry.

HEDDA. I can quite imagine that.

TESMAN. But here's the extraordinary part of it, Hedda. Or rather, the sad part of it, I ought to say. I – I'm almost ashamed to tell you, for Ejlert's sake.

HEDDA. Oh, go on! So – ?

TESMAN. Well, as we were on the way back, you see, I happened to be a little behind the others. Only for a minute or two. You see?

HEDDA. Yes, yes. But what then?

TESMAN. And then, as I was hurrying to catch them up, what do you think I found by the roadside. Eh?

HEDDA. No, how could I know?

TESMAN. Don't say anything about it to anyone, Hedda. You understand. Promise me, for Ejlert's sake. [*Taking a paper parcel out of his coat pocket.*] Just think! I found this.

HEDDA. Isn't that the parcel he had with him yesterday?

TESMAN. It is. It's the whole of that precious, irreplaceable manuscript of his. And that's what he'd gone and lost, without noticing it. Just think, Hedda! Such a sad –

HEDDA. But why didn't you give the packet back to him at once, then?

TESMAN. Well, I didn't dare to. Not in the state he was in.

HEDDA. Didn't you tell any of the others you'd found it, either?

TESMAN. Certainly not. I didn't want to do that for Ejlert's sake, you know.

HEDDA. Then there's no one who knows you've got Ejlert Lövborg's manuscript?

TESMAN. No. And no one must find out, either.

HEDDA. What did you talk to him about afterwards, then?

TESMAN. I didn't get a chance to talk to him again, you see. Because when we got into the streets, he and two or three others got away from us. Just think!

HEDDA. Oh? They must have seen him home, then.

TESMAN. Yes, it looks as if they had. And Brack went off, too.

HEDDA. And where ever have you been since?

TESMAN. Well, I and some of the others went on home with one of the gay lads and had morning coffee at his place. Or night coffee, it would be better to call it. Eh? But as soon as I've had a moment's rest – and when I think Ejlert's slept it off, poor fellow – I must go over to him with this.

HEDDA [*holding out her hand for the package*]. No, don't give it up! Not directly, I mean. Let me read it first.

TESMAN. Oh, Hedda, my dear, I couldn't do that. I really couldn't.

HEDDA. You couldn't?

TESMAN. No. You can just imagine how frantic he will be when he wakes up and misses the manuscript. Because he's got no copy of it, you realize! He said so himself.

HEDDA [*looking searchingly at him*]. Can't a thing like that be written again, then? Re-written?

TESMAN. No, I don't think that would ever work. It's a matter of inspiration, you know.

HEDDA. Yes, of course. I suppose that's it. [*Casually.*] Oh, by the way, there's a letter for you here.

TESMAN. Really?

HEDDA [*passing it to him*]. It came early this morning.

TESMAN. Why, it's from Aunt Julle! [*He puts down the paper package on the other footstool, opens the letter, runs through it and jumps up.*] Oh, Hedda! She says poor Aunt Rina's dying.

HEDDA. Well, that was to be expected.

TESMAN. And that if I want to see her again I must be quick. I'll run across there at once.

HEDDA [*checking a smile*]. Run?

TESMAN. Oh, Hedda dear, if only you could bring yourself to come along, too! Just think!

HEDDA [*getting up and dismissing the matter wearily*]. No, no. Don't ask me to do things like that. I don't want to think of illness or death. You mustn't ask me to have anything to do with ugly things.

TESMAN. Oh well, then. [*Bustling about.*] My hat? My overcoat? Oh yes; in the hall. Oh, I do so hope I'm not going to be too late, Hedda! Eh?

[*Berte comes to the hall door.*]

BERTE. Judge Brack's outside, asking can he come in?

TESMAN. At this moment! No, I really can't see him now.

HEDDA. But I can. [*To Berte.*] Ask the Judge to come in. [*Berte goes out.*]

HEDDA [*quickly, in a whisper*]. The parcel! [*She snatches it from the stool.*]

TESMAN. Yes, give it to me!

HEDDA. No, no. I'll keep it for you till you get back.

[*She crosses to the writing-table and puts it in the bookcase. Tesman is in such a hurry that he cannot get his gloves on. Brack comes in from the hall.*]

HEDDA [*nodding to him*]. Well, you are an early bird.

BRACK. Yes, don't you think so? [*To Tesman.*] Are you going out, too?

TESMAN. Yes, I simply must go and see the Aunts. Just think, the invalid one, she's dying, poor thing.

BRACK. Dear, dear! Is she? Then you certainly mustn't let me keep you. At such a serious moment –

TESMAN. Yes, I really must be off. Good-bye, good-bye! [*He hurries out through the hall door.*]

HEDDA [*coming nearer to Brack*]. It seems to have been rather more than 'gay' at your place last night, Mr Brack.

BRACK. So much so that I haven't had my clothes off, Madam Hedda.

HEDDA. Not you either?

BRACK. No, as you see. Well, what has Tesman been telling you about the night's adventures?

HEDDA. Oh, just a dull story. That they'd gone and had coffee somewhere.

BRACK. I know all about that coffee-party. Ejlert Lövborg wasn't with them, I think?

HEDDA. No, they'd seen him home before that.

BRACK. Tesman, too?

HEDDA. No; but some of the others, he said.

BRACK [*smiling*]. Jörgen Tesman really is a simple soul, Madam Hedda.

HEDDA. Heaven knows he is. Is there something behind this, then?

BRACK. Yes. It's no good denying ...

HEDDA. Well, then let's sit down, my friend. Then you can tell your story.

[*She sits down on the left of the table, with Brack at the long side, near her.*]

HEDDA. Well, now?

BRACK. I had good reasons for keeping track of my guests last night – or rather, of some of my guests.

HEDDA. And I suppose Ejlert Lövborg was one of them.

BRACK. I must admit he was.

HEDDA. Now you are making me really curious.

BRACK. Do you know where he and a few others spent the rest of the night, Madam Hedda?

HEDDA. If it's the sort of thing that can be told, tell me.

BRACK. Oh yes, it can be told all right. Well, they fetched up at an extremely lively party.

HEDDA. Of the 'gay' kind?

BRACK. Of the very gayest.

HEDDA. Go on, please. I want to hear some more.

BRACK. Lövborg had had an invitation beforehand as well. I knew all about that. But he'd refused to go then, because he's turned over a new leaf now – as you know.

HEDDA. Up at the Elvsteds'. Yes. But he went, then, all the same?

BRACK. Yes. You see, Madam Hedda, unfortunately the inspiration took him at my place last night.

HEDDA. Yes, I gather he found inspiration there.

BRACK. Pretty violent inspiration. Anyway, he changed his mind, I imagine. For we men are unfortunately not always so firm in our principles as we ought to be.

HEDDA. Oh, I am sure you are an exception, Mr Brack. But what about Lövborg?

BRACK. Well, to be brief, the end of it was that he fetched up at Mademoiselle Diana's rooms.

HEDDA. Mademoiselle Diana's?

BRACK. It was Mademoiselle Diana who was giving the party. For a select circle of her lady friends and admirers.

HEDDA. Is she a red-haired woman?

BRACK. Precisely.

HEDDA. Some kind of a – singer?

BRACK. Yes, among other things. And, moreover, a mighty huntress – of men, Madam Hedda. You must have heard her spoken of. Ejlert Lövborg was one of her warmest supporters, in his hey-day.

HEDDA. And how did all this end?

BRACK. On a less friendly note, it would appear. Mademoiselle Diana seems to have changed from a most tender reception to downright violence.

HEDDA. To Lövborg?

BRACK. Yes. He accused her or her friends of having robbed him. He declared his pocket-book had gone. And other things, too. In fact, he seems to have made an appalling scene.

HEDDA. And what was the result?

BRACK. The result was a general fight, in which both the ladies and the gentlemen were involved. Luckily the police arrived in the end.

HEDDA. The police, too?

BRACK. Yes. But it looks like being a costly game for Ejlert Lövborg, the crazy fool.

HEDDA. Really?

BRACK. He appears to have put up a violent resistance, and hit one of the constables on the head and torn his coat to pieces. So he had to go to the police station too.

HEDDA. How do you know all this?

BRACK. From the police themselves.

HEDDA [*gazing in front of her*]. So that's how it was? Then he had no vineleaves in his hair.

BRACK. Vineleaves, Madam Hedda?

HEDDA [*changing her tone*]. But tell me, now. What's your real reason for following up Ejlert Lövborg's movements like this?

BRACK. Well, it obviously can't be a matter of complete indifference to me, if it comes out at the trial that he had come straight from my place.

HEDDA. Will there be a trial too, then?

BRACK. Of course. However, that might pass. ... But, as a friend of the house, I felt bound to give you and Tesman a full account of his night's exploits.

HEDDA. And why, Mr Brack?

BRACK. Well, because I have a shrewd misgiving that he means to use you as a kind of screen.

HEDDA. Why, how can you imagine such a thing?

BRACK. Good Lord, we're not blind, Madam Hedda! You watch. This Mrs Elvsted, she won't be leaving town again in a hurry.

HEDDA. Well, even supposing there is something between them, there must be plenty of other places where they can meet.

BRACK. No other home. Every decent house will be closed again to Ejlert Lövborg from now onwards.

HEDDA. And so ought mine to be, you mean?

BRACK. Yes. I admit it would be extremely unpleasant to me if this man were on a firm footing here. If he were to force his way in, superfluous and an intruder, into –

HEDDA. Into the triangle?

BRACK. Precisely. It would simply amount to my finding myself without a home.

HEDDA [*looking at him with a smile*]. Ah yes. The only cock in the yard. That's your idea.

BRACK [*nodding slowly and dropping his voice*]. Yes, that is my idea. And I'll fight for that idea with all the means at my command.

HEDDA [*her smile dying away*]. You are really a dangerous person, when it comes to the point.

BRACK. Do you think so?

HEDDA. Yes, I am beginning to think so now. I'm heartily thankful you've no hold or power over me – and I hope you never will.

BRACK [*laughing equivocally*]. Well, well, Madam Hedda. You may be right there. Who knows what I mightn't prove capable of in that case?

HEDDA. Now look here, Mr Brack. That sounds almost as though you were threatening me.

BRACK [*getting up*]. Oh, far from it! The triangle, you see, is best formed and maintained by free consent.

HEDDA. That's what I think, too.

BRACK. Yes. Well, now I've said what I wanted to and I must see about getting home again. Good-bye, Madam Hedda. [*He goes towards the glass door.*]

HEDDA [*getting up*]. Are you going through the garden?

BRACK. Yes, it's shorter for me.

HEDDA. Yes, and what's more, it's a back way.

BRACK. Quite true. I have nothing against back ways. They can be quite attractive at times.

HEDDA. When someone's practising shooting, do you mean?

BRACK [*at the door, laughing to her*]. Oh, I don't think people shoot their farmyard cocks.

HEDDA [*laughing, too*]. No, not when one has only the one.

[*They nod good-bye to each other, laughing. He goes out. She shuts the door after him.*]

Hedda stands a moment, serious now, and looks out. Then she goes across and peeps in through the curtains over the middle doorway and then goes to the writing-table, takes the packet out of the bookcase and is just going to look through it when Berte's voice is heard, speaking loudly, in the hall. Hedda turns and listens, then quickly locks the package in the drawer and puts the key on the inkstand.

Ejlert Lövborg, with his overcoat on and his hat in his hand, flings open the hall door. He looks disturbed and excited.]

LÖVBORG [*speaking towards the hall*]. And I tell you I must go in and I will. There now!

[*He shuts the door, turns, sees Hedda, controls himself at once and bows.*]

HEDDA [*at the writing-table*]. Well, Mr Lövborg, it's rather late to come and fetch Thea.

LÖVBORG. Or rather early to come and call on you. I apologize.

HEDDA. How do you know that she is still with me?

LÖVBORG. They said at her lodgings that she had been out all night.

HEDDA [*going to the centre table*]. Did you notice anything about the people, when they said that?

LÖVBORG [*looking at her inquiringly*]. Notice anything about them?

HEDDA. I mean, did it look as if they were drawing their own conclusions?

LÖVBORG [*understanding suddenly*]. Oh yes, of course; that's true. I am dragging her down with me. Actually, though, I didn't notice anything. Tesman isn't up yet?

HEDDA. No, I don't think so.

LÖVBORG. When did he get home?

HEDDA. Pretty late.

LÖVBORG. Did he tell you anything?

HEDDA. Yes, I gathered that things had been very merry at Judge Brack's.

LÖVBORG. Nothing more?

HEDDA. No, I don't think so. But anyhow, I was so terribly sleepy –

[*Mrs Elvsted comes in through the curtains in the middle doorway.*]

MRS ELVSTED [*going towards him*]. Oh, Ejlert! At last!

LÖVBORG. Yes, at last. And too late.

MRS ELVSTED [*looking anxiously at him*]. What is too late?

LÖVBORG. Everything's too late now. It's all up with me.

MRS ELVSTED. No, no! Don't say that!

LÖVBORG. You'll say so yourself when you hear.

MRS ELVSTED. I won't hear anything.

HEDDA. Perhaps you'd rather talk to her alone? If so, I'll go.

LÖVBORG. No, you stay too, please. I beg you to.

MRS ELVSTED. Yes, but I won't hear anything, I tell you.

LÖVBORG. It's not last night's escapades I want to talk about.

MRS ELVSTED. What is it, then?

LÖVBORG. Just this: our ways must part now.

MRS ELVSTED. Part?

HEDDA [*involuntarily*]. I knew it!

LÖVBORG. Because I don't need you any more, Thea.

MRS ELVSTED. And you can stand here and say that! Not need me any more! I can still help you, can't I, as I did before? Surely we are going on working together?

LÖVBORG. I don't propose to work in future.

MRS ELVSTED [*in despair*]. What shall I do with my life, then?

LÖVBORG. You must try to go on living as though you had never known me.

MRS ELVSTED. But I *can't* do that!

LÖVBORG. Try to, Thea. You must go home again –

MRS ELVSTED [*protesting fiercely*]. Never in this life! Where

you are, there will I be too. I won't let myself be driven
away like this. I will stay here and be with you when the
book comes out.

HEDDA [*half audibly, in suspense*]. Ah, the book, of course!

LÖVBORG [*looking at her*]. My book and Thea's. For that is
what it is.

MRS ELVSTED. Yes, that's what I feel it is. And that's why
I have the right to be with you when it comes out. I want
to see respect and honour showered on you again. And
the joy – I want to share the joy with you.

LÖVBORG. Thea, our book will never come out.

HEDDA. Ah!

MRS ELVSTED. Never come out!

LÖVBORG. *Can't* ever come out.

MRS ELVSTED [*in agonized foreboding*]. Ejlert, what have
you done with the manuscript?

HEDDA [*looking intently at him*]. Yes, the manuscript?

MRS ELVSTED. Where is it?

LÖVBORG. You'd better not ask me, Thea.

MRS ELVSTED. But I want to know. I've a right to know,
at once.

LÖVBORG. The manuscript ... oh well, then ... I have torn
the manuscript into a thousand pieces.

MRS ELVSTED [*shrieking*]. Oh no, no!

HEDDA [*involuntarily*]. But that's not – !

LÖVBORG [*looking at her*]. Not true, you think?

HEDDA [*controlling herself*]. I suppose it is, of course. If you
say so yourself. ... But it sounded so fantastic.

LÖVBORG. True, all the same.

MRS ELVSTED [*wringing her hands*]. Oh, heavens, heavens,
Hedda! Torn his own work to pieces!

LÖVBORG. I have torn my own life to pieces. So I might as
well tear up my life's work, too.

MRS ELVSTED. And you did it last night, then?

LÖVBORG. Yes, I tell you. Into a thousand pieces. And scattered them out in the fjord. Far out. There at least there is clean sea water. Let them drift in it. Drift with the wind and the tides. And, after a time, they will sink. Deeper and deeper. As I shall, Thea.

MRS ELVSTED. Do you know, Ejlert, this, what you have done to the book – all my life, it will seem to me as if you had killed a little child.

LÖVBORG. You are right. It is like murdering a child.

MRS ELVSTED. But how could you? After all, I had a share in the child, too.

HEDDA [scarcely audible]. Ah, the child. ...

MRS ELVSTED [with a gasp]. It's all over, then. Well, well. I'll go now, Hedda.

HEDDA. But you're not going to leave town?

MRS ELVSTED. Oh, I don't know myself what I'm going to do. Everything is dark ahead of me now.

[She goes out by the hall door.]

HEDDA [standing and waiting for a moment]. So you are not going to see her home, Mr Lövborg?

LÖVBORG. I? Through the streets? Suppose people were to see her walking with me?

HEDDA. Of course, I don't know what else happened to you last night. But is it something so absolutely irreparable?

LÖVBORG. It won't stop at last night only. I know that well enough. But, the point is, I don't *want* to live that kind of life. I don't want to start again, any more, now. It is the courage to live, and to challenge life, that she has broken in me.

HEDDA [looking straight before her]. That pretty little fool has played her part in a human being's fate. [Looking at him.] Still, how could you treat her so callously, all the same?

LÖVBORG. Oh, don't say it was callous!

HEDDA. To go and destroy what has filled her soul all this long, long time! You don't call that callous?

LÖVBORG. I can tell you the truth, Hedda.

HEDDA. The truth?

LÖVBORG. Promise me first, give me your word, that Thea shall never know what I tell you.

HEDDA. You have my word for it.

LÖVBORG. Good. Then I will tell you that that was not the truth – the story I told you just now.

HEDDA. About the manuscript?

LÖVBORG. Yes. I didn't tear it to pieces. Nor throw it into the fjord, either.

HEDDA. Well, but – where is it, then?

LÖVBORG. I have destroyed it just the same. Utterly and completely, Hedda.

HEDDA. I don't understand all this.

LÖVBORG. Thea said that what I had done was as good as child-murder to her.

HEDDA. Yes. That's what she said.

LÖVBORG. But that – killing his child – is not the worst thing a father can do to it.

HEDDA. *That's* not the worst?

LÖVBORG. No. It was that worst thing that I wanted to save Thea from hearing.

HEDDA. And what is that worst thing, then?

LÖVBORG. Suppose now, Hedda, that a man, along towards morning, say, after a wild, riotous night, came home to his child's mother and said: Look here. I have been here and there, in such-and-such places. And I took the child with me. In such-and-such places. And I lost the child. Lost it completely. The devil knows what hands it's fallen into, who's got it in his clutches.

HEDDA. Oh but, when all's said and done, this – well, this was only a book.

LÖVBORG. Thea's whole soul was in that book.

HEDDA. Yes, I understand that.

LÖVBORG. And so you understand also that there is no future before us, her and me.

HEDDA. And what are you going to do, then?

LÖVBORG. Nothing. Only make an end of the whole business. The sooner the better.

HEDDA [a step nearer]. Ejlert Lövborg, listen to me. Could you not see to it that – that it is done beautifully?

LÖVBORG. Beautifully? [Smiling.] With vineleaves in the hair, as you used to imagine once upon a time –

HEDDA. Ah, not vineleaves. I don't believe in that any more. But beautifully, nevertheless. For once. Good-bye. You must go now, and not come here again.

LÖVBORG. Good-bye, Madam. Remember me to Jörgen Tesman. [About to go.]

HEDDA. Wait a minute. You shall have a souvenir to take with you.

[She goes to the writing-table and opens the drawer and the pistol-case. She comes back to Lövborg again with one of the pistols.]

LÖVBORG [looking at her]. Is that the souvenir?

HEDDA [nodding slowly]. Do you recognize it? It was aimed at you once.

LÖVBORG. You should have used it then.

HEDDA. There it is. Use it yourself now.

LÖVBORG [putting the pistol in his breast pocket]. Thanks.

HEDDA. And beautifully, Ejlert Lövborg. Promise me that.

LÖVBORG. Good-bye, Hedda Gabler. [He goes out by the hall door.]

[Hedda listens a moment at the door. Then she goes across to the writing-table and takes out the manuscript in its package. She glances inside the wrapper, pulls some of the sheets half out and looks at them. Then she goes across and sits down in the easy-

chair by the stove with the packet in her lap. After a moment, she opens the stove-door and then the packet.]

HEDDA [*throwing some of the leaves into the fire and whispering to herself*]. Now I am burning your child, Thea. You, with your curly hair. [*Throwing a few more leaves into the stove.*] Your child and Ejlert Lövborg's. [*Throwing in the rest.*] I'm burning it – burning your child.

ACT FOUR

———————— * ————————

[*The same rooms at the Tesmans' house. Evening. The drawing-room is in darkness. The inner room is lighted by the hanging lamp over the table. The curtains are drawn across the glass door.*

Hedda, dressed in black, is walking to and fro in the dark room. Then she goes into the inner room and away to the left side. A few chords on the piano are heard. Then she comes back again and into the drawing-room.

Berte comes in from the right through the inner room with a lighted lamp, which she puts on the table in front of the corner sofa in the drawing-room. Her eyes are red with crying and she has black ribbons in her cap. She goes quietly and discreetly out to the right. Hedda goes across to the glass door, draws the curtain aside a little and looks out into the darkness.

Soon after, Miss Tesman comes in from the hall door, dressed in mourning, with a hat and veil. Hedda goes towards her and holds out her hand.]

MISS TESMAN. Yes, Hedda, here I am dressed in mourning. Because now my poor sister's trials are over at last.

HEDDA. I have heard already, as you see. My husband sent a note out to me.

MISS TESMAN. Yes, he promised he would. But I thought all the same, that to Hedda – here, in the house of the living – I ought myself to bring the news of her death.

HEDDA. It was very kind of you.

MISS TESMAN. Ah, Rina should not have died at such a moment. Hedda's home ought not to be sad just now.

HEDDA [*changing the subject*]. She died very peacefully, didn't she, Miss Tesman?

MISS TESMAN. Ah, it was such a beautiful, peaceful release! And then she had the unspeakable happiness of seeing Jörgen once more, so that she was really able to say good-bye to him. Perhaps he hasn't come back yet?

HEDDA. No. He wrote that I mustn't expect him just yet. But do sit down.

MISS TESMAN. No, thank you, my dear, precious Hedda. I should like to, but I have so little time. She must be prepared and made ready as well as I can. She shall go into her grave looking beautiful.

HEDDA. Can't I help you with anything?

MISS TESMAN. Oh, don't think of that! Hedda Tesman mustn't do that kind of thing. Nor dwell on the thought, either. Not at such a time. Certainly not.

HEDDA. Ah, thoughts ... they are not so easily mastered.

MISS TESMAN [*going on*]. Well, bless us. That's how things go in this world. At home we shall be sewing for Rina. And there will be sewing to be done here too, I think, soon. But that will be a different kind, thank God!

[*Jörgen Tesman comes in by the hall door.*]

HEDDA. Ah, it's a good thing you're back at last.

TESMAN. Are you here, Aunt Julle? With Hedda? Fancy!

MISS TESMAN. I was just going again, dear boy. Well, did you see to all those things you promised to do?

TESMAN. No, I'm really afraid I've forgotten half of them, you know. I must run in and see you again tomorrow. My head is so muddled today. I can't keep my ideas together.

MISS TESMAN. But, my dear Jörgen. You mustn't take it like this.

TESMAN. No? How, then ... do you think?

MISS TESMAN. You must be glad in your grief. Glad of what has happened. As I am.

TESMAN. Oh yes, yes. You are thinking of Aunt Rina, of course.

HEDDA. It will be lonely for you now, Miss Tesman.

MISS TESMAN. Just at first, yes. But that won't last very long, I hope. Dear Rina's little room won't stand empty, I know.

TESMAN. Really? Who do you want to take it? Eh?

MISS TESMAN. Oh, there is always some poor sick person or other who needs care and attention, unfortunately.

HEDDA. Do you really want to take a burden like that on you again?

MISS TESMAN. Burden! God forgive you, my child. It has never been a burden to me.

HEDDA. But if a strange person is going to come, why –

MISS TESMAN. Oh, one soon makes friends with sick folk. And I sadly need someone to live for – I, too. Well, thank God there may be things here, too, of one sort and another, that an old aunt can lend a hand with.

HEDDA. Oh, don't bother about things here –

TESMAN. Just think how happy we three could be together, if –

HEDDA. If – ?

TESMAN [*uneasily*]. Oh, nothing. It'll all come right. Let's hope so. Eh?

MISS TESMAN. Well, well. You two have plenty to talk to each other about, I expect. [*Smiling.*] And perhaps Hedda has something to tell you too, Jörgen. Good-bye. Now I must go home to Rina. [*Turning at the door.*] Dear, dear, how strange it is to think of! Now Rina is with me and with our dear Jochum, too.

TESMAN. Yes, to think of it, Aunt Julle! Eh?

[*Miss Tesman goes out by the hall door.*]

HEDDA [*her eyes, cold and searching, following Tesman*]. I almost think the death has affected you more than it has her.

TESMAN. Oh, it's not only Aunt Rina's death. It's Ejlert; I'm so worried about him.

HEDDA [*quickly*]. Has anything fresh happened to him?

TESMAN. I meant to have run over to him this afternoon and told him that his manuscript was in safe keeping.

HEDDA. Well, didn't you find him, then?

TESMAN. No, he wasn't at home. But afterwards I met Mrs Elvsted, and she told me he had been here early this morning.

HEDDA. Yes, directly you'd gone.

TESMAN. And he seems to have said that he had torn up the manuscript. Eh?

HEDDA. Yes, he insisted he had.

TESMAN. But, good heavens, he must have been absolutely off his head! And so, of course, you didn't dare give it back to him, Hedda?

HEDDA. No, he didn't take it.

TESMAN. But you told him, all right, that we had it?

HEDDA. No. [*Quickly.*] Did you tell Mrs Elvsted we had?

TESMAN. No, I didn't quite like to do that. But you ought to have told him himself. Suppose he goes off in despair and does himself some injury? Let me have the manuscript, Hedda. I will dash over to him with it at once. Where is the parcel?

HEDDA [*cold and immovable, leaning against the easy-chair*]. I haven't got it any longer.

TESMAN. You haven't got it. What on earth do you mean by that?

HEDDA. I have burnt it. Every scrap of it.

TESMAN [*with a start of terror*]. Burnt it! Burnt Ejlert Lövborg's manuscript!

HEDDA. Don't scream like that. The maid might hear you.

TESMAN. Burnt! But, good God! No, no, no! This is simply impossible!

HEDDA. Well, it's true, all the same.

TESMAN. But do you realize what you have done, Hedda? It's against the law, to treat lost property like that! Think of it! You just ask Judge Brack and he'll tell you.

HEDDA. I shouldn't advise you to talk about it either to the Judge or to anyone else.

TESMAN. But how could you go and do anything so unheard of? How could such an idea come into your head? How could it come over you? Tell me that. Eh?

HEDDA [suppressing a scarcely perceptible smile]. I did it for your sake, Jörgen.

TESMAN. For my sake!

HEDDA. When you came home in the morning and told me that he'd been reading to you –

TESMAN. Yes, yes, what about it?

HEDDA. You admitted then that you envied him his work.

TESMAN. Good heavens, I didn't mean it literally!

HEDDA. All the same, I couldn't bear the thought of someone else throwing you into the shade.

TESMAN [in an outburst of mingled doubt and joy]. Hedda! Is it true what you're saying? Yes, but ... but ... I've never known you show your affection in this sort of way before.

HEDDA. Oh well, you'd better know, then, that – just at present – [Breaking off, violently.] No, you can go and ask Aunt Julle. She'll tell you all about it.

TESMAN. Ah, I rather think I understand, Hedda! [Clasping his hands together.] Good heavens! Can it be possible? Eh?

HEDDA. Don't shout so. The maid might hear you.

TESMAN [laughing, beside himself with joy]. The maid! No,

you really are priceless, Hedda! 'The maid'! Why, it's only Berte! I'll go out and tell Berte myself.

HEDDA [*clenching her hands in desperation*]. Oh, it'll be the death of me. It'll be the death of me, all this!

TESMAN. What will, Hedda? Eh?

HEDDA [*cold and controlled*]. All this grotesque nonsense, Jörgen.

TESMAN. Nonsense! That I'm so delighted? But, all the same ... perhaps I had better not say anything to Berte.

HEDDA. Oh yes, why not that, too?

TESMAN. No, no, not yet. But Aunt Julle must certainly know about it. And then, too, that you are beginning to call me Jörgen! Think of it! Oh, Aunt Julle *will* be so glad! So glad!

HEDDA. When she hears that I have burnt Ejlert Lövborg's manuscript, for your sake?

TESMAN. No, that reminds me. That business with the manuscript – no one must get to know about that, of course. But that you feel like this towards me, Hedda, Aunt Julle must certainly hear that! Still, my dear, I should like to know myself whether this kind of thing is usual with young wives. Eh?

HEDDA. You'd better ask Aunt Julle about that, too, I think.

TESMAN. Yes, I certainly will some time. [*Looking worried and dubious again.*] But ... but that manuscript. Oh heavens, it's dreadful to think of poor Ejlert, all the same!

[*Mrs Elvsted, dressed as on her first visit, with her hat and outdoor clothes, comes in by the hall door.*]

MRS ELVSTED [*greeting them quickly and speaking in agitation*]. Oh, Hedda, dear, I hope you won't mind my coming again?

HEDDA. What's the matter, Thea?

TESMAN. Is it something to do with Ejlert Lövborg again? Eh?

MRS ELVSTED. Yes, I'm so terribly afraid some accident has happened to him.

HEDDA [*seizing her by the arm*]. Ah – do you think so?

TESMAN. Bless me, whatever makes you think that, Mrs Elvsted?

MRS ELVSTED. Why, because I heard them talking about him at the boarding-house, just as I came in. Oh, there are the most incredible rumours about him in town today!

TESMAN. Yes, do you know, I heard that too. Yet I could swear that he went straight home to bed. Just fancy!

HEDDA. Well, what did they say at the boarding-house?

MRS ELVSTED. I didn't gather anything definite. Either they didn't know very much or ... They stopped talking when they saw me. And as for asking – I didn't dare do that.

TESMAN [*walking about restlessly*]. We'll hope – we'll hope you misunderstood them, Mrs Elvsted.

MRS ELVSTED. No, no, I am certain it was he they were talking about. And, as I heard it, they said something about the hospital, or –

TESMAN. The hospital!

HEDDA. No! That can't be true.

MRS ELVSTED. Oh, I was so dreadfully frightened about him. So I went to his lodgings and asked for him there.

HEDDA. Could you bring yourself to do that, Thea?

MRS ELVSTED. Yes, what else was I to do? I didn't feel as if I could bear the uncertainty any longer.

TESMAN. But you didn't find him either, did you? Eh?

MRS ELVSTED. No. And the people didn't know anything about him. They said he hadn't been home since yesterday afternoon.

TESMAN. Yesterday! Fancy their saying that!

MRS ELVSTED. Oh, I think there's only one explanation – something dreadful must have happened to him!

TESMAN. Hedda, my dear, suppose I were to go in and make some inquiries?

HEDDA. No. Don't mix yourself up in this business.

[*Brack, with his hat in his hand, comes in by the hall door, which Berte opens and shuts after him. He looks grave and bows silently.*]

TESMAN. Oh, it's you, my dear Judge? Eh?

BRACK. Yes, it was imperative for me to see you this evening.

TESMAN. I can see that you have had Aunt Julle's news.

BRACK. Yes, I have heard that, too.

TESMAN. Isn't it sad? Eh?

BRACK. Well, my dear Tesman, it depends how you look at it.

TESMAN [*looking doubtfully at him*]. Has anything else happened?

BRACK. Yes, something else.

HEDDA [*in suspense*]. Anything sad, Mr Brack?

BRACK. That, too, depends on how you look at it, Mrs Tesman.

MRS ELVSTED [*breaking out, involuntarily*]. Oh, it's something about Ejlert Lövborg!

BRACK [*glancing at her*]. What makes you think that, Madam? Do you happen to know anything already?

MRS ELVSTED [*confused*]. No, no; not at all! But –

TESMAN. But, good heavens, man, tell us!

BRACK [*shrugging his shoulders*]. Well, I'm sorry to say Ejlert Lövborg has been taken to the hospital. As a matter of fact, he's dying.

MRS ELVSTED [*crying out*]. My God! My God!

TESMAN. In hospital? And dying?

HEDDA [*involuntarily*]. So quickly, then!

MRS ELVSTED [*wailing*]. And we parted in anger, Hedda!

HEDDA [*whispering*]. Come now, Thea! *Thea!*

MRS ELVSTED [*without taking any notice*]. I must go to him! I must see him alive!

BRACK. It won't be any use, my dear lady. Nobody's allowed to see him.

MRS ELVSTED. Well, at least tell me what's happened to him. What is the matter?

TESMAN. Why, surely he never did it himself! Eh?

HEDDA. I'm sure he *did*.

TESMAN. Hedda, how can you?

BRACK [*with his eyes fixed steadily on her*]. Unfortunately, you have guessed quite right, Mrs Tesman.

MRS ELVSTED. Oh, how terrible!

TESMAN. So he did it himself! Think of it!

HEDDA. Shot himself!

BRACK. Rightly guessed again, Mrs Tesman.

MRS ELVSTED [*trying to control herself*]. When did it happen, Mr Brack?

BRACK. This afternoon. Between three and four.

TESMAN. But, dear, dear – where did he do it, then? Eh?

BRACK [*a little uncertainly*]. Where? Why, I suppose at his lodgings.

MRS ELVSTED. No, that can't be right. Because I was there between six and seven.

BRACK. Well, somewhere else, then. I don't exactly know; I only know that he was found. ... He had shot himself in the chest.

MRS ELVSTED. Oh, how dreadful to think of! That he should end like this.

HEDDA [*to Brack*]. Was it in the chest?

BRACK. Yes, as I said.

HEDDA. Not in the temple, then?

BRACK. In the chest, Mrs Tesman.

HEDDA. Yes, well ... the chest is a good place, too.

BRACK. How do you mean, Mrs Tesman?

HEDDA [*evasively*]. Oh, nothing – nothing.

TESMAN. And the wound is dangerous, you say? Eh?

BRACK. The wound is absolutely fatal. Most likely it's all over already.

MRS ELVSTED. Yes, yes, I feel sure it is. It is all over! All over! Oh, Hedda!

TESMAN. But tell me, how did you find out all this?

BRACK [*shortly*]. From one of the police. Whom I had occasion to speak to.

HEDDA [*in a ringing voice*]. Something done, at last!

TESMAN [*horrified*]. Good heavens! What are you saying, Hedda?

HEDDA. That there is an element of beauty in this.

BRACK. Hm. Mrs Tesman –

TESMAN. Of beauty! Fancy that!

MRS ELVSTED. Oh, Hedda, how can you talk of beauty in a thing like that!

HEDDA. Ejlert Lövborg has balanced his account with himself. He has had the courage to do ... what had to be done.

MRS ELVSTED. No, don't ever believe that it happened in that way. What he has done was done in a moment of madness.

TESMAN. Done in despair.

HEDDA. It was not. Of that I am certain.

MRS ELVSTED. Yes, it was. In a moment of madness. Just as when he tore up our manuscript.

BRACK [*in surprise*]. Manuscript? The book, do you mean? Has he torn that up?

MRS ELVSTED. Yes, he did it last night.

TESMAN [*whispering softly*]. Oh, Hedda, we shall never get clear of this business.

BRACK. Hm. That was odd.

TESMAN [*walking about the room*]. Fancy Ejlert going out of the world like that! And not even leaving behind him the book that would have made his name immortal.

MRS ELVSTED. Oh, if only it could be put together again!

TESMAN. Yes, just think if it could! I don't know what I wouldn't give –

MRS ELVSTED. Perhaps it can, Mr Tesman.

TESMAN. What do you mean?

MRS ELVSTED [*looking in her handbag*]. Look here. I have kept the loose notes that he used for dictating from.

HEDDA [*a step nearer*]. Ah!

TESMAN. You've kept them, Mrs Elvsted! Eh?

MRS ELVSTED. Yes, I have them here. I took them with me when I came away, and here they've been, lying in my handbag.

TESMAN. Just let me see them!

MRS ELVSTED [*passes him a stack of small sheets*]. But they're in such a muddle. All mixed up together.

TESMAN. Fancy, if we could get it straight, though! Perhaps if we help each other –

MRS ELVSTED. Oh yes! Let's try, at any rate!

TESMAN. It *shall* be done! It *must!* I will give my life to this.

HEDDA. You, Jörgen? Your life?

TESMAN. Yes. Or, rather, all my spare time. My own stuff must wait for the present. You understand, Hedda? Eh? It's something I owe to Ejlert's memory.

HEDDA. Perhaps it is.

TESMAN. And so, my dear Mrs Elvsted, we will pull ourselves together. Heaven knows, it's no use brooding over what's done. Eh? We must try to make our minds as calm as possible, and –

MRS ELVSTED. Yes, yes, Mr Tesman. I will do the best I can.

TESMAN. Well, come along. We must look over the notes

at once. Where shall we sit? Here? No, in there in the
back room. Excuse me, my dear Judge. Now come with
me, Mrs Elvsted.

MRS ELVSTED. Dear God! If only it could be done!

[*Tesman and Mrs Elvsted go into the inner room. She takes off
her hat and overcoat. They both sit down at the table under the
hanging lamp and become absorbed in concentrated examination
of the papers. Hedda goes across to the stove and sits in the
easy-chair. Shortly afterwards Brack goes across to her.*]

HEDDA [*half-aloud*]. Ah, Mr Brack, what a feeling of
release it gives one, this business with Ejlert Lövborg.

BRACK. Release, Madam Hedda? Well, it certainly is a
release for him –

HEDDA. I mean for me. A feeling of release, in knowing
that there really can be such a thing in the world as free
and fearless action. Something irradiated with spon-
taneous beauty.

BRACK [*smiling*]. Hm. My dear Madam Hedda –

HEDDA. Oh yes. I know what you are going to say.
Because you're a professional man too, in your way,
like ... Oh well!

BRACK [*looking steadily at her*]. Ejlert Lövborg meant more
to you than you are perhaps willing to admit to yourself.
Or am I wrong there?

HEDDA. I don't answer that kind of question. I only know
that Ejlert Lövborg had the courage to live life in his own
way. And now – this great deed, with all its beauty? That
he had the strength and will to break away from the feast
of life ... and so early.

BRACK. I am very sorry, Madam Hedda, but I must deprive
you of your pretty illusion.

HEDDA. Illusion?

BRACK. Which you would have been deprived of soon, in
any case.

HEDDA. And what is it?

BRACK. He did not shoot himself intentionally.

HEDDA. Not intentionally?

BRACK. No. This affair of Ejlert Lövborg did not happen quite as I described it.

HEDDA [*in suspense*]. Have you been keeping something back? What is it?

BRACK. For poor Mrs Elvsted's sake I did make one or two slight modifications.

HEDDA. What were they?

BRACK. In the first place, he is actually dead already.

HEDDA. In hospital?

BRACK. Yes, and without regaining consciousness.

HEDDA. What else did you keep back?

BRACK. The fact that the thing didn't happen at his lodgings.

HEDDA. Well, that doesn't really make much difference.

BRACK. It does, rather. For I must tell you Ejlert Lövborg was found shot in – in Mademoiselle Diana's boudoir.

HEDDA [*half gets up, but sinks back again*]. That's impossible, Mr Brack. He can't have been *there* again today!

BRACK. He was there this afternoon. He came to demand something that, he said, they had taken away from him. Talked wildly about a child that had been lost –

HEDDA. Ah! So that was why ...

BRACK. I thought perhaps it might have been his manuscript. But I gather that he destroyed that himself. So it must have been his wallet.

HEDDA. It must have been. And it was there, then, that he was found?

BRACK. Yes, there. With a discharged pistol that had gone off in his breast-pocket. The shot had wounded him fatally.

HEDDA. In the chest – yes.

BRACK. No. It hit him in the stomach.

HEDDA [*looking up at him with an expression of disgust*]. That too! The ridiculous and the sordid lies like a curse on everything I so much as touch.

BRACK. There is something more, Madam Hedda. Something that can also be classed as 'sordid'.

HEDDA. What is that?

BRACK. The pistol that he had on him –

HEDDA [*breathless*]. Well! What about it?

BRACK. He must have stolen it.

HEDDA [*jumping up*]. Stolen! That's not true! That he did not!

BRACK. No other explanation is possible. He *must* have stolen it. ... Hush!

[*Tesman and Mrs Elvsted have got up from the table in the inner room and come into the drawing-room.*]

TESMAN [*with papers in both hands*]. Look here, Hedda, it's hardly possible for me to see in there under the hanging lamp. Just think!

HEDDA. Yes. I am.

TESMAN. I wonder if you would mind our sitting at your writing-table for a little while. Eh?

HEDDA. I don't mind. [*Quickly.*] Wait a minute! Let me tidy it up first.

TESMAN. Oh, you needn't do that, Hedda. There's plenty of room.

HEDDA. No, no. Just let me tidy it, I tell you. I'll take all this in and put it on the piano for the time being. There!

[*She has pulled out something covered with music paper from under the bookshelf, puts some more sheets on it and carries it all in to the left in the inner room. Tesman puts the loose papers on the writing-table and moves the lamp there from the corner table. He and Mrs Elvsted sit down and settle to work again. Hedda comes back.*]

HEDDA [*behind Mrs Elvsted's chair, ruffling her hair gently*]. Well, my precious Thea, how is Ejlert Lövborg's memorial getting on?

MRS ELVSTED [*looking up dispiritedly*]. Oh dear! It looks as if it's going to be terribly difficult to straighten out.

TESMAN. It *must* be done. There is nothing else for it. And this – getting another man's papers in order – it's just the job for me.

[*Hedda goes over to the stove and sits on one of the footstools. Brack stands over her, leaning against the easy-chair.*]

HEDDA [*whispers*]. What was it you said about the pistol?

BRACK [*softly*]. That he must have stolen it.

HEDDA. Why, precisely, stolen?

BRACK. Because any other explanation ought to be impossible, Madam Hedda.

HEDDA. Really?

BRACK [*glancing at her*]. Of course, Ejlert Lövborg was here this morning. Wasn't he?

HEDDA. Yes.

BRACK. Were you alone with him?

HEDDA. Yes, for a time.

BRACK. Didn't you go out of the room while he was here?

HEDDA. No.

BRACK. Think it over. Were you never out of it for a moment?

HEDDA. Well, perhaps just for a moment – out in the hall.

BRACK. And where was your pistol-case in the meantime?

HEDDA. I kept that in ... I had it locked in ...

BRACK. Well, Madam Hedda?

HEDDA. The case was there on the writing-table.

BRACK. Have you looked since to see whether both pistols are there?

HEDDA. No.

BRACK. Well, there's no need. I saw the pistol Lövborg had

on him. And I knew it again at once, from yesterday. And from longer ago too.

HEDDA. Have you got it?

BRACK. No, the police have it.

HEDDA. What will the police do with the pistol?

BRACK. See if they can trace the owner.

HEDDA. Do you think they can find out?

BRACK [bending over her and whispering]. No, Hedda Gabler. Not so long as I keep silence.

HEDDA [looking askance at him]. And if you do *not* keep silence – what then?

BRACK [shrugging his shoulders]. There is always the other way out: the pistol was stolen.

HEDDA [firmly]. Rather death!

BRACK [smiling]. That is the kind of thing one *says*. One doesn't *do* it.

HEDDA [without answering]. And suppose, now, the pistol isn't stolen. And the owner is discovered. Then what happens?

BRACK. Well, Hedda, what happens then is a scandal.

HEDDA. Scandal!

BRACK. Scandal. Yes! The thing you have such a deadly fear of. Of course you will have to appear in court. Both you and Mademoiselle Diana. She will have to explain how the thing happened. Whether it was accident or homicide. ... Did he try to pull the pistol out of his pocket to threaten her? And is that how it went off? Or did she snatch the pistol out of his hand, shoot him and put it back in his pocket again? She's quite equal to that. She's a hefty young woman, that same Mademoiselle Diana.

HEDDA. But all these repulsive details don't concern me.

BRACK. No. But you will have to answer the question: Why did you give Ejlert Lövborg the pistol? And what conclusions will people draw from the fact that you did give it him?

HEDDA [*drooping her head*]. That's true. I didn't think of that.

BRACK. Well, fortunately there is no danger, so long as I say nothing.

HEDDA [*looking up at him*]. So I am in your power, Mr Brack. From now on, you have a hold over me.

BRACK [*whispering softly*]. My dearest Hedda, believe me I shall not abuse the position.

HEDDA. In your power, all the same. At the mercy of your will and demands. And so a slave! A slave! [*Getting up impatiently.*] No! That thought I cannot tolerate. Never!

BRACK [*looking at her half mockingly*]. And yet one usually manages to tolerate the inevitable.

HEDDA [*returning his look*]. Yes, possibly. [*She goes across to the writing-table.*]

HEDDA [*suppressing an involuntary smile and imitating Tesman's intonation*]. Well, is it getting on all right, Jörgen? Eh?

TESMAN. The Lord only knows, my dear. In any case, there's months of work here.

HEDDA [*as before*]. Well, fancy that! [*Letting her hands stray gently through Mrs Elvsted's hair.*] Doesn't it feel strange to you, Thea? Here you are sitting with Jörgen Tesman just as you once sat with Ejlert Lövborg.

MRS ELVSTED. Well, if only I could inspire your husband too –

HEDDA. Oh, that will come all right – in time.

TESMAN. Yes, do you know, Hedda, I really think I am beginning to feel something of the kind. But you go back and sit down with Judge Brack again.

HEDDA. Is there nothing here I can help you two with?

TESMAN. Not a thing in the world. [*Turning his head.*]

Would you be so kind as to keep Hedda company for the time being, Judge Brack?

BRACK [*with a glance at Hedda*]. It will give me the very greatest pleasure.

HEDDA. Thanks. But I'm tired tonight. I will lie down for a little while on the sofa in there.

TESMAN. Yes do, my dear. Eh?

[*Hedda goes into the inner room and draws the curtains after her. There is a short pause. Suddenly she is heard playing a wild dance tune on the piano.*]

MRS ELVSTED [*jumping up from her chair*]. Oh! What is that?

TESMAN [*running to the doorway*]. But, Hedda, my dearest – don't play dance music this evening. Think of Aunt Rina! And of Ejlert, too!

HEDDA [*putting out her head between the hangings*]. And of Aunt Julle. And of all the rest of them. I will be quiet in future. [*She pulls the curtains to again after her.*]

TESMAN [*at the writing-table*]. It upsets her to see us at this sad task, of course. I tell you what, Mrs Elvsted. You shall move into Aunt Julle's and I'll come over in the evenings. And then we can sit and work there. Eh?

MRS ELVSTED. Yes, perhaps that would be the best plan –

HEDDA [*in the inner room*]. I can hear perfectly well what you are saying. But how am I going to get through the evenings out here?

TESMAN [*turning over the papers*]. Oh, I'm sure Judge Brack will be kind enough to come out and see you.

BRACK [*in the easy-chair, calling gaily*]. Willingly! Every single evening, Mrs Tesman. We shall have a very pleasant time together here, you and I.

HEDDA [*clearly and distinctly*]. Yes, that is what you are looking forward to, isn't it, Mr Brack? You, as the only cock in the yard.

[*A shot is heard within. Tesman, Mrs Elvsted, and Brack jump up.*]

TESMAN. Ah! Now she's playing with the pistols again.

[*He pulls the curtains aside and runs in. So does Mrs Elvsted. Hedda is lying lifeless, stretched out on the sofa. Confusion and cries. Berte comes in distractedly from the right.*]

TESMAN [*shrieking to Brack*]. Shot herself! Shot herself in the temple! Think of it!

BRACK [*half-collapsed in the easy-chair*]. But, merciful God! One doesn't *do* that kind of thing!

CURTAIN

NOTES

I HAVE thought it advisable to add notes on some half-dozen passages, so that readers who are interested in the treatment of the original may see the kinds of reasons that have led to my renderings and modifications. I have not written a note on every case that deserved it, but only one or two, to serve as illustration, on each kind of problem that arose.

The Pillars of the Community

(Pp. 25, stage directions; 31, 32.) I have translated 'bue' as 'toy gun' because a 'cross-bow' would be meaningless to modern readers, and to call it a 'bow' would make some confusion later, when Hilmar talks about there being a 'shot' in it. The cross-bow, which was common in 1877 and is still, I am told, used by children in country districts in Norway, could be restored to the text in production, and Olaf would have one as a property in this scene.

(Pp. 28, 50.) The Fallen Sisters have given translators a great deal of trouble. The original is 'Disse moralsk fordaervede', which could be rendered literally as 'These morally depraved'. A modern euphemism must be found, such as a modern Rörlund would use. 'Lapsed and lost' was a brilliant rendering in the 1890s, but I doubt whether its overtones would be recognized today. I am not altogether satisfied that even our Rörlunds today talk about 'fallen sisters'; but the advance of the social sciences has made it unlikely that we produce any Rörlunds. The trouble becomes worse when Lona, in Act III, says that she has been up in the market-place and met 'et par af de moralske', 'a few of the moral ones'. If we have not kept 'moralsk' in some form in our translation of the passage in Act I, the glancing allusion, with its double meaning, is gone. We must then choose between preserving Lona's contemptuous dislike of their self-righteousness or her humorous reference to the untoward circumstances of her arrival the day before. The Scottish 'unco guid' seemed to me the kind of phrase a modern Lona might use, but it is, I gather, becoming less familiar in England. Finally, I have chosen 'virtuous sisters', containing both her meaning and her allusion, though not very pithily.

(P. 101.) The stage direction to Krap's first speech is omitted by the 1930 edition. I have supplied it from the Minneutgave (1908).

The Wild Duck

(P. 195.) 'Harryson' is Hedvig's own substitute for 'Harrison' and I have let it stand.

P. 199, l.9.) Gina confuses the common word 'dividere' (divide) with the less common 'divertere' (to amuse), which she has, no doubt, overheard. I owe to my friend Illit Gröndahl the suggestion that this confusion should be represented in English by 'divergence' and 'diversion'.

(P. 208, l.3.) What Gina actually says is 'ressenser om mig'. It has been suggested to me that she is confusing 'ressenser' (to 'review' or 'criticize'), a literary word of French origin, with the common intransitive 'raesonere' (to 'argue', 'discuss') and perhaps also with the transitive 'raesonere' (to 'find fault with'). Altogether a pretty mixture, and just what we should expect, when she is flustered, from the unfortunate Gina, who is 'not altogether without education', having picked it up from the conversation of Hjalmar and his friends. The substance of what she says is 'Don't stand there talking about me!' The translator who wants to convey the muddle as well as the meaning can use the word 'argufying' or 'making an aspersion of me' or some such turn.

(P. 238, end.) Worse still is Gina's 'intrikate fordringen' at the end of Act IV. She has a confused memory of a word that Hjalmar and Gregers have bandied to and fro in the discussions of the last few hours. It is hard to follow the track of her mind, but a friend suggests that the word she is feeling for is 'ideale'. If this is so, then a translator must find a word that sounds like 'ideal' but is not – and yet makes some kind of sense. 'Idea', 'idle', 'idol' all suggest themselves. I have chosen 'idol' because it represents best her particular mixture of sense and nonsense and is yet within the range of an English Gina's vocabulary.

Hedda Gabler

(P. 277, l.33.) The word 'fogd' presents the kind of difficulty a translator always finds in presenting the institutions of one country (such as local government) in terms of another where they have no precise equivalents. There are several instances in these three plays, and I have chosen this one to illustrate the problem. A 'fogd' is a resident government official, something between a magistrate, a Chief Constable and a Lord-Lieutenant of a county, except that, like a judge on circuit, he from time to time travels through his district administering justice in the local courts. The nearest equivalent in English seems to me to be 'District Magistrate'. This office does not occur in England, but it is familiar to most English readers because of its frequency in India and the Crown Colonies.

*

This is the fittest place to acknowledge certain specific debts to my predecessors. There are, inevitably, many coincidences of word, phrase and sentence of which I am unaware. But in certain notorious difficulties I naturally consulted the earlier versions and adopted what I found there if I was convinced that I could not get nearer to Ibsen's meaning. Moreover, there are one or two strokes in the first versions which the future is not likely to better, such as Relling's outburst to Molvik, 'Shut up, you fool! You're drunk', or Hedda's 'I still have one thing to kill time with'. These are the classical passages of the translations and the future will probably leave them untouched; I, at least, prefer to do so. My conscious borrowings in both these kinds do not amount to more than half-a-dozen sentences in the three plays, and those who are familiar with the translations will recognize them readily enough.